BY THE AUTO EDITORS OF CONSUMER GUIDE®

Publications International, Ltd.

Louis Weber, C.E.O.
Publications International, Ltd.
7373 North Cicero Avenue
Lincolnwood, Illinois 60646

Permission is never granted for commercial purposes.

Manufactured in U.S.A.

8 7 6 5 4 3 2 1

ISBN: 0-7853-1228-5

Library of Congress Catalog Card Number: 95-69019

CREDITS

Photography:
The editors gratefully acknowledge the cooperation of the following people who supplied information and photography to help make this book possible.

Special thanks to:
Kate Godar; Floyd Joliet; Klaus Parr, photo archivist with Porsche AG, Stuttgart, Germany; Mirco DeCet.

Nicky Wright: 7, 29, 33, 42, 50, 51, 56, 57, 72, 73, 191, 200, 204, 205; Gary Versteege: 79, 80; Bud Juneau: 92, 135; David Gooley: 102, 180; Thomas Glatch: 49, 104, 105, 191, 199; Jerry Heasley: 108, 109, 184, 185, 207; Dan Lyons: 197; Vince Manocchi: 117, 178, 179; Sam Griffith: 125, 184, 185;

Chris Poole: 127, 165; Hidden Image: 127, 215; Milton Gene Kieft: 41, 136, 137; Doug Mitchel: 149, 201; Mitch Frumkin: 182.

Owners:
Special thanks to the owners of the cars featured in this book for their enthusiastic cooperation.

C.A. Stoddard: 7, 29, 33, 41, 50, 51, 56, 57; 191, 200, 204, 205; Tom Mittler: 42, 72, 73; Jonathan Phillips: 49; Bob Briggs: 92; Barbara Hendrickson: 104, 105; Otis Chandler: 108, 109, 207; Michael F. Hartmann:135; P. Garvey: 136, 137; Lynn Larson: 191; Michael Graham: 197; Robert Baker: 199.

Contents

Sports Cars Like No Other

This book traces the evolution of the Porsche company and its cars over their nearly 50 years of existence. And an eventful story it is, full of irony and innovation, persistence and daring, remarkable achievements by the score, and a few puzzling failures. Through these pages, we hope you'll come to appreciate why these sports cars are like no other in the world.

The Porsche saga may be relatively recent history, but it really begins in the automobile's earliest days with Dr. Ferdinand Porsche, so this book begins with him. That's only right, for every Porsche reflects the great legacy of his stunningly successful 75-year pursuit of excellence. His fierce dedication would be passed on to son Ferry (Ferdinand Porsche II), who would carry it forward into the modern Porsche company.

Despite his title of *Herr Doktor*, the elder Ferdinand never earned a formal engineering degree. Equally ironic, he barely lived to see the cars bearing his name and only glimpsed the potential of his most monumental creation, the Volkswagen. But though he spent most of his life working for others, Porsche gifted the world with concepts so advanced that they wouldn't be commonplace for decades. No wonder that Porsche cars and the company have always been at the forefront of technology.

Ferdinand Porsche staunchly believed that "racing improves the breed," so it's no surprise that his heirs did, too—or that Porsche has compiled an incredible competition record that continues to this day. Though it has not been unerringly successful, no make has won more races or more *kinds* of races, which testifies not only to Porsche's constant search for perfection but its historic reliance on competition as the absolute crucible for new technology.

Yet Porsche has never embraced change for its own sake, and never will. Today's sophisticated all-wheel-drive 911 Turbo reflects the same philosophy that guided Ferry in shaping the first, humble 356: Start with the best possible design, test it in competition, use what you learn to improve it, then keep improving it year after year until you either run out of ideas or come up with something truly superior.

Following the path of evolution, not revolution, tends to breed cars that defy the ravages of time, so the 911's long 30-plus-year lifespan is no real surprise, either. Indeed, it bespeaks the engineering artistry that is part and parcel of the great *Herr Doktor*'s legacy. As Ferry said in 1984: "You must not change every year. If you do, you have the nicest car [only] at the beginning. . . ."

With that, Porsche has become almost synonymous with cars having rear-mounted horizontally opposed air-cooled engines. Yet the elder Dr. Porsche, his son, and their colleagues have produced fours, V-8s, flat-eights, V-12s, and even V-16s; engines with water and air/water cooling; and cars of mid- and front-engine configuration. So Porsche has never been bound to a single design concept or technology; rather, it employs those best suited to particular needs.

Those needs, as anyone who has ever driven a Porsche surely knows, include the highest standards of performance but not at the expense of durability or practicality. Porsches are built to take it because that's what the race track and Porsche's own engineering ethics demand. And though they are sports cars designed for "driving in its purest form," as Ferry once said, you can live with them happily day in and day out. For proof, look no further than the many 10-, 15- and even 20-year-old 911s still in daily service—and still bringing broad smiles of satisfaction to their owners.

With all this, it may truly be said of Porsche that the more things change, the more they stay the same. Alas, world economics and an auto industry increasingly interested in upscale customers conspire to make owning a new Porsche an increasingly rare privilege. Yet exclusivity is another Porsche tradition. After all, the price of excellence is never cheap, and Porsche has never readily compromised on the dubious altar of cost.

Excellence, exclusivity, an unrivaled engineering heritage, race-bred performance—all make up the Porsche chronicle, and our *Porsche Chronicle*, as well. It's a remarkable story we know you'll enjoy.

Ferdinand Porsche: The Artistic Genius

Like most of the great automotive pioneers, Ferdinand Porsche was special. From the first, he viewed cars not as toys for the rich but universal conveyances designed to be afforded by anyone. In this he was like Henry Ford. He was certainly as complex a personality: "wayward, brilliant, contradictory and utterly single-minded," with "a firm belief in his own ideas," in the words of historian David Owen—and even more naive about politics. Both were mechanical geniuses possessed of enormous native skill. Both were primarily "engine men." And though not always right, both ultimately succeeded through a relentless drive that invariably inspired loyal associates who contributed more to each man's legend than is generally appreciated.

But while Ford was a technician, Porsche was an artist who had "more in common with a painter than a designer of machinery," according to Owen. Historian Leonard Setright notes, Porsche was "one of those creatively fecund individuals whose vision penetrated the obscurantist orthodoxy of more than mere cars." His advanced concepts and lifelong pursuit of mechanical excellence are reflected in today's Porsche company and its cars, neither of which can be fully appreciated without an account of the man's extraordinary life.

Ferdinand Porsche was born on September 3, 1875 (a dozen years after Henry Ford), in the Austrian village of Maffersdorf, located in Bohemia near the town of Reichenberg, in what used to be Czechoslovakia. Reichenberg (now called *Liberec*) is located southeast of Dresden and northeast of Prague. The Hapsburg Empire, stretching from the Carpathians to the Alps and embracing scores of nationalities among its 50 million subjects, was at its zenith at the time of Porsche's birth. At least five generations of Porsches had lived and worked around Reichenberg as tailors, weavers, carpenters, and metalsmiths. Among the last was Ferdinand's father, Anton.

In 1890, Anton Jr., the eldest of Papa Porsche's three sons, died in an accident, leaving Ferdinand heir apparent. The 15-year-old soon began an apprenticeship to prepare him to one day assume control of the family business. But to his father's chagrin, Ferdinand had no talent for metalworking. Worse, he hated it. Ferdinand's mother ultimately intervened, persuading Anton Sr. to let their son attend the Imperial Technical School in Reichenberg.

It was there that young Ferdinand discovered the compelling mysteries of electricity. It wasn't long before he secreted an array of wires and batteries in the family attic, where, after a 12-hour day, he'd experiment with a form of power that Bohemia had hardly heard of. Anton was furious when he found out about his son's only hobby, considering it a frivolous waste of time. On one occasion, he even stomped on Ferdinand's batteries, ruining a shiny new pair of boots and suffering severe acid burns.

But Ferdinand persisted. By 1893, again with his mother's encouragement, he'd designed, built, and installed a complete electrical system in the family home, including a generator, switchboard, incandescent lighting fixtures, door chimes—even an intercom. Greeted one evening by the blaze of the new electric lights, Anton Porsche realized there might be more to this "frivolousness" than he had believed. Accordingly, he allowed Ferdinand to go to Vienna to find work; the youngest son, Oskar, became the apprentice metalsmith.

Ferdinand's formal education would be spotty. He'd done poorly at the Imperial School and couldn't afford university training. But in Vienna he became a handyman at Bela Egger, an electrical-equipment maker that later became the giant Brown Boveri concern. After sweeping floors and oiling machinery, Ferdinand would sneak into lecture classes at a nearby university. His enthusiasm so impressed college authorities that he was allowed to continue his "auditing" even after he had been found out. The only trouble was, Ferdinand wasn't a registered student and thus couldn't take formal examinations. But his determination was rewarded at Bela Egger, where by 1897 he was manager of the test department and first assistant in the calculating section.

Then, a turning point came. In 1898, Ferdinand Porsche signed on as an engine designer with Jakob Lohner, the patron Viennese coachbuilder to the Hapsburgs and other rich and famous personages. Two years before, Lohner had begun moving

Engineer, risk-taker, visionary: Ferdinand Porsche, photographed in 1950, near the end of his life. He approached automotive engineering with the precision of a watchmaker and the instincts of a fine artist. Perhaps his most important quality was his imagination, which led Porsche to constantly challenge himself. That the company he founded survives today is the best testament to his uncommon vigor and talent.

into the production of newfangled horseless carriages. Now, deciding that gasoline engines were too crude for his high-class customers, he wanted someone to design an electric auto. Young Porsche was only too happy to oblige.

The result was the Lohner "Electric Chaise." Built on the *Radnabenmotor* principle, it employed an electric motor at each front wheel, thus eliminating the need for a transmission, gears, driveshafts, and all their weight. Accordingly, it was also the world's first car with front-wheel drive—Ferdinand's first "first"—and could travel up to 50 miles on one charge. Porsche demonstrated it in 1900 on a run to Versailles from the Universal Exposition in Paris, a feat that earned him a Grand Prize. In short order, the electric Lohner began selling well from England to Prussia. The Rothschilds had one. So did Archduke Franz Ferdinand.

But despite Ferdinand's weight-saving innovations, the Lohner remained heavy (2156 pounds, of which 990 pounds were batteries) and thus slow. Porsche duly modified it, then went to the Semmering hillclimb course on September 23, 1900, where he set a new record time of 14 minutes, 52 seconds, handily beating the previous best of 23:27.

Striving for even better performance, Porsche reduced battery weight by developing a "mixed-drive" Lohner—what we'd now call a hybrid-power car—with a small gasoline engine to drive a generator feeding the hub motors. Even if the engine failed, the car still could travel 38 miles on its batteries alone. But Jakob Lohner, now earning tidy profits, wasn't interested in improving his cars and sold his patents to Emil Jellinek in 1906. Ferdinand decided it was time to seek new opportunities.

He found them at prestigious Austro-Daimler, the Austrian branch of the German Daimler company. By 1908, Porsche had completely redesigned A-D's four-cylinder "Maja" (honoring one of Emil Jellinek's daughters, a sister of Mercedes, a name with which Porsche would soon be familiar), giving it a few extra horsepower and a four-speed transmission with either shaft or chain drive. A trio of racing versions was entered in the 1909 Prince Henry Trials (named for Prinz Heinrich, the car-enthusiast brother of the German Kaiser). They were unsuccessful there, but Porsche himself drove one to victory in the Semmerling Hillclimb on September 19. That same day, his wife gave birth in Neustadt, in suburban Vienna, to a son: Ferdinand Anton Ernst Porsche, later most always called Ferry.

Austro-Daimler made an eight-car assault on the 1910 Trials with the Porsche-designed 27/80. Its 5.7-liter (348-cubic-inch) racing four was patterned after one of A-D's aircraft engines, with steel pistons, inclined valves, and a single overhead camshaft. Though considered "small," it produced a remarkable 95 horsepower. Porsche took great pains to make the cars the engine powered as light as possible to counter the brute force of the competition's over-20-liter (1220-cid) engines. He also took pains with aerodynamics, evident in *tulpenform* (tulip-shaped) bodywork: rounded at the front, tapered at the rear, curved upward and outward on the sides. There weren't any wind tunnels then, but these A-D racers must have been quite slippery, for their top speed was near 90 mph—amazing for 1910. The result was a 1-2-3 finish, with Porsche himself in the winning car.

But 1910 would be the high point for the Austro-Daimler team. Indeed, it was one of the last times that the old Hapsburg Empire would win an honor of any kind. Big-power rivalries—beginning with the Kaiser's decision to match Britain's navy, then France's alliance with Russia—were about to plunge the world into a cataclysm that would sweep away the old royal houses and redraw the map of Europe. War came in August 1914, though the Great Powers had been preparing long before (Britain and Germany with their naval race; France, Russia, and Austria-Hungary with their stockpiling of armaments).

Meantime, Ferdinand Porsche had been designing aero engines at Austro-Daimler. First came a water-cooled inline six, which was followed by his first air-cooled horizontally opposed design, a four-cylinder unit with pushrod-operated overhead valves. He'd later devise several V-type engines, a rotary (though nothing like the late-Fifties Wankel), and even a W-type engine, with three rows of cylinders on a common crankshaft.

Perhaps anticipating the war, in 1913 Austro-Daimler had acquired Skoda, the great armaments firm that survives today as an automaker in that part of the former Czechoslovakia that then still belonged to Franz Josef. Skoda was naturally assigned to produce army artillery, and Ferdinand Porsche was assigned there. His first task: find a way to move Skoda's big guns. Drawing on his Lohner experience, he devised a four-wheel-drive tractor with gas/electric power for hauling a monstrous 305mm mortar. This gun leveled the fortress of Naumaur, helping the Central Powers roll through Belgium in August and September of 1914.

Soon afterward, Porsche conceived an incredible "land train" comprising a mixed-drive tractor that

Ferdinand Porsche's skill at automaking was firmly grounded in his experience in the decidedly unglamorous aspects of engineering. While working for the mammoth Skoda armaments firm in 1913, he designed a four-wheel-drive gas/electric tractor dubbed "Big Bertha" (top), capable of hauling Skoda's mammoth 420mm mortars. Earlier, while working for engine designer Jakob Lohner in 1898, Ferdinand developed the "Electric Chaise" (bottom right), which could travel 50 miles on a single charge of its 990 pounds of batteries. It was the world's first front-drive vehicle. A more sophisticated Lohner (bottom left) was built two years later for a Briton named E. W. Hart; the car caused a sensation at the 1900 Paris World's Fair. At age 35 in 1910, Porsche was a handsome figure (middle right). Two years later, he was appointed to Knight of the Order of Franz Joseph I. The November 12, 1912, ceremony in Vienna was officially noted by this certificate (middle left).

pulled as many as eight self-steering cars, each with electric front-wheel hub motors receiving power from the tractor via cable. It was ideally suited to one of the war's most devastating weapons, the enormous 420mm Skoda mortar that weighed 26 tons and fired one-ton shells. Thanks to these and other achievements, Porsche was awarded an honorary doctorate from the Technical University of Vienna in 1917; the following year, he became Austro-Daimler's managing director.

But the walls came tumbling down with war's end in 1918. With the Treaty of Versailles carving up the old Austro-Hungarian empire, Porsche found himself the boss of a car company with bleak prospects. He also found himself, at least technically, a citizen of another country, as his native Bohemia had been handed to the new Czech Republic.

Though Porsche never cared much about politics, he couldn't ignore the new social and economic realities. Indeed, he recognized that no European automaker could survive by returning to the big, extravagant products of prewar days. Small, affordable cars were what the struggling new war-formed nations needed most, and he was determined to supply them.

An opportunity came in 1921 when Count Sascha Kolowrat, a wealthy Austrian filmmaker, asked Porsche to design a small 1.0-liter (61-cid) car, all expenses paid. The result, inevitably called "Sascha," was a lightweight, open two-seater with a single-overhead-cam four capable of pushing the Sascha to an astounding 90 miles an hour. In that year's Targa Florio road race, standard Saschas driven by Kuhn and Poecher finished 1-2 in the 1100-cc class. A third car with a slightly larger engine placed seventh in the hands of driver Alfred Neubauer, who would soon follow Porsche to Daimler in Germany, where he became legendary as Daimler-Benz's racing manager. Interestingly, Ferry Porsche, then only 12, helped his father run-in one of the Saschas.

Meanwhile, dissension and decline were setting in at Austro-Daimler, which was still wedded to *luxus* automobiles and wealthy clients. In 1922, the board decided to withdraw from racing, ostensibly because an A-D driver had been killed in an accident. But the real reason was money—or rather, the lack of it. A-D's foreign-exchange earnings were being converted into rapidly devaluing Austrian schillings, and the resulting need to economize led the board to inform Ferdinand that development funds for a Porsche-designed 2.0-liter racing Sascha capable of 106 mph had been cut off. Never one to suffer fools gladly, Porsche hurled a

gold cigarette lighter at the directors and stormed out of the board meeting.

Given his small-car dreams—and the board's opposition—he was probably right to react as he did. Though Karl Rabe, later Porsche's right-hand man, replaced him at Austro-Daimler, the firm would be out of business within 10 years. Porsche, meantime, had gone to Germany, where he became technical director and a board member at Daimler in Stuttgart. It was another timely move.

It's unclear how much Porsche actually contributed to his first assignment at Daimler. Before he arrived, the firm had built a new 2.0-liter supercharged engine with competition in mind. David Owen has written that Porsche spent nine months transforming it from also-ran (at the 1923 Indianapolis 500) to class champion (1-2-3 at the 1924 Targa Florio), but Leonard Setright claims Porsche only inherited it. Regardless, the University of Stuttgart recognized this achievement by awarding Porsche his second honorary doctorate in 1924.

There's much less argument over the big supercharged sixes that Porsche conceived for the K- and S-Series Mercedes of the late Twenties and early Thirties: They rank among the greatest engineering feats in automotive history.

The late Michael Frostick wrote, "brute force and bloody ignorance is hardly a fair description" of those cars, yet there was some of both in their engines. Each was a masterpiece in light alloy, a veritable King Kong among period European powerplants. All stemmed from Porsche's basic 6.0-liter racing six with which D-B won the 1926 German Grand Prix.

But the blower was each car's Achilles' heel, for driving with it engaged for even a few miles could easily destroy the engine. Distinguished collector Connie Bouchard once left a bit of a magnificent 540K engine on Woodward Avenue after answering a village hot-rodder's challenge. It's been said that the blower was never intended to run on gasoline; it was to be filled with benzol instead. And in fairness, the owner's manual advised against prolonged use. Yet even with its assistance, these supercharged Mercs were more sluggish than their spectacular looks suggested, because their bodies and chassis were ponderous.

Setright has written that on the basis of these cars' handling, Ferdinand Porsche was "utterly hopeless on chassis design." But Setright took pains to note, "occasional errors can be forgiven in anybody; even though a man might be a divine creation, his design has shown the need for some developmental work. . . . Let us at least give

The Porsche family home in Maffersdorf (top left), photographed in 1888, when Ferdinand (front, far left) was 13 years old. In 1916, Porsche greeted officers of the army of Franz Joseph at Austro-Daimler headquarters (top right). In 1921 a wealthy Austrian filmmaker, Count Sascha Kolowrat, commissioned Austro-Daimler and Porsche to create an automobile for his personal use. The 1.0-liter, two-seat "Sascha" (middle left) was Porsche's first lightweight car. It was capable of a 90-mph top speed—truly eye-opening for the day. That's the Count himself behind the wheel. A 1922 Sascha (middle right) was perhaps the last, for Austro-Daimler pulled out of racing that year, enraging Ferdinand and prompting him to quit the firm. By the mid-Thirties, Ferdinand had developed supercharged sixes that turned Mercedes cars (bottom) into true powerhouses. The older car parked next to the Mercedes is an eight-cylinder Horch of about 1928 vintage.

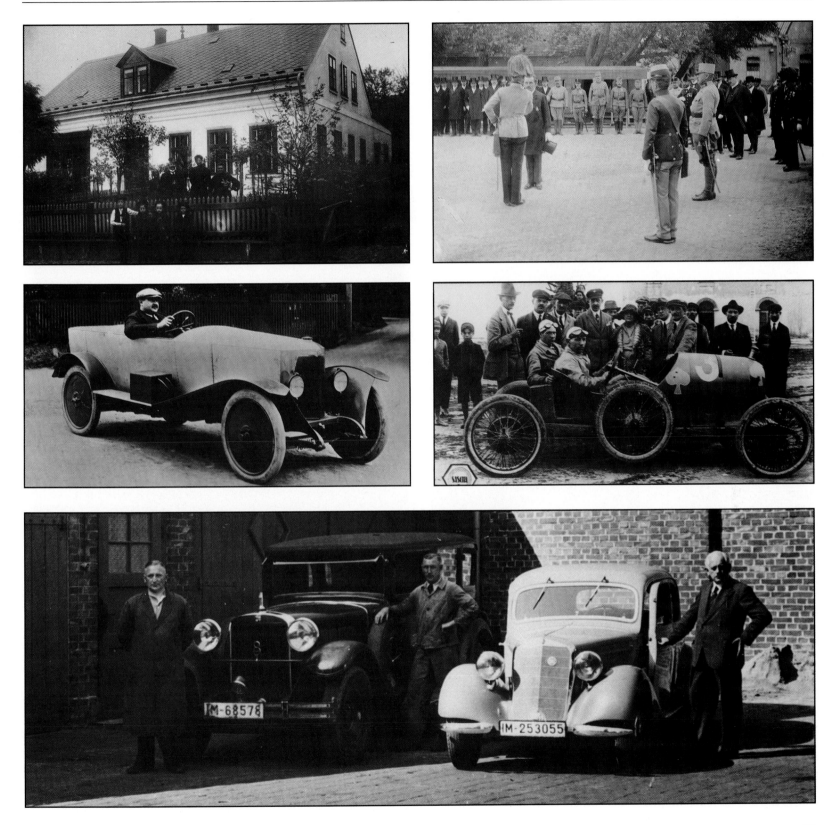

The awesome Mercedes SSK racers (above and top) *that ran with supercharged engines designed by Ferdinand Porsche typify the unrestrained aspect of Germany in the Twenties. With maximum horsepower of 300, these cars could reach speeds of up to 150 mph—unbelievable figures for the period and plenty potent even today. Ferdinand's son, Ferry, followed his father into the auto business; here (above right), he strikes a natty pose next to a Porsche Project 7, the first car Ferdinand produced after forming* Porsche Konstruktionsburo *in 1930. A year later, Ferdinand began preliminary work on a* Wagen fur das Volk (right), *an affordable "people's car."*

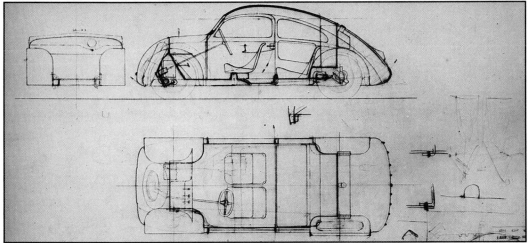

Porsche development of the Type 32 "people's car" (above and below) continued in 1932, by now in conjunction with motorcycle manufacturer NSU. Adolf Hitler, who rose to absolute power in Germany in 1933, reportedly had a hand in the car's general configuration. The 32 ran with a four-cylinder "boxer" engine displacing 1.45 liters. A variation, the Type 60 of 1934 (left), is an obvious ancestor of the Volkswagen Type I "Beetle."

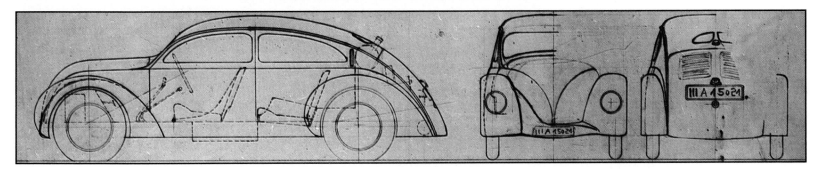

[Porsche] the credit for having been, in an admittedly special sense, an artist."

It would be well here to sort out the various Porsche-designed Mercedes. The first was the Model 24/100/140, a huge touring car of relatively little aesthetic appeal. It quickly evolved into the K (for *kurz* or "short" wheelbase), also known as the 24/110/160. Arriving in 1926, the year Daimler merged with Benz, it packed 160 DIN horsepower at 3000 rpm and could reach 90 mph.

The Model S followed a year later, its engine bored from 6.25 to 6.79 liters for 120/180 bhp normal/supercharged, good for up to 100 mph. The SS of 1928 saw displacement boosted to an even 7.0 liters, horsepower to 225, and top speed to nearly 100 mph—impressive considering the car's great size. The SSK, with a shorter chassis and somewhat lighter body, was commensurately faster. The final development, in 1931, was the fabulous SSKL (for *sehr schnell, kurz, leicht*)—very fast, short wheelbase, light. Offering 300 bhp at 3200 rpm with the supercharger, it could reach an unprecedented 140-150 mph.

The Mercedes SSK/SSKL still often appear on "great cars" lists. No matter that they were mighty handfuls to drive, that they managed only five mpg with all stops out, that their cable brakes were useless against the lofty speeds made possible by that unbelievable engine, or that only a handful of people could afford them. They were otherworldly beasts, part of the razzmatazz that was the Roaring Twenties. And roar they did, on road and track, to the astonishment and delight of all who appreciated things mechanical. The SS won the 1928 German GP; the SSKL simply won everything in sight.

Great though they were, these mighty Mercedes were a long way from a people's car—the *Volkswagen* that Ferdinand Porsche continued to think about. He'd been waiting for another chance at one since the Sascha's untimely demise, but Daimler-Benz was no better place than Austro-Daimler for realizing his dream. Indeed, some D-B managers (mostly conservative former Benz people) viewed him as something of an idealist in this regard and were predictably cool toward him.

The closest Porsche came to a universal car while at D-B was the medium-priced "Stuttgart," forerunner of the production early-Thirties 370S Mannheim. In early 1929, managers asked him to prove that he'd finally licked its cold-starting problems by firing up any of 15 prototypes that had been left outside through a cold night. Porsche failed, flew into a fury, told the managers to go to the devil, and resigned on the spot. (Ironically,

someone else succeeded with a similar test just three weeks later.) Nobody tried to coax him back.

Returning quickly to Vienna, Porsche developed a Stuttgart-like car for Steyr, which was a big hit at that year's Paris Auto Show. Then the failure of a Vienna bank, one of Steyr's main shareholders, made a merger with Austro-Daimler inevitable, and Porsche was on the move again. The last thing he wanted was another bout with A-D.

But why suffer bosses at all? Porsche didn't really need to by now and so decided to set up his own engineering and design company back in Stuttgart at 14 Kronenstrasse. The date was December 1, 1930, which son Ferry would always regard as the start of the modern Porsche company (hence its 50th anniversary observance in late 1980).

The firm opened under an appropriately imposing name: *Dr. Ing. h.c. Ferdinand Porsche, G.m.b.H., Konstruktionsburo fur Motoran-, Fahrzeug-, Luftfahzeug- und Wasserfahrzeugbau*—literally, "Doctor Engineer (honoris causa) Ferdinand Porsche, Limited, Design Office for Motors, Motor Vehicles, Aircraft and Ships." Porsche's nine-man team was equally impressive. He brought in Karl Rabe from Austro-Daimler and added Adolf Rosenberger, a financier who liked motor racing. Also on hand were Joseph Kales, a specialist in air-cooled engines with experience at Skoda and Tatra (the latter being Czechoslovakia's other automaker); body designer Erwin Komenda, who would later design the first Porsche car; son Ferry, a skilled technician in his own right (he'd already worked at Bosch and Steyr, too); and gearbox expert Karl Frohlich.

Of course, this was hardly an auspicious time for starting any new business. The worldwide Depression was in full swing, and a vehement politician named Adolf Hitler was telling Germans he could wipe out their miseries.

Nevertheless, Porsche had a client even before opening his doors. It was Wanderer, the German maker of medium-price cars, for whom Porsche conjured up a smaller 1.8-liter model with overhead-valve engine and swing-axle rear suspension. Though this was his firm's first job, Porsche labeled it Project 7, fearing that "Project 1" might convey an unhelpful, neophyte image. But the little Wanderer was such a success that Porsche was asked to do an upsized eight-cylinder version. Alas, that was left stillborn when Wanderer merged with Audi, DKW, and Horsch in 1932 to form Auto Union (whose linked-rings emblem survives on today's Audis).

By April 1931, *Porsche Konstruktionsburo* was registered in Stuttgart, and Ferdinand was busy laying out his dream car. It would be a *Wagen fur das Volk*, a

Development of the "people's car" continued during 1934-37. Ferry Porsche drove a topless Type 60 prototype (top left) in 1935, while father Ferdinand (top right) supervised refinements to the racing Auto Union P-Wagen that same year. Development of the latter had begun in 1932, and by '35 it was called the Type B Auto Union. Although quite difficult to control, the Type B ran with 375 horses that rocketed it to Grands Prix wins in Italy and Tunisia. Racing was all well and good, but the car Hitler really wanted was a refined Type 60 for the masses. The VW-3 of 1936 (middle row) was rapidly approaching the familiar Type I configuration; note the hatch hinges and sharply cut vents. Professor Porsche chats with a technician in 1937 (bottom left), the same year he observed tests of the VW Type 30 in Stuttgart.

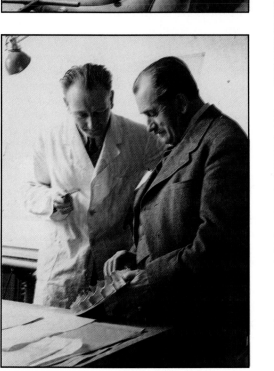

new car any German could afford. The engine would be mounted in back to avoid a long, heavy driveshaft and to allow plentiful interior and luggage space; air-cooled to obviate the need for a weighty water-cooling system; and made of light alloy to preclude a severe rear weight bias. Porsche also decided it should be a horizontally opposed four—compact and thus ideally suited to the small body size envisioned. Further, it would hook up easily to Frohlich's proposed aluminum-case transaxle.

Looking to aircraft techniques used at Austro-Daimler, Porsche envisioned unit construction, the body welded to a central-backbone platform chassis to avoid the weight of a conventional frame. Suspension would be by simple, low-cost swing axles, springing by the torsion bars that Porsche would perfect in 1932, located transversely front and rear. Styling would be aerodynamically efficient, again for best performance and fuel economy.

Though certainly ambitious, this *Volksauto* was long overdue. At the time, America had a car for every six people; Germany had one for every 200. Porsche's car could change all that—*if* he could find a backer with the same vision.

He found one in Dr. Fritz Neumeyer, head of the Zundapp motorcycle company in Nuremberg. Zundapp had wanted to get into auto manufacturing since 1925 but hadn't been motivated to do so until the Depression put a big dent in his company's motorcycle sales. Neumeyer had heard of Porsche and paid him a visit, offering to foot the bill for the *Volksauto*'s production development—provided Porsche made a few changes. Porsche complied within four weeks, and Project 12 was underway.

Three prototypes were soon run up in nighttime secrecy at the Reutter coachworks in Stuttgart. All had rear engines, but the powerplants were water-cooled five-cylinder radials, rather too elaborate for a low-cost "people's car." Porsche himself favored a three- or four-cylinder but was overruled. Not that it mattered, for numerous failures cropped up once prototype tests began in early 1932. With that and a sudden upturn in motorcycle sales, Zundapp lost interest.

Later that year, Porsche visited Russia at the invitation of dictator Joseph Stalin, who wanted to make him "state engineer," effectively the czar of the country's motor industry. Carte blanche authority and an unlimited budget were promised to sweeten the offer, but Porsche soured when he learned that he wouldn't be allowed to leave Russia without direct permission from the Kremlin.

Upon his return to Germany, Porsche was greeted

by the head of another motorcyle firm: Dr. Fritz van Falkenhayn of NSU in Neckarsulm. The result was a new small-car project, the Porsche Type 32, a slightly larger version of the Zundapp design but with Ferdinand's favored air-cooled flat four, this time at 1.5-liters. This design suffered far fewer prototype problems, and tests showed a pleasing top speed of over 70 mph. The path to production seemed clear until an agreement with Fiat, under which the Italian company would handle NSU's auto development, put an end to the relationship in 1933. (One Type 32 was discovered in Germany by a NSU employee in 1945 and is still owned by Volkswagen AG.)

Porsche's dream might have ended there had it not been for the aforementioned Herr Hitler. Rising from obscure mediocrity, he came to power in 1933 on waves of jingoistic sloganeering and grandiose theories for rebuilding Germany out of the Depression. Part of the latter involved a network of *Autobahnen*—the world's first superhighways—plus an affordable car for the average German to travel them. Hitler asked his advisors which engineers were best qualified to design such a car. As Erick Eckermann relates, "Somebody foolish got up and mentioned three names: Joseph Ganz, Edmund Rumpler, and Ferdinand Porsche. There followed an icy silence, because Ganz was a Jew and so was Rumpler. That left Porsche."

The apolitical Porsche wasn't concerned about Hitler's demented social philosphy, only his interest in a people's car. Apparently encouraged by that interest, Porsche sent a memo outlining his ideas to Germany's Transport Ministry in January 1934. Three months later, he was summoned by Jakob Werlin, one of Hitler's inner circle, to a meeting with *Der Fuhrer* at Berlin's Hotel Kaiserhof.

Hitler laid down his requirements: a roomy, rear-engine car with a 100-km/h (62-mph) cruising speed, 30-40-mpg economy, and low maintenance costs. It must be air-cooled, he said, because most Germans don't have garages, and because German winters are harsh. It must seat four, he added, because "we can't separate children from their parents." So far, so good. But when Porsche finally asked about price, he was stunned. "Any price," replied Hitler. "Any price below 1000 Reichsmarks."

In retrospect, it's easy to dismiss these mandates as lunatic ravings—especially that price: equal to about $240 at the time. That criterion, of course, was never met, while the others weren't achieved until many years later, when Germany lay prostrate following the European war she started.

But the fact is that Hitler knew something about cars. He knew about and admired Henry Ford (years

As Germany's preparations for war reached a fever pitch in 1938, Porsche became involved in the development of military vehicles. The chassis and front and rear body panels of the VW Gelandewagen (top left) suggest a well-armored Jeep-like vehicle. Note the machine gun and driver's viewing slit. In late May 1938, Ferry Porsche chauffered Adolf Hitler during a demonstration of the "KdF" Wagen Cabriolet near the VW works in Fallersleben. Pre-production prototypes of VW's Type I had been completed by 1938, when Ferdinand Porsche admired one (middle right). A sedan version was proposed in drawings dated January 20, 1941 (bottom right), but war materiel, such as the Porsche Type 205 Maus mobile gun of 1944 (bottom left), quickly forced the "people's car" to the sidelines.

before he'd read a Ford biography while in Landsberg prison, where he wrote *Mein Kampf*). Then too, he personally attended every Berlin Auto Show; in fact, it was at the 1933 event that he promised *Autobahnen* and *Volkswagens,* as well as lower car taxes, fewer rules, and *Deutschland uber Alles* in racing. He was also the single reason why Mercedes-Benz and Auto Union came to dominate the world's Grand Prix circuits in the Thirties. As a politician, he knew his RM1000 Volkswagen would be well received. As a dictator, he knew he could subsidize the price down to that level even if Porsche's design couldn't be built for so little. So, as in most of Hitler's industrial recovery programs, there was a degree of reason behind the airy rhetoric. Indeed, Dan R. Post has recorded that in mid-1934, when Porsche said he couldn't get the price below RM1500, Jakob Werlin told him that Hitler would solve the problem in "an administrative way."

Porsche had certain advantages in realizing Hitler's people's car, including the Zundapp experience and the NSU prototypes (on which he retained full rights). He also had some disadvantages, chiefly an impatient *Fuhrer* and a doubtful, if not incredulous, RDA (*Reichsverband der deutschen Automobilindustrie;* German Auto Manufacturers Association). Hitler ordered the RDA to sponsor what all Germans now knew as their *Volkswagen,* but the Association offered only a faintly ludicrous $50,000 budget. With that, Porsche could merely revise what he'd already developed. But tests of three new prototypes, designated Type 60 and built at Porsche's home in 1934-35, proved the design well up to claims. By the time testing concluded in late 1936, the RDA grudgingly admitted that this *Volkswagen* deserved further study and support.

Not that anyone in the RDA really wanted to back it. Obviously, a successful small car selling for even RM1500 would be a serious competitor to the economy models on which most German automakers had been working since the Depression. Accordingly, Hitler organized a state-owned corporation, the *Gesellschaft zur Vorbereitung des Volkswagens* (VW Development Company), with Dr. Porsche on its board, and testing went forward from 1937. With unlimited government funding, 60 development VWs were run over a million miles by SS soldiers in secret long-distance tests near the Germany Army barracks at Kornwestheim.

Meantime, Porsche had visited the United States in 1936, talking to rear-engine exponents, including John Tjaarda, and visiting the Fords in Dearborn and touring the Franklin works in Syracuse. He re-

turned with several production experts—of carefully selected Aryan stock—to help set up the *Volkswagen* factory near Castle Wolfsburg in Lower Saxony, a site the Nazis promptly confiscated. Hitler himself attended the dedication ceremonies in May 1938.

In due course, Porsche Project 60 became the VW Series 30 and, finally, the Series 38. The latter was the final production prototype, marked by the now-famous beetle-shape body with its high beltline and tiny divided rear window. Hitler had wanted to call it KdF for *Kraft durch Freude*—"strength through joy"—but even propaganda minister Josef Goebbels couldn't sell *that* one. *Volkswagen* the people called it; Volkswagen it became.

To sell it, the *Deutsche Arbeitsfront* (German government labor organization) issued booklets in which would-be owners pasted stamps, creditable toward the car's purchase price, buying them for a minimum of RM5 weekly. Of course, this money promptly went into the Third Reich's war effort from mid-1939 (hostilities began on September 1 of that year), and nothing but pilot VWs were built through 1945, the final year of the war. But *Volkswagenwerk* did honor the stamps through 1961 to the tune of 600 deutschemarks credit or dm100 cash.

Ironically, it was the British, then the dominant car-exporting people, who got Wolfsburg back into serious postwar production. Heinz Nordhoff, formerly of Opel, was picked to run the place and put VW firmly on its feet. Nordhoff needed 10 years to do it, but the lowly Beetle would ultimately overwhelm the likes of Austin and Morris in world markets, notably the United States. Germany thus accomplished in the auto field what she failed to do on the battlefield: achieve lasting dominance over France and Britain.

Even as the VW drama unfolded, Ferdinand Porsche was accomplishing great things in motorsports—less well known perhaps but a vital part of his story. As we've seen, by the early Thirties he was no stranger to competition cars or their engineering requirements, and it was in 1932 that he began work on his most awe-inspiring creation: the Auto Union P-Wagen.

Its design was prompted by the new 750-kilogram Grand Prix formula of 1934. Typical of Porsche, it emerged as an incredibly sleek single-seater with light-alloy monocoque construction, mid-mounted supercharged V-16 matched to a five-speed transmission, and VW-style all-independent torsion-bar suspension with front trailing links and rear swing axles. Initial DIN horsepower was an incredible 295 on 7.0:1 compression. To ensure all that power got

With war's end in 1945, Ferdinand Porsche found himself interrogated and tossed into a French prison, where he remained until ransomed by son Ferry in 1946. The elder Porsche was by now over 70 and in failing health. Supervision of Porsche company activity thus fell to Ferry, who was determined to make the Porsche name synonymous with superbly engineered performance automobiles. Drawings from 1947 (bottom right) suggest the shape of the Type 356, which existed in prototype form by 1948 (other photos).

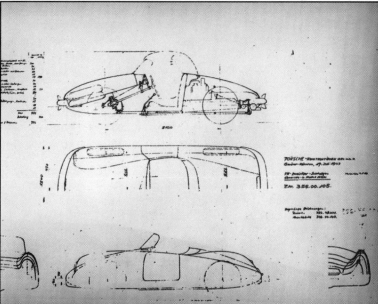

to the ground, Ferry Porsche later conceived the world's first limited-slip differential. Nearly 50 years later, he modestly recalled that his father "became very enthusiastic about it."

Originally conceived for Wanderer, the P-Wagen ended up an Auto Union, thanks to that 1932 merger. The following year, Porsche met with Hitler to request the same $250,000 in racing support that the new Chancellor had just granted Daimler-Benz. Hitler flatly told Porsche that only D-B could produce a champion for Germany. At that, Porsche turned five shades of red and, wrote David Owen, "launched into a typical flood of technical argument, explaining just what his new racing car was, what it could do, and why no other car could do it. Hitler tried to interrupt, but for once in his life he was forced to listen. . . . At first astonished, finally he was impressed. Hitler changed his mind completely and signed an order awarding Auto Union the same government subsidy."

The first P-Wagen, logically called Type A, was completed by late 1933. Hans Stuck drove it to win the Grands Prix of Germany and Switzerland in 1934 as the Auto Unions generally demolished the factory Alfas and even the GP Mercedes. A Mercedes onslaught gave D-B the Manufacturers Cup in 1935, though the squirrely but blindingly fast Type B Auto Union, with 375 bhp, won the Italian and Tunisian events, with Stuck and new team member Bernd Rosemeyer starring.

Rosemeyer was particularly adept at using the car's awesome oversteer to advantage. Indeed, he seemed about the only one who could really control the beast (except for Ferry Porsche, who did much of the development testing). Rosemeyer won the 1936 Italian, Swiss, and German GPs with the 6.0-liter 520-bhp Type C. In 1937, he drove the ultimate 6.3-liter 545-bhp version to win Germany's *Eifelrennen* against Mercedes's best. Before Hitler rang down the curtain on peace, Auto Union won the GPs of Romania (Stuck), France (Muller), and Yugoslavia (the great Tazio Nuvolari). The last would be the final Grand Prix for the duration of the war and was actually run while the Germans were beating down the Poles on September 3, 1939.

The P-Wagens were themselves impressive high-speed record breakers. Rosemeyer set 17 new marks in October 1937, including the flying kilometer at 252.47 mph on the Frankfurt-Darmstadt autobahn. He alternated between the R-Type, a special speed-record version that made the 252-mph run, and a smaller-engine car for the 3000-5000-cc class. The following January he took out after the new 270-mph record of Rudi Caracciola's Mercedes; tragically, a

crosswind sent the devilishly tricky AU out of control, and Rosemeyer was killed.

Unquestionably, the Thirties marked a golden era for motor racing in general and German GP cars in particular. Driven by the likes of Rosemeyer, Caracciola, Nuvolari, Hermann Lang, Dick Seaman, and Werner von Brauchitsch, Germany's silver missles ruled the circuits throughout the decade. The cars were wildly beautiful and truly unforgettable for anyone lucky enough to have seen them. All these immortals—the Auto Unions directly and the Mercedes at least tangentially—owed their concept to the same gifted man.

Sadly, the winds of a new war ended Ferdinand Porsche's brief years at the pinnacle. Wolfsburg was soon given over to military production (one of its first tasks was making stoves to warm the *Wehrmacht* for the frigid invasion of Russia that would be undertaken in June 1941); the Volkswagen was shunted aside.

But Porsche was too talented to be left idle. His first wartime project was the Type 82 *Kubelwagen* ("bucket car"), the German Army equivalent of the American Jeep (without four-wheel drive), a VW variant that carried Rommel's *Afrika Korps* across the Sahara. He then rendered the more successful *Schwimmwagen,* an amphibious derivative with four-wheel drive and detachable propeller.

Porsche also designed the Tiger tank that spearheaded the 1940 invasion of France and the Low Countries, staved off the advancing Russians for months late in the war, and fought the Americans to a standstill at the Battle of the Bulge in December 1944 until the Germans ran out of gasoline. Porsche also had a hand in some of Hitler's "secret weapons," including the improbably named, 20-foot-high *Maus,* conceived as a sort of impregnable, far-ranging mobile fort. In practice, though, the contraption proved *im*mobile on soft ground, and only three were built before the Third Reich collapsed in the spring of 1945.

Shortly before that, at the end of 1944, the Porsche design business was evacuated to Gmund, Austria, when Allied bombs began devastating Stuttgart. Nevertheless, *Herr Doktor* Porsche was arrested by the British, though saved from immediate imprisonment by Albert Speer, the young architect who had interpreted Hitler's grandiose plans for a new Berlin. Speer explained to the Brits that the plain-bolts engineer they had captured cared nothing about politics and was not a Nazi. Porsche was released.

But in November 1945, Porsche was invited to visit French occupation headquarters in Baden-

Proceeds from postwar contracts with Cisitalia and other automakers brought Porsche the funds needed to develop the 356. Early examples, such as the 1948 coupes and Cabriolets seen here, were built in Austria, and made of aluminum hand-formed over wooden bucks. Horsepower was modest at 40, but splendid aerodynamics and a 1300-pound curb weight allowed the 356 to hit 90 mph at full tilt. The grille's vertical "cat's whiskers" vanished when production moved to Germany in 1950.

Baden, ostensibly to discuss an idea from Industry Minister Marcel Paul for a *French* people's car—a VW with a different body. Porsche said he would help, only to be arrested a few days later as a Nazi "collaborator," along with Ferry and son-in-law Anton Piëch (who'd married Ferdinand's only daughter, Louise). The idea was to divert French public attention from the arrest of Louis Renault on the same charge. Porsche was soon marched in chains through Dijon by the French, who nevertheless had the presence of mind to tap his brain at the Renault factory, obtaining suggestions that ultimately produced the postwar Renault 4CV. They then locked the 72-year-old Porsche in an unheated Dijon dungeon and demanded a million francs bail.

Ferry Porsche, released in mid-1946, raised the money by signing a contract with Italian Piero Dusio to develop a new Grand Prix Cisitalia. The result was highly advanced, with four-wheel drive, fully synchronized gearbox, and a mid-mounted 1.5-liter supercharged flat 12 producing no less than 385 bhp. Ironically, it would never race, but it did help to bring the elder Porsche home. Ferdinand was later tried in absentia by a French court and acquitted of all charges, but the million-francs ransom was never returned.

Ferdinand Porsche continued working, but war, politics, and betrayals had broken the indomitable spirit that had stood up to countless setbacks and even Adolf Hitler. In November 1950, barely two months after his 75th birthday, he suffered a stroke from which he would not recover. When he died the following January 30, the first sports cars bearing his name were just starting to excite the motoring world.

Their basic design reflected engineering tenets he'd espoused for decades, though their direct predecessor dated only from 1939 (the Type 114 F-Wagen, conceived with Ferry as sporty VW). Though Ferry would produce the first Porsche cars, his father was the true founder of the marque. Today, the great man's spirit lives on in every Porsche ever built.

Ferdinand Porsche was mercurial and at times violently temperamental. He could not abide slipshod engineering—or engineers—and he expressed his dislikes in the bluntest of terms. Yet as David Owen notes, "he was a child" politically. He saw Hitler only as a sponsor, and a useful one at that. He was never a Nazi, and the evidence is that Nazi practices abhorred him. Ironically, he prevented the Gestapo from arresting and probably killing Jean-Pierre Peugeot (after the French Resistance bombed the occupied Peugeot factory), only to be branded a "collaborator" by Peugeot after the war, resulting in needless imprisonment.

Fortunately, Porsche lived long enough to see his two greatest dreams fulfilled: an efficient small car for the masses and an unbeatable competition car. Owen relates that Ferry drove his father to Wolfsburg for a 75th-birthday celebration in September 1950. "On the way [they] passed shoals of VWs crowding the *autobahns*. For [the elder] Porsche, coming at the end of his captivity and illness, it was too much. He broke down and wept. Yet if Porsche was an artist—and he was—he was unusually fortunate. Not many artists are lucky enough to see their work valued at its true worth before they die."

In 1950, Ferdinand Porsche posed with his nephew (and secretary) Ghislaine Kaes during an Alpine road trip taken in a production Volkswagen Type I. Ferdinand died that same year. In 1951, the Porsche team assembled for a portrait; seated from left: designer Erwin Komenda, Ferry Porsche, and technician Karl Rabe. Others are Franz Reihe, Franz Sieberer, Emil Soukup, Leopold Schmid, Leopold Janschke, and Egon Forstner.

Porsche During World War II

Adolf Hitler's "people's car"—a *volkswagen*—began to be developed by Ferdinand Porsche in Stuttgart in 1934. Plans for a production version were shelved with the onset of war five years later, when a prototype dubbed Type 60 was adapted for the military. Porsche was asked to tweak the 26-horse VW engine to allow it to function effectively at high altitudes. The added power was also to be sufficient for the engine to act as a generator, if necessary. Porsche went about the task via supercharging, initially tested by hooking a standard VW engine to a Roots fan, which gave 45-50 horsepower.

The military version of the VW was called the *Kubelwagen*, and while it met the military's powerplant requirements, it lacked 4-wheel-drive and was no match overall for the Allies' jeep. An amphibious variant, the *Schwimmwagen*, was more successful.

After being named an honorary professor by the Technical University of Stuttgart in 1940, Porsche designed the Tiger tank, a 56-ton monster that utilized a gasoline engine running a generator. Porsche also submitted designs for an upgraded variant, the Tiger II, but lost out to the Henschel organization.

Undeterred, Porsche convinced the German military to use his Tiger II chassis as the basis of the *Jagdpanzer Elefant*, a thickly armored tank destroyer fitted with an 88mm cannon. Ninety Elefants were built in 1943.

A year later, Porsche's 180-ton Type 205 *Maus*, a gargantuan rolling gun mount, was unveiled.

Stuttgart came under heavy bombing late in 1944, and the German High Command ordered Porsche and his people to move to Czechoslovakia. Ferry Porsche found two sites in Austria instead, Zell am See and Gmund, where work continued until the arrival of British occupation troops in 1945.

The 356 Chronicle: Beginning a Dynasty

With its Nazi-ordered departure from Zuffenhausen, which was a tempting target for Allied bombs, *Porsche Konstruktionsburo* seemed to have vanished by May 1945. So imagine the surprise of a detachment of British troops entering the sleepy Austrian village of Gmund, where a makeshift Porsche operation—complete with most of the firm's top engineers—was discovered.

Gmund was a useful, out-of-the-way headquarters for the Stuttgart refugees. But the Porsches had decided they could no longer risk keeping all their valuable equipment in one place. Though some tools were shipped to Gmund, others were left in Zuffenhausen or secreted at the family estate at Zell am See, Austria.

The first postwar priority was to get the Porsche business going again, and Ferry threw himself into the task as soon as the French released him from prison in mid-1946. In a 1979 interview with veteran journalist Jan P. Norbye, he recalled, "matters became quite serious for me . . . since it all came down to my own initiative. My father was [still] interned at Dijon. . . ." Ferry's sister, Louise Piech, held things together in the interim, with help from the loyal Karl Rabe.

Yet despite what Ferry termed "very primitive conditions in Gmund," progress was swift. Author Karl Ludvigsen notes, "By December of 1946 the works employed 222 people, 64 more than it had a year earlier. . . . Their total 1946 business volume was 1,319,000 Reichsmarks, only 17 percent less than it had been in 1938." One of the first and most important contracts was the four-wheel-drive Cisitalia GP car, which Ferry used to secure his father's release on August 1, 1947.

Ferry and his father first thought of a sports car based on their Volkswagen as early as 1937, when they devised the Type 64, essentially a VW with a special body and a hotter engine. But the project ran afoul of the convoluted Nazi bureaucracy, so the Porsches tried again the following year. The result was the direct forerunner of the production Porsche, the Type 114 F-Wagen.

An astounding technical achievement, the 114 was largely finalized by transmission specialist Karl Frohlich, with chassis design completed by early 1939. Like the all-conquering Auto Union P-Wagens, its engine sat ahead of the rear axle, with a Frohlich-designed five-speed gearbox behind. But that engine was a complex water-cooled V-10 displacing 1493cc on a bore and stroke of 58.0 X 56.5mm. Typical of Porsche, it had aluminum block and cylinder heads, six main bearings, domed pistons, hemispherical combustion chambers, and a single overhead camshaft per cylinder bank. Magneto ignition was provided for each bank, driven off the intake cams. Three one-barrel downdraft units squeezed within the 72-degree valley provided the carburetion. Radiator and cooling tubes were initially placed up front and later moved to the rear. Suspension was again VW-like, with swing axles, trailing arms, and torsion bars aft; parallel trailing arms and transverse torsion bars at the front—all on a tubular chassis. Unsurprising for a Porsche design, the two-passenger body looked like a teardrop. Wheelbase was initially 106.3 inches, later 108.3.

Three Type 114s with special coupe bodies were built for racing. Designated Type 60K10, they were blessed by *Korpsfuhrer* Huhnlein of the Nazi Motoring Corps (NSKK) after *Herr Doktor* Porsche convinced him to show them off in a special Berlin-Rome road race. The event was scheduled for September 1939—and was thus fated for cancellation in the wake of Hitler's September 1 invasion of Poland. But Ferdinand Porsche used one of these cars, modified for the road, as a daily driver during the early war years, and Ludvigsen records that Porsche's capable chauffeur, Josef Goldinger, once averaged 85 mph on a trip from the VW factory to Berlin.

The Porsches were obviously quite adept at building remarkable sports cars from ordinary components, but it would be left to Ferry to realize the first production Porsche. As he related to *CAR* magazine's Steve Cropley in 1984: "During the war I had an opportunity to drive a supercharged VW convertible with about 50 horsepower, which was a lot of power then. I decided that if you could make a machine which was lighter than that, and still had 50 horsepower, then it would be very sporty indeed."

Ferry and Karl Rabe again turned to a VW-based

Arguably the most coveted body style in Porsche's seminal 356 Series, the racy Speedster bowed in September 1954, just over a year before the original line gave way to improved 356A models. This period photo shows an A-Series version looking a bit incongruous with the whitewall tires that some American owners preferred in those days. The Speedster introduced the one-piece curved windshield that would be featured on 356A coupes and cabriolets. The vertical rearview mirror mounting bar was retained from earlier models.

sports car in 1947. By the time Ferdinand rejoined them in August, they had the specifics firmly on paper. Ferry recalls his father being "very interested . . . of course. He took an interest in everything, but didn't have the energy anymore. . . . I had to assume the risk myself."

What ultimately emerged was Project 356, a smooth, aerodynamic open two-seater with an 85-inch-wheelbase tubular chassis, air-cooled VW engine, and dry weight of about 1300 pounds. The chassis was a sturdy affair, anchored by bulkheads in the cowl and behind the seats that turned inward at each end to connect by hefty transverse tubes.

The chassis was influenced by the Type 114 and Karl Frohlich's Auto Union concepts. As the flat-four was amidships, the VW's rear suspension was reversed so that the transverse torsion bars sat at the back and the trailing arms became leading arms. In theory, this meant wicked oversteer that was reduced by careful attention to weight distribution, which ended up nearly even, and by an ultra-low center of gravity. Front suspension was stock VW, as were steering and the cable-actuated 9-inch-diameter drum brakes. Special Porsche-modified cylinder heads with larger intake valves and ports, plus higher compression (7.0 versus 5.8:1) boosted brake horsepower from 25 (DIN) stock to near 40 (at 4000 rpm). Displacement remained at 1131cc on a 75 X 64mm bore and stroke.

"We built that car only for experience," Ferry recalled in 1984. "It was to see how light we could go and how many VW parts we would need." He and a bright young engineer named Robert Eberan von Eberhorst first tested the running chassis in March 1948 on a natural proving ground not 20 miles from Gmund: the daunting 32-percent grade of the Katshberg Pass. It easily passed every test, confirming that the VW hardware could withstand the most demanding conditions.

Retrospectively known as 356/1, the first prototype Porsche received its aluminum roadster body, designed by longtime Porsche hand Erwin Komenda, in April 1948 and was completed a month later. Smooth and low, with a two-piece unframed windshield, it set the pattern for the future production 356 but had many unique touches. For example, there were no air grilles in back, and engine access was via a long front-hinged lid instead of a small hatch. Behind the engine was room enough for a spare wheel, six-volt battery, and a small amount of luggage. Inside were a rudimentary semi-contoured seat and the only instrument, a speedometer, though a clock was built into the

glovebox at the far right. Up front, the Porsche name was proudly spelled out in letters not unlike those used today.

In all, the 356/1 was attractive, sporty, obviously aerodynamic, and different from anything else on the road. Only one problem surfaced on a shakedown run from Gmund to Zell am See: A rear frame tube bent from pounding the rugged pavement of Grossglockner Pass. With the 356/1 limping into the village, Ferry and his riding engineer fashioned a two-piece metal sleeve to cover the weakened nub, a reinforcement later applied to production 356s. A July showing at Berne in Switzerland earned good reviews from the British and European press. That same month, the 356/1 captured a 1000-1200-cc road race in Innsbruck, Austria—the first of many 356 victories to come.

Next came the 356/2, which historian Ludvigsen determined "was developed in parallel with the space-frame roadster and not as a successor to it, as has often been maintained. Planned in both coupe and cabriolet models, [the 356/2s] differed sharply in design [with] new frame construction, body style and engine position." They were, in fact, the first production Porsches.

And once they appeared, little was heard of the 356/1. Komenda moved closer to the definitive 356 look, while retaining aluminum construction for both body types. The engine now sat firmly behind the rear-wheel centerline, which produced even more oversteer that was only partly countered by reverting to normal mounting for the VW rear suspension.

But of course, these changes were not without rationale. "We felt the mid-mounted engine had little interest for the customer," Ferry explained later. He also believed that even a sports car should have good passenger and luggage space; a more "out of the way" engine provided it within the same overall package size. Besides, "our goal has always been to build cars for normal purposes, that can go on all kinds of roads and in all weathers"—hence, the beetle-like fastback coupe.

Backed by encouraging good-faith orders from Swiss enthusiast-businessmen R. von Senger and Bernhard Blank, *Porsche Konstruktionen GmbH* planned to build 50 Type 356/2 chassis, of which 10 would have coupe bodies. Publicity brochures announced the coupe at $3750, the cabrio at $4250—stiff pricing for the time. Americans could buy two 1947 Chevys with that money, and VWs sold in Germany for about half as much.

But the issue of hefty price tags was very nearly moot, for Gmund couldn't turn out many cars very

The direct progenitor of the first production Porsche was the "356/2" coupe (top, and middle row), of which four were built in 1948 at the fledgling firm's facilities in Gmund, Austria. A distinctive "beetle" shape and an air-cooled rear-mounted engine betrayed design origins in Ferdinand Porsche's Volkswagen, but would fast become familiar to sports-car devotees the world over. The very first car to bear the Porsche name was the "356/1" (bottom row), a true mid-engine design completed in April 1948 but also based on VW components. Essentially a prototype for the production 356, it wore a smooth aluminum body with unframed windshield designed by Erwin Komenda. After Ferry Porsche proved its inherent ruggedness on a mountain shakedown drive, the car won a road race at Innsbruck in July— the first in the long skein of Porsche victories that continues to this day.

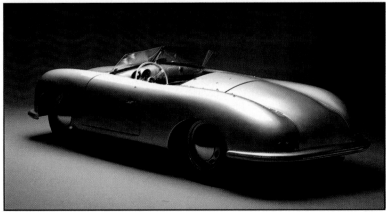

quickly. Only four 356/2s were built in 1948—all by hand— then 25 the next year and 18 in 1950. By spring 1951, just 51 had been sold. But then, as Ferry Porsche later declared, "It seems almost a miracle to me that we managed to build [cars] in Gmund. . . ." The coupe/cabriolet breakdown has been variously quoted as 45/5 and 42/8; the latter seems more likely, as six cabrios bodied by Beutler of Switzerland are known.

Most of these early Porsches were sold by the aforementioned Bernhard Blank, a successful Zurich dealer. A few had a bore of 73.5mm, instead of 75mm, to keep displacement below 1100cc for class racing purposes. Historians doubt the published 7.0:1 compression ratio; 6.5:1 is more like it. But it's interesting that the Porsche was at least as economical as a VW, maybe more so. Despite its piddling 40 bhp, the 1300-pound curb weight and slippery body allowed near 90 mph all out with economy (according to contemporary road tests) of no less than 27 mpg—and usually closer to 35. (Testers commonly reported 30 mpg at a 70-mph cruise.) This unusual frugality would characterize later roadgoing Porsches capable of far higher speeds.

As noted, most 356/2 cabrios were bodied by Beutler in Thun, near Berne, using bare chassis shipped from Gmund. These were slightly longer than the coupes, undoubtedly the coachbuilder's doing. The last one was delivered in August 1949.

As months passed and word spread about the Porsche, a minor sales demand developed. Rabe had promised 150 units by the end of 1948, but conditions just wouldn't allow it. Bodies, for instance, had to be hand-hammered over wooden forms. Engines varied slightly from car to car because everything was in such short supply. Still, the ledgers were being written in black, even if the numbers weren't large.

Seeking firmer footing for his company, Ferry Porsche concluded a multifaceted deal in September 1948 with VW's Heinz Nordhoff, whom the British had installed to lead the rebuilding effort at Wolfsburg (which fell within the British zone of the new postwar West Germany). The Porsche organization agreed on a new license for the VW design, as well as on a consulting contract that reestablished the prewar Porsche/VW relationship. Additionally, Porsche became the import agency for Austria, gaining favored status on delivery of VW parts used in its own cars. Finally, Porsche enjoyed joint use of the worldwide VW sales organizations. All of this, Ferry noted, "was the basis for our fresh start." The Marshall Plan and subsequent recovery of the German economy would do the rest.

Suddenly, the village of Gmund posed a thorny problem: It was too small, too remote, and completely removed from the car-building heart of industrial Germany. Porsche needed to return to Zuffenhausen. Trouble was, the Americans had been using the old Porsche premises for military motor pools. But when the GIs reluctantly agreed to leave in mid-1950, Porsche began preparing to close up at Gmund and move back home.

The decision was not made lightly. VW work was Porsche's bread-and-butter then; sports cars were but a hobby by comparison. Conceivably, Porsche viewed returning to Zuffenhausen as a tax write-off against earnings from VW. But sports cars were more fun than people's cars, and there was no question of designing tanks or any other new military hardware. The one fly in this ointment was a big one: Production start-up in Stuttgart would be far costlier than any likely amount of VW income could cover.

The problem was solved when Alfred Prinzing, Ferry's wily business manager, took a Porsche coupe on a tour of Germany's main VW distributors and returned with orders totaling DM200,000. Adding that to VW receipts gave Porsche at least a fighting chance. Thus, by April 1950, Porsche was building cars in Zuffenhausen.

"We signed a contract with Reutter to build bodies for the 500 cars we planned to start with," Ferry Porsche recalled 29 years later. "Since Reutter had no experience with welding light alloy, we had to change to steel for the coupe. We had only perhaps $50,000 on hand to start production and never dreamed we would eventually reach . . . 78,000 of the 356-model cars."

Reutter Karosserie was right next door, which was a stroke of good fortune. Porsche had to rent 5000 square feet of the coachbuilder's plant for chassis fabrication and final assembly because its own factory wasn't immediately usable. A short time later, Porsche bought a nearby 1100-square-foot building for administrative offices and design space. The company soon changed its name again, to *Dr. Ing.-h.c. F. Porsche KG* (*KG* denoting the German term for limited partnership).

"Having Reutter nearby was a great advantage for us," Ferry said later. "In those days, chassis and body construction were far more separated than they are today. Later we took over the Reutter firm so that we could build the bodies, which are the most expensive part of an automobile, ourselves."

In preparation for an ambitious tenfold production boost, Komenda revised the 356/2 coupe and

Porsche built just 25 cars in 1949 and a mere 18 in 1950, by which time the 356 had progressed to this definitive early form. Differences from the "356/2" include lack of door vent windows and generally smoother contours. This particular car, part of the Porsche Museum collection and shown in restored original condition, was one of the first built in Stuttgart following Porsche's return to its hometown in 1950. It was nicknamed "Ferdinand" by company hands because it was given to Dr. Ferdinand Porsche for his 75th birthday on September 3, 1950. Though he passed away five months later, his namesake 356 spent the next eight years covering nearly 400,000 kilometers as a test bed for later production-model features like radial tires, rack-and-pinion steering, and even the first of the high-performance Carrera engines.

cabriolet into the now-familiar shape of what was simply called the 356. The windshield remained divided but was enlarged; side-window area was reduced via a higher beltline; and vent wings were eliminated. An oil temperature gauge appeared inside, and the clock moved from the glovebox to beside the speedometer. A gas gauge was still lacking, though, as Porsche relied on VW's reserve-tank system and its thoroughly un-modern measuring device, a wooden dipstick.

The engine was still the 40-bhp (DIN) Type 369 air-cooled flat-four but now with twin carburetors (Solex 32 PBI). Chassis changes followed those of the 1950 VW, which meant hydraulic shock absorbers (in steel towers) and hydraulic drum brakes. The latter proved inadequate in the Porsche and thus gave way by 1951 to twin-leading-shoe Lockheed front drums supplied by the German Alfred Teves company (Ate). At the same time, the previous lever-arm rear shocks were replaced with modern tubular units.

Porsche completed its first Stuttgart car on Good Friday 1950 and never looked back. Deliveries were underway by April, with the coupe priced at DM9950 (about $2030). By midyear, sales were 33 a month, versus the eight or nine projected in the Reutter contract. By year's end, sales totaled 298. Sadly, the great Dr. Ferdinand Porsche died in late January 1951, but he did live long enough to see the rapid progress of the cars and company that bore his name. By the time of his passing, the factory's claimed output was 60 a month.

Meantime, Porsches were gradually getting into the hands of non-German testers, who would presumably render the harshest verdicts. But the folks in Zuffenhausen needn't have worried. Consider this excerpt from Britain's weekly *The Autocar* in April 1951: "Even a short run serves to give the characteristic impression of a really well streamlined car. The acceleration above 50 mph is quite beyond what would be expected from the engine size, and is achieved in extraordinary quietness. About 60 mph is available in third gear. . . . It is a rare car these days in which the designer has gone all out for certain qualities . . . and has accepted certain disadvantages instead of trying to achieve a well-balanced mediocrity. . . . It is not a car for everyone's taste, but it offers a unique combination of comfort, performance and economy, for which some people will pay a very good price."

That same month at the Frankfurt Automobile Show, Porsche introduced the 356/1 and 356/3, its first 1300-cc models. Their new engine—precisely 1286cc (78.5 cubic inches) on a bore and stroke of

80.0 X 64mm (3.14 X 2.52 inches)—was a bored-out Type 369 with aluminum instead of cast-iron cylinders, chrome plated on their working surfaces for greater durability. The 369's compression may be disputed, but this Type 506 engine definitely ran 6.5:1. This plus the extra displacement, it was claimed, lifted horsepower to 44 (DIN) at the same 4200 rpm. Reflecting Porsche's traditional concern for craftsmanship, each engine was assembled by a single worker, a job that took 25 hours.

More modest compression made the 1300 engine more amenable to Europe's low-grade fuel than the 1100 version, yet performance actually improved slightly by about 2-3 mph, to 92 mph all out, according to factory records. Also announced at Frankfurt as across-the-board changes were improved defrosting, an optional tachometer, and the new VW-based suspension, tube shocks, and Lockheed-Ate brakes. In all, the 1300 was a step forward that helped it earn more good marks from the press.

Volume began taking off in 1951. Porsche completed its 1000th Stuttgart car on August 28, and that year's 1103 total units earned the company a $3 million profit. Though not widely known at the time, Porsches were built in Gmund through March 1951, after which production centered solely in Zuffenhausen.

A small part of 1951 revenue came from the United States, home of hard currency, the bigger-is-better philosophy, and many well-heeled buyers. Much of this Stateside sales activity was owed to Max Hoffman, the veritable godfather of postwar America's import-car business, who in 1950 added Porsche to the select nameplates displayed at his Park Avenue showroom.

Hoffman was dubious at first, perhaps because some customers thought the 356 curious: small and "funny," yet as costly as a Lincoln. But he had a weakness for Porsches, being Austrian-born and a great admirer of Ferry and his father. Hoffman had brought the VW to America, selling two in 1949 before giving up the franchise—one of his greatest mistakes, he later admitted. But Hoffman did sell Porsches—up to 10 a week by 1954. He later acknowledged that sales—and his own opinion—rose considerably in 1953, when Porsche dumped the VW-based "crashbox" for its own four-speed synchromesh transmission.

This gearbox stemmed from a design patented in 1947 and conceived for the GP Cisitalia. Gear synchronization was its most unique feature, accomplished by intermediate servo rings instead of conventional cones. Each pinion had a servo ring

One of the rarest and most coveted of early 356 models, the America roadster (top) was instigated in 1952 by U.S. Porsche distributor Max Hoffman as a lighter, simpler open model than the standard Reutter-built cabriolet. Glaser supplied a more rakish body rendered in aluminum instead of steel. The cockpit (lower left) was predictably more Spartan that of other 356s; the normal divided windshield could be replaced by a low, racing windscreen. Power (lower right) came from the then-new 1500 Super version of Porsche's air-cooled flat-four with 55 initial horsepower, soon upped to 60. Unfortunately, costly construction and high price—a steep $4600—limited demand. Just four Americas were built in all of '52, and production ended the following year at between 20 and 50 units total (experts disagree on the exact number).

revolving with it at equal speed; as a shift was made, the appropriate servo ring matched the clutch ring's rate of rotation to that of the rear output shaft. The result was quicker shifts, owing to the shorter gear braking/acceleration time. The arrangement was also more compact. Synchromesh was eventually extended to all Porsches, and other carmakers were quick to copy the design of this superior system, including Alfa Romeo, BMW, Ferrari, even Daimler-Benz (beginning with the racing 300SLR of 1952).

If the 1100/1300 could perform well while sipping tiny amounts of fuel, why not a 1500? Porsche began work on it in mid-1950 once 1500cc became the upper displacement limit for several racing classes. Moreover, it seemed an ideal size for a small, light sports car like the 356.

Since the 1100 had been bored to get 1300cc, it was logical to lengthen stroke to achieve 1500. The Hirth company of Stuttgart devised a connecting rod compact enough to allow a 10-mm increase (to 74), giving 1488cc. Hirth also supplied a new crankshaft with roller bearings, which reduced friction but soon had Max Hoffman and others complaining about durability. Prolonged low-rpm running or delayed oil changes most always led to early crank failure. Avoiding it was as easy as reading the owner's manual—which, of course, not everyone did. Interestingly, the 1488-cc engine began the practice of "keeping the revs up" that many Porschephiles (especially 911 owners) happily perpetuate, even though it's long been unnecessary.

Initially, the 1500 used the small twin carbs and developed 55 bhp (DIN) at 4500 rpm. However, only 66 of these Type 502 engines were built before Porsche switched to a Type 547 derivative with Solex 40BPI instruments and 60 bhp (the smaller carbs could be fitted if desired). The original Solex 32s reflected caution on Porsche's part rather than engineering error. The company felt the gearbox might not be up to the extra power, but the new all-synchro transmission ended that concern.

A squad of 356s, 1100s, and 1500s, went to Monthléry, France's huge banked oval track for some speed-record attempts in September 1951. All performed brilliantly. The 1100s set three new marks, averaging over 100 mph for 500 miles, 1000 kilometers, and six hours. The 1500s, including a mildly modified car from Volkswagen dealer Walter Glockner, broke no fewer than 14 records. The factory car raised official averages to over 97 mph for 3000, 4000, and 5000 kilometers; 2000, 3000, and 4000 miles; and 24 and 48 hours. It also averaged 95.75 mph for 10,000 kilometers and 94.6

mph for 72 hours. The "Glockler," a streamlined roadster, ran 500 and 1000 kilometers and the six hours at 114-116 mph, breaking three more records. The 72-hour mark came despite a disabled top gear that forced drivers to run in third at 90 mph with the engine whirling at a busy 4500 rpm. It was a tremendous performance that conclusively proved the 356's mettle.

Ferdinand Porsche once said it makes no difference where a car's engine is located, so long as it's light. The 1500 unit weighed a mere 160 pounds, while early 356s rarely exceeded 1750 pounds at the curb. Fore/aft weight balance was around 780/970 pounds, but this wasn't the drawback it might seem. In unofficial tests conducted by an unnamed Southern California aircraft company, the 356 body generated 175 pounds of front aerodynamic downforce that effectively equalized weight distribution.

Balance of another kind impressed editor Dick von Osten of America's *Auto* magazine during a test of a Porsche 356/1500: "The top-speed runs were made with two different drivers on a level, measured quarter-mile at sea level. I expected to clock slightly over 100 mph, [but I] reached that figure with no apparent effort and kept on going. [We] both managed to hit the maximum speed of 111.1 mph on both an east and west run. Five mph were probably added to the top speed by the perfect wheel balance, a typical detail of this car: all Porsches come from the factory with the wheels and tires in a perfect state of dynamic and static balance. Dr. Porsche once said that . . . wheel balance can add or subtract 500 engine rpm at top speed." (Incidentally, von Osten's reported maximum speed was 15 mph above the factory claim and indicative of the conservatism that marks official Porsche performance figures even today.)

Despite the more-powerful engine, fuel economy was hardly affected. Von Osten covered 329 miles (75 in city traffic) on one tankful, including top speed, acceleration, and braking tests, plus a 70-75 mph highway run. All this required just 11 gallons of gas for an overall average of close to 33 mpg. With figures like these, you wonder if we've learned all that much in the last 45 years.

Significantly, von Osten was also taken with his test Porsche's "unmistakeable quality. From the gentle 'click' of the door to its smooth paint, from the handling ease to the engine's performance, the Porsche reflects genius in design and pride in craftsmanship. . . . Although it is not a low-priced car (approximately $4284 for the coupe and $4560 for the convertible), it is a car to which every

Prefiguring both the America and the Speedster, this one-of-a-kind 356 roadster (top) was built in 1951 by a small shop near Stuttgart for Heinrich Sauter, a young Porsche enthusiast. Besides a then-new 1300 engine enlarged to 1.5 liters, the two-seater had a steel body with rear-hinged doors (note the front-mount door handles) and a racing windscreen, which suggested its intent. Alas, the car did not do well for either Sauter or French racing driver Francois Picard, who later owned it and called it "le petit tank." Thoughts of a larger 356 (middle left) surfaced as early as 1952 in a pair of experimental 2+2s dubbed Type 530. This coupe and a similar cabriolet were built with mild 1.5-liter engines and an extended 94.5-inch wheelbase (same as the VW Beetle's), but "marketing and technical reasons" precluded production. Another look at the 1952-53 America roadster (bottom left) shows its distinctive dipped beltline. Karl Rabe (right) was the brilliant engineer and longtime friend of the Porsche family who figured as much as Ferry Porsche in the 356's considered development.

owner can point with pride. . . ."

Even in these early days, the 356 reflected the Porsches' belief in the perfectability of a given design—provided it was good to begin with. By mid-1952 all 356s wore a one-piece windshield (albeit with a vertical central bend), perforated disc wheels, and deeper bodywork beneath the bumpers. A large 6000-rpm tachometer replaced the clock, and both it and the speedo were newly hooded for better legibility.

The ultimate developments of the original 356 were the 1300S and 1500S—"S" for Super. The latter came first, in October 1952. Its new Type 528 powerplant had the same displacement as the 502/507 but ran 8.2:1 compression, good for a rated 70 DIN horsepower and 80 pounds/feet of torque at 3600 rpm. That torque peak hinted at Porsche's intentions—production-class racing—and the Super was inevitably less powerful below 3500 rpm than the normal 1500. Both the 1500S and 1300S (announced in November '53; same CR, 60 bhp) benefited from a revised camshaft designed by future Porsche chairman Ernst Fuhrmann, a Gmund engineer who'd been involved with the GP Cisitalia. The factory assigned the 1300S an official top speed of 100 mph, the 1500S 105 mph. But again, the evidence is that these were conservative claims.

Perhaps the most important of the early 1500 Supers was the America, a rakish roadster with aluminum bodywork by Glaser, marked by an ultra-low beltline. Though almost unknown in Europe, it was hardly familiar in the United States either, thanks to a lofty $4600 price.

Like many of the more-interesting Fifties imports, the America sprang from the fertile mind of Max Hoffman, who wanted a lighter open Porsche without the heavy top and side windows of the standard cabrio. Of course, he had racing in mind, and so the America was designed with weight-saving touches that prevented overall weight from exceeding 1600 pounds. These features included light aluminum-frame seats, Plexiglas side curtains, thin snap-on canvas roof, no glovebox door, and a divided windshield that could be replaced by a racing windscreen. With all this, the America was even more exciting than the regular 1500S. *Auto Age* magazine's test showed a 110-mph top speed, 0-60 mph in 9.3 seconds, and the standing quarter-mile in 17.9 seconds.

Regrettably, not many Americas were built, largely because of *how* they were built. Reutter sent rolling chassis to Glaser in Ullersricht, north of Munich, where artisans hand-hammered the aluminum bodywork and welded it to the chassis. The semi-finished cars were then trucked back to Zuffenhausen for final assembly. Only four were sold in the United States in all of 1952, and production ended the following year. One Porsche expert puts the total built at 20, another at 50. Regardless, the America remains a rare and highly collectible Porsche. A seemingly limited market and high production costs (aggravated by transportation expense) condemned it to an early grave, though it would not be forgotten.

A literal symbol of Porsche's progress marked the 1953 models: the now-famous Porsche crest. This, too, was prompted by Max Hoffman, who thought all cars should wear emblems. He suggested it while lunching in New York one day with Ferry, who quickly sketched out a bit of heraldry on a napkin. As finalized by freelance graphic designer Eric Strenger (who at the same time developed the Porsche logotype still used today), it bore the Stuttgart coat of arms: a rampant black horse on a yellow shield representing an old part of the city (*Stuotgarten*) where a stud farm had once been; surrounding this were the colors and six staghorns from the crest of the state of Baden-Wurttemburg.

Other Porsche changes for 1953 were more obvious. Parking lamps moved inboard to beneath the headlamps, taillamps became circular pairs on each side instead of circle/oblong duos, and a separate trip odometer joined the total mileage recorder. Engines stayed essentially the same. The 1500 Super gave up its Hirth crank for one of forged steel, as Rabe was able to shorten the original rod design by making a diagonal cut across the big end, thus leaving adequate clearance for the longer stroke. The 1500 Normal had 6.5:1 compression and only 55 bhp at 4400 rpm, but the factory claimed that good for 96 mph all out. It was an ideal foil for the 1500S as it was more tractable at lower speeds and thus better for everyday driving. All these engines (except the 1100, which vanished after 1954) were available in coupe or Cabriolet, and would run through 1955.

Only the 1500s came to the United States in '53, where the Normal was called *America* and attractively priced at $3445 for the coupe and $3695 for the cabrio—the most affordable Porsches yet. (The upmarket Supers listed at $4284 and $4584.) Maxie had struck again, but he wasn't offering an entirely free lunch, for he had Porsche delete the reclining seatbacks, wheel trims, the fold-down provision for the vestigial back seat, the radio, passenger-side sunvisor, and the tachometer, all standard on European 1500s.

A 1953-model 356 cabriolet poses with its immediate predecessor to show that year's minor styling alterations, which included parking lamps mounted a bit inboard of the headlights and a new Porsche crest on the chrome hood spear. The latter was suggested by U.S. importer Max Hoffman, who thought all cars should wear emblems. Ferry Porsche sketched the basic heraldry, but it was finalized by freelancer Eric Strenger, who also rendered the basic Porsche logotype still used today. Engines were carried over from 1952: basic 1100 (dropped after '54) and 1300 and 1500 in Normal and top-power Super tune.

Porsche passed a production milestone on March 15, 1954, with Zuffenhausen car number 5000, which nearly coincided with another batch of running changes. Parking lamps now sat within tiny grilles that, despite their size, efficiently channeled cooling air to the brakes and opened up hooting space for new twin Bosch horns. Inside were a semicircular, Detroit-style horn ring, passenger grab handle and instrument-lighting rheostat. A windshield washer and oil filter were also adopted.

Porsche's big event of 1954 arrived in September: the charming, sporty Speedster. It was still another bit of marketing magic from Max Hoffman, who, despite his experience with the '52 America, didn't think U.S. demand for roadsters was quite so limited—and that an inexpensive model should be a permanent part of the Porsche line.

The Speedster was actually evolved from the Glaser-built America, and even had the same Type number (540), but was designed by Reutter for minimum production cost. For example, it used the regular cabriolet body but had none of its accoutrements. Like the America, the Speedster arrived with only a simple canvas top and side curtains instead of a built-in padded top and roll-up door windows, though its windshield was cut about 3½ inches shorter for extra raffishness. The cockpit was as Spartan as a Triumph TR2's. Seats were simple buckets with fixed backrests. Instrumentation was limited to speedo, tach, and temperature gauge; technically, the tach and heater were extras, but it was hard to find a car without them, so they were effectively "mandatory options" that pushed the typical delivered price over $3000. But Hoffman realized his target base price of $2995 POE (Port of Entry) New York.

Exterior appearance was standard Porsche from the waist down save the aesthetically pleasing, nearly full-length bodyside chrome strips that ran neatly through the door handles. Still, the Speedster was invariably likened to an inverted bathtub, and it looked a bit bizarre buttoned up.

Not surprisingly, the 1500 Normal engine was standard for the Speedster, but the Super spec was available for about $500 more. Speedsters weren't immediately sold in Europe but were well received in the United States. After an exploratory 200-unit run for 1954, the factory increased output. By the time the last one was delivered in 1958, the total exceeded 4900.

Visually, the 1954 and '55 Speedsters were quite similar, the differences confined mainly to gauges, bonnet handle, and emblems. Like all 356s since the first, they rolled on 16-inch-diameter wheels and tires.

The Speedster seemed born to race and was certainly quick enough for it. The base model weighed nearly 200 pounds less than a 1500N coupe and was thus about a second faster in the 0-60 mph sprint, though superior aerodynamics let the coupe pull away after about 80 mph. The 1500S version was commensurately faster but could not catch its coupe counterpart at the top end. Comparing Super and Normal Speedsters, respective 0-60 mph times were 10 and 14 seconds; figures for the standing quarter-mile were 17.5 seconds at 100 mph versus 19 seconds at 95 mph.

Of course, being Porsches, the Speedsters *did* race, and with distinction. John von Neumann, Porsche's West-Coast counterpart to Max Hoffman, started running them in SCCA events in November 1954, when his 1500S finished eighth overall in a six-hour enduro at Torrey Pines, near San Diego, and won its class the following day. In 1955, Bengt Sonderstrom drove one to win the national SCCA F-Production championship.

Walt Woron waxed enthusiastic after testing a Speedster for the July 1955 issue of *Motor Trend*: "Its size, power, easy shift and steering make it fun to drive. . . . The brakes are extremely good . . . they get you out of situations where you may have delayed too long. . . . For a sports car, and especially such a small one, the Porsche Speedster has a very smooth ride. . . . There's absolutely no wallowing when it comes out of a dip. . . ."

Like most drivers, Woron felt slightly claustrophobic in the Speedster. "With the top up . . . you have to jackknife in; the top is extremely low [overall height was a mere 48 inches] and if you're over six feet, your head is going to touch. It doesn't leave much room between the top and doors for seeing out; and with the side curtains on, you may as well be content with just looking forward."

Though rudimentary next to the cabrio roof, the Speedster top was high-tech next to the Erector-set affairs of British contemporaries. "Putting up the soft top is absurdly easy," said Woron. "You reach behind you, grab the top's forward bow, pull forward so that it reaches the windshield and snap the two locks in place." He also noted that Reutter had managed to sneak a little padding between the top's inner and outer layers, an advance unknown in darkest Coventry.

Summing up the Speedster's appeal, Woron rhetorically asked, "Where else are you going to get a sports car that has the performance, the ride and the workmanship of this one? . . . Sure, it lacks certain features like roll-up windows, but if . . . you

Porsche production rose fairly fast in the early Fifties. After completing its 1000th Stuttgart car in August 1951, the firm rolled out number 5000 (lower right) less than three years later in March 1954. Just as newsworthy was the September arrival of the natty Speedster (top), another Max Hoffman idea engineered by body builder Reutter to sell for much less than Maxie's '52 America—initially $2995 POE. An abbreviated windshield limited top-up head room, and the car looked a bit bizarre buttoned up, but critics loved the Speedster, which soon proved its mettle in competition. Appropriately, cockpit furnishings (middle left) were less lavish than on other 356s, but U.S. models were sold with tachometer and heater as "mandatory options" that pushed delivered price above $3000. Another $500 replaced the standard 60-bhp 1500 Normal engine with the 70-bhp Super unit. The original 356 line closed out in 1955 (coupe shown, bottom left) with engines that were more uniquely Porsche yet more reliable and easier to service.

drive for the fun of driving, you'll *love* this one."

Soon after the Speedster's debut, Porsche introduced a wholesale engine revamp for 1955. Though the 1100 was dropped, the four remaining units became "/2" types (for example, 546/2 and 528/2 for the 1500 Normal and Super). Among the changes: improved valvegear, strengthened castings, virtually square cylinder dimensions on 1300s (74.5 X 74.0mm), and three-piece, 4.5-liter aluminum sumps (replacing two-piece, 3.5-liter magnesium types).

The "/2" engines put further distance between Porsche and VW engineering, being designed for easier servicing and quicker camshaft swapping under race conditions. Though fewer parts interchanged with VW's, that was okay with Ferry Porsche. His cars were rapidly becoming more specialized and thus increasingly removed from their humble origins, marking his firm's emergence as a manufacturer in its own right and, no less important, reducing its reliance on VW components. Porsche didn't make much of these changes (indeed, they're listed mainly in factory documents), but they reflected the continual quest for perfection that remains a fact of life at Zuffenhausen.

There was one other change for '55. Again at Hoffman's behest, U.S. models were called *Continental* that year—and that year only, because Lincoln owned the name and was about to bring out its new Continental Mark II.

The Autocar captured much of the early Porsche essence in its November 1953 test of a 1500: "By virtue of its very low build and fine aerodynamic lines it attracts immediate attention and interest from young and old. It is so obviously a car designed by [those] who knew what they wanted and were able to carry out their ideas. Its very appearance suggests speed, and as soon as one is seated . . . any desire to loiter is quickly [forgotten]. The Porsche [holds the road] in no uncertain manner, the soft torsion-bar springing allowing it to hurry round main road corners without roll, while the rather direct steering gives the driver exact control over the front wheels."

Atypically, the editors admitted to extending their seat time simply because the 1500 was so much fun: "The high top gear makes cruising effortless, with an indicated 75-80 on the speedometer. One can imagine the car being thoroughly at home storming Alpine passes, where the admirable third gear and also second could be used to advantage. At night there is the impression of being in an aircraft cockpit, with the close curved windscreen and discreet lighting from the fascia,

the suspension ironing out any sudden undulations in the road surface and no squeal being evident from the tyres [sic] when cornering fast. There is a feeling of rushing through space with the road disappearing rapidly immediately in front and the subdued beat of the engine from the rear." That was about as lyrical as the conservative British weekly ever got.

As the final '55s came off the line, Porsche could look back on a successful quarter century. The company had certainly come far since the great Ferdinand opened the doors on Kronenstrasse in 1930. Calendar-year production was a satisfying 2952 units. Even more important, Porsche was back in its original premises, restored by the West German government on December 1. But though few would have believed it, even greater things lay ahead.

They began with 1956 models that looked little different at first glance but actually represented a thorough update. Per established Porsche custom, the new 356A bowed at the Frankfurt Show, in September 1955, entering production a few weeks later.

Coupe, cabrio, and Speedster body styles continued (again supplied exclusively by Reutter), but styling was subtly altered. Most obvious were slim rocker rub rails and a one-piece curved windshield without a vertical crease. The Speedster's windshield and top-frame bows rose about 2½ inches to improve headroom (a running change actually made in mid-1955). Less noticeable, but a key chassis improvement, was a switch from 16- to 15-inch-diameter wheels with a new "super-wide" 4.5-inch breadth. Tires were correspondingly fatter: 5.60 X 15s versus 5.00 X 16s.

Inside, the all-metal center-bulge dash of yore gave way to a new flat-face panel with padded top and, Speedsters excepted, a radio mounting slot. Ahead of and readily visible through the steering wheel were a large central tachometer flanked by an equal-size speedometer on the left and a combination fuel level/oil temperature gauge on the right. Headlight flashers were standard, again Speedsters excepted, and handbrakes were more conveniently located. Entry/exit and front legroom improved via a 1½-inch lower floor, and the ignition switch gained a starter detent. Car for car, more thorough sound insulation in strategic places made A-models quieter than 356s.

The A also sported major revisions to the now-familiar 356 chassis that stemmed from a prototype (nicknamed "Ferdinand" after the elder Dr. Porsche) used for testing since 1954. Suspension

Bulky "top stacks" are a familiar feature of German convertibles, and Porsche's 356 cabriolet is no exception, as seen on this circa-1954 example (top). But the bulkiness here only reflects full padding and lining that make for unusually comfortable top-up motoring (lower left). The Porsche company observed its Silver Anniversary in 1955. A U.S.-trim cabrio (lower right) displays the "Continental" badges worn by all American-market 356s that year—and that year only, as Ford Motor Company "owned" the name and would use it on a new 1956 Mark II hardtop. Rocker rub strips also appeared on 1955 U.S. 356s, prefiguring a style point of the following year's heavily revised A-Series.

Porsche's race-bred 1500GS Carrera engine bowed with the 356A Series in September 1955. This Speedster (top and above) is so equipped— and all the more desirable for it. The 356 coupe looked better than ever in A-Series form (left). A new one-piece curved windshield made it easier to see out of. Chrome wheels with center-lock hubs (opposite page) remained optional for 356As.

was modified for more travel, and a softer ride was achieved by removing leaves from the laminated front torsion bars and by making the rear bars both longer (from 21.8 to 24.7 inches) and thinner (by 1mm, to 24). These changes and the chunkier rolling stock were found to improve roadholding. Shock absorbers were suitably stiffened and repositioned, the rears mounted vertically instead of angled. Up front, suspension mounts were beefed up and a stiffer, thicker anti-roll bar appeared. Outer suspension-arm bearings changed to the needle-roller type. Steering geometry was altered and a small hydraulic damper was added to absorb road shock and reduce kickback through the wheel. While the chassis tuning definitely aided ride, roadability was unaffected, so a 356A feels considerably more modern than a 356.

Road & Track described the A as "an impressive combination of control and true riding comfort. The inbuilt oversteer, an old story to those who know Porsches well, can still make the novice a little jumpy until he is sure just what the car is going to do. Then he will find himself hunting up sharp curves for the sheer pleasure of being in control of so exceptionally maneuverable a car."

Inevitably, Porsche also improved its flat-four engines, which now numbered five: 1300 Normal and Super, a new 1600N and 1600S, and the 1500GS. Only the last three came to America. All were available in the three body styles save a nonexistent 1300N Speedster. They remained air-cooled, of course, and all but the 1500GS retained overhead valves actuated by pushrods and rocker arms. The GS was nothing less than a detuned version of the twincam 550 Spyder unit from Porsche's 1954 sports-racing model—the heart of the soon-to-be-legendary Carreras that were sufficiently different to warrant separate coverage at the end of this chapter.

The brace of 1.6-liters was prompted by a new 1600-cc competition limit. The engines were created by simply fitting larger cylinder barrels that widened bore on the existing 1500 block by 2.5mm, giving bore/stroke of 82.5 X 74mm and precisely 1582cc. Higher compression yielded 60 DIN horsepower (70 SAE) at 4500 rpm for the Type 616/1 Normal engine; the 616/2 Super delivered 76 bhp (DIN) at 5000 rpm (88 bhp SAE). With their extra cc's, both mustered more low-end torque for even better tractability at low and midrange speeds. Incidentally, transaxles received longer-lasting mounts, and the clutch was redesigned.

Motor-noters generally judged the 1600 better behaved than previous Porsches. It responded,

said Britain's *Autocar,* "more like an orthodox high-performance sports car, although a certain skittishness at the rear, partly attributable to the the swing-axle rear suspension, can still be felt. . . . Stability remains very good indeed, and the design as a whole gives a liveliness to the controls of which the skilled driver can take advantage."

Porsche's workforce continued to grow, but so did output per worker. Yet there was no compromise in the by-now-famous Porsche workmanship. The Germans' painstaking attention to detail must have been as mind-boggling to the British as it was to Americans, perhaps more so. For example, all steering mechanisms were run-in "on the bench," lock-to-lock, for the equivalent of 5000 kilometers. Trim, upholstery, and paint were a noticeable cut above the norm even for Porsche's price class.

The Autocar made this conclusion: "The superbly controllable Porsche brings back to motoring some of the joy that those privileged to drive sports cars in the earlier spacious days must have experienced. At the wheel one feels to be one up on the other fellow in all the things that matter in driving for its own sake. The imposition of duty and purchase tax make the total price formidable for British buyers [and Americans, at $5300 for the 1600 coupe] but the car remains, nonetheless, highly desirable."

Having made such a long leap, Porsche was content to let the 356A carry into 1957 unchanged, then made some detail refinements in the spring of that year. The speedometer exchanged places with the combination gauge, the four round taillights gave way to horizontal teardrop types, the license plate/backup-lamp bar moved from above to below the plate, and padded sun visors became standard.

Evolution was again the watchword on the '58 models, designated T-2. Vent wings appeared in cabriolet doors, and coupes could sprout extra-cost windwings on the outside of their window frames. Exhaust tips on all models now poked through the lower part of the vertical rear bumper guards, and a double-bow front bumper overrider replaced the former single-bow design. Larger rear windows improved top-up vision in Speedster and cabriolet, and both open models were offered from late '57 with a lift-off fiberglass top as a factory option (made by Brendel in Germany for Europe, Glasspar in California for America). Though controversial, that Cadillac-style exhaust routing was practical in that it better protected the tips and raised exhaust-system ground clearance.

On the mechanical front, the 1300 engines were

The 1956 Speedster naturally shared the improvements accorded that year's revised 356A coupe and cabriolet, including new 1.6-liter pushrod engines, 15-inch rolling stock, modified suspension, better leg room and entry/exit, more sound insulation, and a new flat-face dash with central tachometer. The Speedster windshield remained unique, but was slightly taller for a bit more head clearance with the top in use. As before, that was skimpier than the normal cabriolet roof, though that meant neater folding for a smoother top-down look.

dropped, the 1600s reverted to plain bearings, and cast-iron cylinders returned on the 1600 Normal to reduce both cost and noise for what was basically a touring Porsche. Carburetors were now Zenith NDIX devices. A Hausserman diaphragm clutch replaced the coil-spring Fitchel & Sachs unit, and the shift linkage was reworked for shorter throws. The old worm-and-peg VW steering gave way to a Ross-type mechanism by ZF and, from late '58, progressively wound single valve springs replaced dual springs in all pushrod engines.

Along the way, Porsche also instituted better door locks, a one-piece aluminum transaxle (ousting cast magnesium), redesigned oil coolers and, for the 1600N, offset-wristpin pistons (to eliminate cold-engine piston slap) and fiber camshaft gears. Later came racing-homologated gear ratios and a 5.17:1 final drive. Convenience and appearance were served by repositioned heater controls, new outside door handles and inside window winders, revised rear package shelf, optional gasoline heater, slim-back bucket seats, larger-diameter steering wheel, and new hubcaps bearing the Porsche crest.

A change in sales tactics was evident in August 1958, when Porsche got a head start on model year '59 by replacing the Speedster with the Speedster D, retitled *Convertible D* shortly before its public debut. The "D" denoted Drauz of Heilbronn (about 20 miles from Stuttgart), which built the bodies. Still a two-seater but priced $500 higher, the Convertible D had a taller chrome-framed windshield and a top somewhere between the original Speedster's low, simple design and the cabrio's deluxe padded top. Also featured were roll-up windows (no more side curtains) and reclining front seats, as on other models. Retained was the unique Speedster dash with no glovebox (kick-panel map pockets substituted) and a hood over the instruments. The Speedster's bodyside chrome strips were also retained, giving the D some of its visual character, but the taller top was far more practical.

The rationale for the Convertible D was simple: Ferry had never liked the Speedster. He felt a "stripper" didn't really fit the make's image, and he cited low sales in making a case against it on cost grounds, as well. As usual, he was right. Though more like the regular cabrio and thus, perhaps, less charming than the Speedster, the Convertible D earned plenty of press praise. *Road & Track* called it "the best buy in a highly desirable line [offering probably] more driving pleasure per dollar than almost any car you can buy." Which

was saying something, considering that it cost only some $200 less than a '59 Corvette.

Apparently noting that narrow price spread, *Motor Trend* conducted an odd comparison test between the Convertible D and a fuel-injected example of America's sports car. While concluding that both were great buys, writer Wayne Thoms admitted that the Porsche was superior on most counts: fit and finish, handling, braking, low-speed tractability, passenger comfort, and fuel economy. The 'Vette won points only for acceleration (7.8 seconds 0-60 mph versus 15.2) and more readily available service.

R&T seemed amazed at "how a company can continue to improve a car so much over a period of years with only detail refinements." This was simply Porsche's way, of course, but planning for the 356's successor had already begun—back in 1956, in fact, just as the first As were reaching customers.

Still, the basic 356 design had a lot of life left in it. As if to prove that, Porsche trotted out the 356B in time for the Frankfurt Show in late '59. It was as close as Zuffenhausen ever got to a GM-style face-lift. Indeed, General Motors itself could have devised the cowl-forward makeover that seemed pretty frightening to old Porsche hands. Erwin Komenda, still an active company designer, conjured a more massive front bumper with jumbo guards, then elevated it four inches for better protection. Rear bumpers were larger, too, and higher by the same amount. Headlamps became more upright, prompting near-straight front fenders and blowsier lower front sheetmetal. A more garish chrome handle adorned the hood, phallic parking lamps sprouted from the outboard ends of the horn grilles, and a pair of brake-cooling slots was cut in below the front bumper. Some reviewers who fancied themselves styling purists carped that Porsche had "done a Detroit." But like most of the factory's changes, these were soon accepted. As Karl Ludvigsen later wrote, many people had come to think that if Porsche did something, it *must* be right no matter how it looked.

Regular engines now encompassed a trio of 1600-cc Type 616s: the Normal with 60 bhp (DIN) at 4500 rpm and a claimed top speed of 100 mph; the 110-mph Super with 75 bhp (DIN) at 5000 rpm, and thus sometimes called *Super 75*; and the new Super 90, with 90 bhp (DIN) at 5500 rpm and an official 116-mph maximum. The last, though announced at Frankfurt, didn't reach production until March 1960. Bodies (designated *T-5*) carried over from the last 356As: coupe, cabriolet, and Convertible D. The last was renamed *Roadster* in

Recalling the wartime VW-based Kubelwagen and Schwimmwagen, this amphibious vehicle (middle and top left and right) was Porsche's bid to supply a "hunting car with off-road capabilities" to a newly constituted West German army. Designated Type 597 and first tested in late 1954, it used the new 1.6-liter engine from the 356A, detuned to 50 DIN horsepower, which drove the rear wheels or all four wheels via a five-speed gearbox. Top speed was just 62 mph, but the vehicle would float for towing on water. Though 71 were built for evaluation, the 597 did not see regular production because Porsche's Zuffenhausen factory had all it could do to fill orders for sports cars. Farm equipment was another potential source of ancillary business that Porsche had eyed from its earliest days in Gmund, where at least five tractors were designed. One of the few that reached fruition was this so-called "Type Junior" (bottom). Aptly nicknamed Schlepper, it was built in 1957 but went no further than this prototype. As the nameplate implies, it used a small purpose-designed two-stroke diesel, which was also intended at one point for the VW Beetle.

1960. As before, all were available with any engine, giving a total of nine separate models (save Carreras).

Aside from the more-blatant changes already mentioned, the B arrived with a stubbier gearlever and a lower rear seat that gave added head room. The latter's fold-down backrest, a feature since the earliest 356s, was newly split so that three persons and some luggage could be carried inside. All models wore door vent windows, and defroster vents appeared inside below the backlight.

Alterations to chassis and running gear were subtle but notable. Porsche's synchromesh transmission, with an easier-to-engage first gear, was carried over from late 356As, while the drum brakes became cast-aluminum units with 72 radial fins (instead of circumferential ones) and cast-iron liners secured by the Al-Fin process. They were not only stronger but better sealed against moisture. After the first 3000 cars, transaxles reverted from single to dual mounts.

In a March 1960 test for *R&T*, Hansjoerg Bendel observed that the Super 90 was "developed because Porsche wanted to [provide] performance similar to that of the original Carrera, using the simpler, less expensive pushrod [engine], which is also less exacting in maintenance than the sophisticated 4 ohc engine." Its power was accordingly produced through conventional means: a higher-lift cam, improved carburetion (two twin-choke Carrera-style Solex 40 P-II-4s with larger throats and high-performance jets) and tighter compression (9.1:1, versus 8.5 for the Super 75 and 7.5:1 for the Normal).

In all, the changes brought precise but unexotic tuning (typical of the Porsche philosophy) and no loss of flexibility. *Sports Car Graphic* reported that the Super 90 was "tamer in traffic and [the] lower speed ranges than the 1600 Super. Getting off the mark fast from a standing start takes some practice, as the big carburetors can't be dumped open too fast. Once the biggest chunk of inertia is overcome, you can [floor the accelerator] and start moving out very fast indeed. In fact, one of the most impressive things about this engine is the feeling of torque—the sheer push in the shoulders—that one gets on booting the throttle...."

Objectively, the Super 90 *was* quick: under 10 seconds 0-60 mph in *SCG*'s test. Bendel, however, managed only 12.5 with his Roadster. Still, he found "the level of performance ... remarkably close to that of the Carrera, though.... the acceleration times are not quite as good as those of [our 1958] Super Speedster ... because the new body is

heavier and because 4th gear is now 3.78 instead of 3.91."

Testers generally praised the B's handling, especially in 1961 when Koni shock absorbers became standard for both Supers, matched by suitably lower spring rates. More significant was a reduction in rear roll stiffness via 23-mm torsion bars (one mm thinner than previously) and the addition of a transverse leaf spring—sometimes called a "camber compensator"—as standard for S90s (optional elsewhere). "Normal procedure," said *SCG*, is "letting the front end plow to compensate for the rear coming out ... [which] net you a trip through the tules. It must be set into a high drift attitude before the corner and varying amounts of power applied." This was on German Dunlop Sports tires; with harder racing tires, handling was more like what Porsche drivers were accustomed to.

Nevertheless, *R&T*'s Bendel stated, "the present chassis remains practically neutral up to very high cornering speeds. This means the driver is in control of a most responsive car, which goes around corners with deceptive ease and stays on its course even when the road surface is decidedly bumpy and/or cambered. The springing is a good compromise between firmness and comfort, damping is good and [the suspension] never bottoms.... The steering is wonderful, highly accurate and yet light.... It gives superb contact with the road without undesirable feedback...."

Super 90s could be revved about 800 rpm higher than other 356B 1600s thanks to a special cooling layout that gathered in more air, plus nitrided crank and cam-bearing surfaces, a lighter flywheel, stiffer valve springs, light-alloy rockers, larger-diameter (by 5mm) main bearings, and cylinders lined with Ferral, a coating of steel over molybdenum. S90s also had a unique oil pickup system that allowed the engine to draw lubricant from the sump's full side in hard cornering, thus ensuring proper lubrication at all times. It was an important advance that Porsche racers had wanted for several years and was especially welcome in the high-performance 90.

Meantime, models and coachbuilders proliferated. Bodies for the Drauz-built Roadster, which continued into the early part of model-year 1962, were also supplied by D'Ieteren Freres, and Karmann in Osnabruck began production of a new fixed-roof notchback coupe looking much like the cabriolet with optional lift-off top in place.

Subtle body changes marked the '62-model T-6 356Bs. Coupe windows were enlarged, and twin grilles appeared on a bigger engine lid. The front

The 356A received a host of changes in 1957, and more followed for 1958 models internally designated T-2. Examples shown on this '58 cabrio (top left and right) include door vent windows, exhausts ported through the rear bumper guards rather than below it, and (middle right) an optional lift-off fiberglass hardtop for the cabriolet. Not visible here, but welcome, were improved carburetors for 1.6-liter engines (the 1300 units were dropped) and better clutch and shift linkages. Interior upgrades included resited heater controls, an optional gasoline heater, and a larger steering wheel. The '58 Speedster (bottom left and right) naturally shared these changes, including a new "double bow" design for the optional rear-bumper "overrider." Regrettably, days were numbered for the Speedster, which would be replaced by the more practical, if less romantic, Convertible D starting with model-year '59.

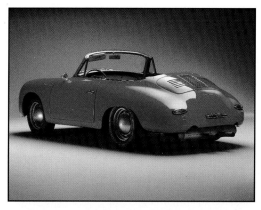

lid acquired a flatter lower edge, an external gas filler appeared (under a flap positioned in the right front fender), and a cowl vent was added ahead of the windshield. The series then continued in this form through July 1963, when the 356Cs appeared; these were the last and arguably best of the early pushrod Porsches, available in steadily diminishing numbers through 1965.

Apart from new flat-face hubcaps and a still-larger coupe backlight, the Cs were visual twins to the Bs. Even so, constant improvement was again quite evident. For instance, a lever replaced the clumsy VW-derived heater knob (VW itself made this change a few years later), and seats were more "buckety" than before.

A significant mechanical update was the arrival of standard four-wheel disc brakes (as on the previous year's Carrera 2). It was quite typical of Zuffenhausen—and inevitable. Porsches were getting faster, and they needed to stop with equal authority.

Since 1958, Porsche had experimented with a pair of disc systems: its own (ultimately used on the Carrera 2) and a Dunlop design made under license by Ate. The technologies forced a choice between pride and cost. The latter won, and Dunlop's cheaper system was the one selected.

Though the C-Series lost the 60-bhp Normal engine, the 75 returned as the 1600C. The Super 90 was renamed 1600SC and given higher compression (9.5:1) to achieve 95 DIN horsepower. Positive crankcase ventilation was adopted for the U.S. versions of both, along with reshaped ports that improved airflow. The 1600C benefited from a higher-lift cam, while the SC gained small-diameter intake valves and larger exhausts. For 1964, the SC's Ferral cylinder coating gave way to a new Biral treatment that provided more efficient heat dissipation at less cost. Similar to the Al-Fin brake process, it comprised a finned aluminum shell cast around a cast-iron sleeve.

With the Roadster's demise, the 356C lineup was composed of C and SC fastback coupe, cabrio, and the Karmann notchback coupe. A corporate move with lasting implications for enthusiasts generally and Zuffenhausen in particular occurred in 1963, when Porsche absorbed Reutter and spun off a seat-making division that's still world-famous as *Recaro* (from *Re*utter *Caro*zzerie).

As the most refined of a long line, the 356C is as close to perfect as cars get. Karl Ludvigsen records that in the C's last season, warranty costs averaged only $8.38 per car, "the lowest in history for Porsche and incredibly low for any car." The other side of the coin is that 356s of all kinds have long been collectible and thus very pricey today.

After more than 15 years and precisely 76,303 units, the 356 Series was honorably retired in September 1965. Production by type is as follows:

Type	Production	Yearly average
356	7627	1090
356A	21,045	5261
356B	30,963	7741
356C	16,668	8334

Those figures wouldn't occasion toasts at General Motors, but for Porsche, which had started from ground zero with this basic design, they told a remarkable story: one of constant evolution and steady, satisfying growth within the original 1947 concept laid down by Ferry Porsche and Erwin Komenda. Moreover, the ever-improving 356 had brought Porsche international respect as a builder of durable, superbly engineered performance machines at home on road and track alike.

Prosperity naturally accompanied Porsche's growth and growing renown. The firm had needed four years to build its first 5000 cars (April 1950 to March 1954), yet by the time of the 356B, sales were running far above that in every calendar year:

Year	Unit Sales
1960	7598
1961	7664
1962	8205
1963	9692*

* incl. 356C

Of course, the cars themselves had come a long way from the Gmund days and even the early Zuffenhausen 356s. As *Road & Track* observed: "Gradually, and part by part, Porsche adopted bits, pieces and complete assemblies of its own. Today nothing remains in the way of VW parts, though there are many similarities in arrangement and construction. The modern Porsche is unique, it has had a tremendous success, and it deserves it."

The Mighty Carreras

Natural progression now brings us to the first of the immortal Porsche Carreras, the ultimate 356. Introduced with the A-Series in late 1955, it combined a supremely capable basic design with an advanced engine developed expressly for racing. The result was a true "giant killer" that achieved through elegant, efficient engineering what rivals

This 356A Speedster (opposite, top) lacks the usual chrome bodyside strips and rocker rub rails but packs the four-cam 1500GS Carrera engine with 100 DIN horsepower and virtually the same specifications as the racing 1500 Spyder unit. Though that power sounds modest, an early Carrera coupe turned 0-60 mph in 11.5 seconds for Road & Track. Cockpit (lower left) was functional in expected Porsche fashion, but the Speedster's narrow side curtains (middle right) were far less practical, especially in the rain. Rear aspect (lower right) shows how the exhaust on early Carreras exited below the bumper, not through it as on other 356As after 1957.

September 1959 brought yet another 356 update in new
T-5 B-Series models, most readily recognized by higher
front bumpers and headlamps. Here, an early coupe
(bottom left) and three views of the cabriolet.

Besides 4.5-inch higher bumpers, the 356Bs featured more glass area, standard door vent windows, lowered front seats for extra head room, a newly split folding rear seatback, and stouter Alfin aluminum brakes. Engine choices were unchanged from the last 356As.

could manage only through sheer bulk.

The late Dean Batchelor recorded that the Carrera engine originated in 1952: "Ferry Porsche and his team of engineers had wondered what the potential of the air-cooled four-cylinder boxer engine might be, and Dr. (later Prof.) Ernst Fuhrmann was told to find out. A figure of 70 horsepower per liter [was mentioned] and Fuhrmann's calculations indicated [it] was possible—with four camshafts instead of the single camshaft and pushrod/rocker-arm valve actuation.

"The Fuhrmann design followed the basic configuration of the standard Porsche engine but differed in almost every detail. It had four camshafts (two per side, called double overhead or dohc), twin ignition, dual twin-choke Solex carburetors, dry-sump lubrication, and roller bearings on both mains and rods.

"Fuhrmann's new design was tested on Maundy Thursday, 1953. It was a happy day for several reasons: It was three years to the day after the first Stuttgart-built Porsche . . . and the new [1498-cc] engine produced 112 hp at 6400 rpm on the first test . . . 74 hp per liter."

The four-cam was developed mainly for the racing Type 550 Spyder (see Chapter 7), but in March 1954, as Batchelor recorded, a developmental unit "was installed in [Ferry] Porsche's personal car, *Ferdinand,* to evaluate the engine/chassis combination. . . ." A year later, a similar engine was tried in another of Ferry's cars, a gray cabrio. The enthusiasm of Porsche personnel was unanimous, but only Fuhrmann had seen the possibilities early on.

The model name honored the *Carrera Panamericana,* the famed Mexican Road Race where Type 550s had distinguished themselves in 1953-54. The first roadgoing Carrera was internally designated 1500GS, the letters signifying "Grand Sport." Normal 356s already had plenty of that; the Carrera simply delivered more.

Differences between the production four-cam engine (officially 547/1) and its competition counterpart were few. Compression was initially lowered from 9.5:1 to 8.7:1 but was soon restored to 9.0:1. Also, the twin distributor drives were placed at the opposite ends of the intake cams for easier access. On its '55 Frankfurt debut, the Carrera packed a rated 100 DIN horsepower (115 SAE gross) at 6200 rpm (versus 110 bhp for the racing version). The engine was such an easy-revver, though, that it could be routinely taken to 7000-7500 rpm without harm.

Though the 356 chassis could handle this extra power without major change, Porsche took its typi-

cally thorough approach and gave the Carrera wider tires (5.90s), an 8000-rpm tachometer, and a 180-mph speedometer. External clues were limited to discreet gold namescript on front fenders and engine lid, making this a "Q-car" par excellence. Because their engine was slightly heavier, Carreras weighed about 100 pounds more than equivalent 356As.

Again per Porsche practice, the quadcam was sold in all three body styles, Speedster included. Fuhrmann accurately described the Carrera as "a detuned version [of the Spyder] providing extra performance for high speed, Gran Turismo competition, with more power than the pushrod engine could produce."

Critic John Bentley timed the gray prototype at under nine seconds 0-60 mph and less than 20 seconds 0-100 mph. He was disappointed that the extra weight in back made handling even more squirrely than on his 356 coupe, but the production Carrera benefited from the suspension upgrades accorded the 356A.

Road & Track noted that these "do not appear important in detail [but] have made a considerable improvement in the handling. In addition, the Carreras appear to be coming through with about 1° of negative camber at the rear wheels, with no load. This and the larger 5.90-inch section road-racing tires give as close to neutral steering as is conceivable. With the tremendous power available, a burst of throttle in a corner (in the correct gear) will give oversteer, just as it does with any machine of comparable power-to-weight ratio [18.5 lbs/bhp for the test coupe]. High-speed stability at over 100 mph in a cross wind still leaves something to be desired in our opinion, but this applies to almost any well-streamlined coupe with [a] preponderance of weight on the rear wheels. In any event, the steering is accurate and quick and requires only common sense and alert attention at over the magic century mark." Jesse Alexander largely concurred, after driving a Carrera Speedster for *Sports Cars Illustrated,* but observed that the "use of factory-recommended tire pressures seems to be the answer for making a Porsche handle satisfactorily. . . ."

Both magazines used similar words to sum up the Carrera. "Without a doubt, this was one of the most interesting cars we have ever tested," said *R&T.* "It completed the vigorous performance tests as if it were out for a Sunday drive . . . ." Some Sunday drive: 0-60 mph in 11.5 seconds, the standing quarter-mile in 17.7, and a top speed of just over 120 mph.

Opposite page: The Abarth-Carrera GTL was named for its 356B Carrera chassis and bodywork by Italy's Carlo Abarth. Fewer than 20 were built, originally with 1.6-liter engines, but some were later fitted with 2-liter units. This model won Porsche the World GT racing crown in 1961-63. Flat-face hubcaps and revised T-6 body styling marked the 356C models that Porsche began building in July 1963 (bottom). Go-power was better than ever, but the real news was standard four-wheel disc brakes—a production-Porsche first—to provide equally strong stopping power.

But automotive excitement is rarely cheap, and the Carrera delivered in the U.S. for a minimum $5995. On the other hand, *R&T* stated, "the price doesn't seem quite so steep" considering the Carrera's performance, its "fool-proof, if not ultra-rapid" gearbox and "tremendously powerful" brakes.

May 1957 saw a new Carrera Deluxe replace the "standard" offering. This mainly meant a heater that really heated instead of blowing tepid air at your feet. Announced at the same time was a no-cost GT option for coupe and Speedster, with an extra 10 bhp (and a higher, 6500-rpm power peak). The fuel tank now had a 21-gallon capacity instead of 14, and the car's stopping ability was enhanced via Spyder front brakes with 128 square inches of lining area (versus 115). Spyder worm-gear steering was another significant alteration. Again, the intent was competition, so GTs were literal strippers, shorn of heater and undercoating and fitted with plastic windows and lighter bumpers. By 1958, they'd acquired aluminum doors, hood, and engine lid, and lightweight bucket seats, all of which pared 150 pounds from the coupe and 100 pounds from the Speedster.

Journalist John Bentley bought and tested a Carrera Speedster GT in 1958, ordering it in a silver-grey metallic that matched the finish of the prototype that had won him over to Porsches. His car naturally had the latest running changes: new crankshaft distributor drive, ram-type air intake (via engine-lid louvers), built-in rollbar posts, and Fren-do competition brake linings. Bentley was too early for the Koni adjustable shock absorbers that later became standard, but he installed a set post-purchase.

Bentley's report can still stir your blood: "Low gear [with the standard 5.17:1 U.S. final-drive ratio] is a shade too low; but in second gear the GT leaps forward with a wild, exhilarating surge. . . . The muffler is noisy, but that noise is music of a delightful kind. As the tach needle leaps to 5200 rpm and peak torque, the car seems to grab hold and a terrific surge of power becomes available. The savage bark of the exhaust levels off to a high-pitched snarl, and before you know it the tach is indicating 7500 rpm."

Everything ever hung onto the evolving 356 seemed to work that much better on the Carrera. Both the brakes and all-synchro gearbox were not only smooth and precise but light to the touch; the bucket seats provided ample support. Handling, in Bentley's view, was now beyond criticism: "With 26 lbs [of air] in the front [tires] and 27 in the rear

you can break the tail loose in the secure knowledge that the machine will respond to correction in the normal manner. There is no danger that the slide will become an uncontrollable spin, as in former years."

Plug fouling was the Carrera's one serious flaw. A week of town driving was usually enough to gum up the plugs—and changing them, as Bentley said, took "the dexterity of an octopus and the tenacity of a leech."

Still, most agreed that the Carrera was one impressive car. "What an enthusiast's dream," Bentley concluded. "It is in a class by itself." Even better, it was as reliable as any 356 when carefully run-in. John Batchelor wrote that all Carrera engines were bench-tested at 4000 rpm for several hours, then given full throttle for several minutes before installation.

With that, the Carrera was rather unhappy in relatively low-speed American driving. After all, it was basically a race car in road dress, which helps explain the changes instituted for 1958 under technical manager Klaus von Rucker. Included were the new distributor drive already mentioned, a plain-bearing Alfing crankshaft to replace the roller-bearing Hirth, and twin oil radiators (located behind the horn grilles) to compensate for the higher oil temperatures produced by the plain bearings. This revised 1500GS engine was designated Type 692/1; a roller-bearing version, Type 692/0, was devised for competition. Nominally rated at 110 bhp (DIN) at 6400 rpm, they weren't common: just 14 and 20 were built, respectively.

Von Rucker had left room for a bore increase, and it arrived during 1958 with the new Type 692/2 engine. An 87.5-mm bore and the existing 66-mm stroke made for 1588cc but "only" 105 DIN horsepower (121 SAE) at 6500 rpm—still more than sufficient, though.

The GT version, designated 692/3, got 9.8:1 compression (versus 9.5 on the Deluxe), Weber 40DCM2 carburetors, a 12-volt electrical system, a free-flow muffler, and sodium-cooled exhaust valves, the last a real competition touch. Output was a smashing 115 bhp (132 SAE), over 1.4 bhp per cubic inch.

But the Carrera wasn't nearly so potent on the sales chart: just 700 deliveries through January 1960—far less than Porsche had hoped—this despite the addition for 1959 of a plusher, 2100-pound 1600GS. What's more, as Batchelor noted, 692/2 engines totaled just 45 in 1958, 47 in '59, and a mere two in 1960. The declining production was due mainly to two big problems. First, the "cook-

356Bs built after September 1961 like this cabriolet (top and lower right) sported new T-6 body styling, identifed by a squared-off lower edge on the front trunklid. The same look would continue on 356Cs, but engines (lower left) were revised yet again to encompass new 1600C and SC versions, replacing the 1600N and Super 90 units from late Bs, plus the rare, 2-liter Carrera unit. Porsche interiors (upper left) were no longer so stark by the early Sixties—and quite comfortable with it.

ing" 356A was pretty high-strung; the Carrera was even more so, thus limiting appeal that much further. Second, it cost a bundle, and those most able to afford one usually didn't understand how to drive and care for it—a regrettable paradox. So if you lived in America and didn't race, owning a pushrod Porsche made far more sense.

Acknowledging this state of affairs, Porsche offered only detrimmed Carrera GT coupes for 1960-61 with lightweight Reutter bodywork, simplified bumpers without guards, aluminum hubcaps, and a more Spartan interior. The 1960 models retained the 692/3 power unit. An evolution, the 692/3A model, arrived for '61 with larger main-bearing journals, stronger con rods, and redesigned cams with a total of six small flywheels to quell harmonic vibration in the valvetrain.

But sales continued to be disappointing, so the final roadgoing 356 Carreras bowed at the Frankfurt Show in late 1961 for the '62 model year. Based on the 1960 B-Series, they included a steel-bodied 1600 coupe with a 1582-cc engine packing 90 bhp at 5500 rpm; a lighter 1600GS with 115 bhp at 6500 rpm from 1588cc; and a new 2000GS, also known as the *Carrera 2*. The last featured the new four-wheel Dunlop disc brakes, and all three had the latest body modifications except the bumper-guard exhaust outlets (the tips exited below the bumper, as before, but within a protective apron).

The Carrera 2's most prominent selling point was its Type 587 engine. An expansion of the Type 547, it was decidedly oversquare at 92 X 74mm—1966cc in all. Horsepower was 130 DIN at 6200 rpm (150 SAE), close to 1.3 bhp per cubic inch. The torque curve was broad and flat, and peaked at an impressive 131 pounds/feet at 4600 rpm. Reflecting lessons learned in the marketplace, the Carrera 2 had plain bearings rather than the roller type, and its top two gears had longer-striding ratios for lazy Americans. This alteration to gearing was not a major one but gave the U.S. Carrera 2 that fraction of extra power that made the difference between lugging and strong pull off the line. For this reason, not to mention the car's innate civility, it proved the most popular Carrera yet.

Indeed, civility was the key. Hansjoerg Bendel lauded the "notable innovation" of a combination fresh-air intake and heater fan (via an optional gasoline heater), the comfortable Reutter seats, the quick shifter, and, above all, the unmistakable quality of a car built for the connoisseur. He also approved of the chassis: "The steering gave improved response with reduced vibration, the car seemed to stick better to the road and stay stuck during hard acceleration, and the disc brakes, added late to the Carrera 2 specification, were more than adequate."

Acceleration, which Bendel termed "exhilarating," was more than adequate, as well. He noted, "The clutch takes quite a bit of throttle without protest, and when one finds that it is time for 2nd gear, down comes the stick in a flick, more acceleration, and other cars pass by as if in reverse. High up in the speed range, this is it—the effortless superiority of the true high-performance machine."

Bendel complained that the Carrera was still too noisy—and for a hefty $7595, it probably was. Also, the engine had a "certain roughness well remembered from older Carreras." Finally, and perhaps telling in 1962, was the near 20-year-old basic design: "Even the accustomed eye begins to notice some signs of age. The instrument panel, for example, is higher up than is usual nowadays, and visibility could only benefit from a lower waistline." But he should have been more patient. The 911 was on its way.

But not before a short run of 356C-based Carrera 2s in 1963. Like the '62s, they were available with Porsche's usual vast assortment of competition equipment: a larger fuel tank, a limited-slip differential, and special weight-saving body and chassis components—virtually anything a would-be racer might want.

Bendel aptly summed up the Carrera 2 as "one of the most desirable GT cars" of its day, one to "delight the owner looking for a car of high quality and exceptional roadworthiness." But like most good things, it was short-lived, built mainly to homologate the Type 587 engine for competition, initially in production-based cars and later in the factory's more specialized racers such as the 2000GS/GT and the lovely 904 (see Chapter 7).

But the ultimate 356s left their mark as the first of a grand roadgoing line that persists through the 911 Series to this day. Every indication is that that pedigree will be perpetuated well into the future.

Many critics regard the end-of-the-line C-Series as the best of the standard 356s. They were certainly the most civilized. Twin engine-lid grilles (upper right) were a feature of B- and C-models, as were standard door ventwings on coupes (upper left). With cancellation of the Roadster (nee Convertible D) early in the '62 model year, the cabrio (bottom) became the sole open Porsche. It would also be Porsche's last full convertible until 1982. Though 356 production was halted in September 1965 to make way for the new 901/911, some 10 cars were built for special customers in 1966.

The 911 Chronicle: The Essence of Porsche

For most enthusiasts, the 911 remains the one "true" Porsche, the only one with a direct link to the original 356, yet longer-lived by far. Though Ferry Porsche thought his first six-cylinder production car would have a good long run when he showed it in late 1963, even he couldn't have forseen that it would endure into a new millenium.

But this seeming immortality is not without reason. Over the years, the 911 has been put in a coffin more times than Dracula—mainly by the press, though certain forces in Zuffenhausen also wanted to kill it at various times. Yet, as the Beetle once was for Volkswagen, the 911 became such a strong symbol of everything Porsche that it overshadowed—and outsold—its intended successor, the 928 (see Chapter 6). VW finally made its great model change, but Porsche has not. The 911 became too profitable, too vital for survival to be cast aside—one reason you can buy a new one today.

Another reason is nearly four decades of Porsche-style honing that have kept the 911 fresh, exciting, and quite extraordinary. The result is both a living legend and a perpetual classic—a car that seems like it's always been around, yet in many ways is even more relevant now than it was in the beginning.

Of course, the 911 *was* very good to start with, preserving the essence of earlier Porsches while setting a new and entirely higher standard of engineering and design. Mechanically it was a sharp break with Porsche practice in several areas. For example, it was the first production Porsche without front trailing arms or rear swing axles, though it retained 356-style torsion bars. It was the first roadgoing Porsche with more than four cylinders, yet its engine was still a horizontally opposed air-cooled type placed behind the rear wheels. Also unlike the 356, the 911 engine was supported at both ends: by the transaxle in front and by a transverse mount in back. An all-synchromesh gearbox with overdrive top gear was no surprise, but instead of four ratios buyers could have five, which provided greater low-speed flexibility and higher top-end potential.

The 911 originated as Project 695, which also produced the 356's disc brakes. Planning began in 1956, a mere six years after Zuffenhausen began production. At first, the new model was seen not as a 356 replacement but as a larger four-seat car with performance comparable to that of the charismatic Carrera. It was intended that other 356s carry on even after the "big Porsche" was launched, as indeed some did for a time. But Ferry Porsche changed his mind about the size, fearing a full four-seater would put his firm in the unaccustomed and uncomfortable position of competing with much-larger outfits, notably Daimler-Benz.

By 1959, work was underway on what emerged as the T-7 prototype (T-6 was the last 356 body, appearing in 1961). Styling was entrusted to one of Ferry's four sons, Ferdinand Porsche III, known as "Butzi." Ferry wasn't a body designer per se, but he knew what he wanted. A family resemblance to the 356 was a must, but so were (as he later described) "more space inside" and a "luggage space that could take an owner's golf clubs."

High performance was naturally a given, too, but Ferry put new emphasis on smooth, quiet running: "We decided on a 2.0-liter six-cylinder engine because sixes are more comfortable and refined," he said in 1984. "We studied the concept of a mid-mounted engine . . . but we could not give it enough interior room for the outside size we wanted." What they *did* want, in short, was a roomier, smoother, quieter, more practical, and somewhat more luxurious Carrera. In that regard, it's interesting to note that the late Dean Batchelor observed "the four-cam Carrera engine was considered briefly as an across-the-board replacement for the pushrod-and-rocker-arm engine, but was too costly and too complicated to be considered seriously for general use."

Without greatly extending the wheelbase, Butzi did a remarkable job of providing near four-seat interior room. Outside, T-7 showed a low beltline, lots of glass, and a sharply sloped "hood." Front fenders remained high and prominent, something Butzi considered vital to Porsche identity.

With a huge wrapped backlight and stubby semi-notchback tail, the T-7 looked a bit unorthodox, but its styling from the B-pillars forward would appear almost unaltered on the production

If one model sums up the essence of Porsche, it's the 911. Timeless, aggressive, and beautiful, its says "performance machine" like no other automobile in the world. Seen opposite is a 1972 911 Carrera RS, a Rennsport model specially lightened and bereft of emissions equipment. It was not street legal in the United States, but did race there.

911. When Ferry decided on a more evolutionary look with Porsche's traditional 2+2 seating, Butzi revised the T-7 from the doors back, creating the now-familiar fastback with ovoid rear side windows and back-slanting B-posts. Batchelor recorded that Ferry decreed a wheelbase of no more than 2200mm, 100mm longer than the 356's, and that's about how it worked out: 2211mm (87.0 inches) versus 2100 (82.7) for the 356.

Designated *Type 901*, the new Porsche greeted the world at the Frankfurt Automobile Show in September 1963. Porsche allowed that it was being shown early; production wouldn't begin before the summer of '64. *Road & Track*'s John R. Bond reported "there were so many rumors circulating they were forced to show it."

The new design and the 901 designation weren't linked. The Porsche organization has never been strictly sequential in assigning project numbers and has skipped quite a few; "901" was chosen simply to suggest a new direction. And, of course, it didn't last. Peugeot claimed a "right" to three-digit model numbers with middle zeros and threatened to prevent a "901" from being sold in France, so "911" badges were substituted before sales began. (Zuffenhausen got the last laugh by giving middle-zero numbers to a half-dozen of its competition cars, including the beautiful 904 GTS.)

As Ferry specified, the 911 had a split fold-down rear seatback for greater cargo/passenger-carrying versatility. And despite having a more streamlined tail than the T-7, it still offered enough rear room for one adult or two small children.

Yet for all its newness, *R&T*'s John Bond reported that the chrome-yellow Frankfurt show car was "not as much different from the 356 as it appears in the photos. . . . The big difference is the elimination of the broad-beam hip effect that results in a trimmer, narrower look and a roofline that, in [overhead] view, no longer tucks in at the rear. The net result of these appearance changes is a car 2.7-in. narrower overall, and more head, shoulder, and leg room for rear-seat passengers."

Though again all-independent, the 911 suspension broke new ground for Porsche with front MacPherson struts on single transverse A-arms connecting to longitudinal torsion bars. Rear suspension comprised transverse torsion bars and semi-trailing arms, a logical progression from swing axles. After its inaugural test in 1965, *R&T* judged the 911 "neutral in its behavior and perfectly controllable throughout the whole speed range and even on atrocious road surfaces. True, the suspension is on the firm (not to say harsh)

side, but for a high-performance car like this, it appears a small price to pay. . . ."

Steering design also parted company with the past, as ZF rack-and-pinion steering ousted the VW-based worm-gear mechanism, one of the last remnants of the old Porsche/VW kinship. The new system was not only more direct, with virtually no play at the wheel, but light, full of feel, and virtually shock-free (thanks, as usual, to a hydraulic damper).

Porsche also took pains to provide effective heating, ever difficult in air-cooled cars. Air was drawn from the cooling fan to a heat box, then fed to the cockpit via under-dash and dash-top vents. Still optional was a gasoline heater with an electric fan to force more air into the heater boxes, but it was rarely needed once the car was warmed up and moving. Interior ventilation improved with the addition of extractor slots above the backlight to speed cockpit flow-through.

But the big attraction was the new 1991-cc flat-six, designated *901/01*. Developed by Ferdinand Piech, Ferry's nephew, and Hans Tomala, it was quite oversquare (bore and stroke: 80 X 66mm/3.15 X 2.60 inches). With twin triple-choke Solex 40 PI carburetors and 9:1 compression, rated output was 130 DIN horsepower (148 SAE gross) at 6100 rpm and 140 pounds/feet of torque at 4200 rpm. Unlike previous Porsche fours, the 901 six employed a single overhead camshaft per cylinder bank. Each operated two valves per cylinder (arranged in V-formation) via rocker arms and was driven by a pair of roller chains instead of the complex train of bevel gears used on 356 Carrera engines.

Enhancing the greater inherent smoothness of the "boxer" six was a six-throw, forged-steel crankshaft with no fewer than eight main bearings. A countershaft mounted beneath carried impulses to twin chain sprockets at the crank's rear end, each sprocket driving a camshaft. Ahead of the countershaft were two oil pumps: a large scavenger for circulating oil between the dry sump and a separate, remote reservoir, and a smaller pump for maintaining oil pressure. An oil cooler was also specified, reflecting Porsche's passion for proper lubrication as one aid to overall engine cooling. The factory said that oil temperature should never exceed 130 degrees, and no tester ever recalled that it did, which was only to be expected from a system developed in the literal heat of competition.

Again per Porsche practice, the 911 engine had a cast-aluminum crankcase and separate cylinders with hemispherical combustion chambers of cross-flow design. Cylinder construction was rather

The 911's origins can be traced to the 695 (top), a project begun in 1956. The 695 seen here dates from 1961-62. The 911 was originally slated to be called the 901 (middle row) but the name was changed late in 1963 to appease Peugeot, who claimed "ownership" of three-digit designations with a zero in the middle. The Type 901 bodyshell was immensely strong, with a low beltline and plenty of glass. From the start, Porsche was determined that the 911's 2.0-liter 6 (bottom row) be smooth and quiet.

exotic for 1963, comprising aluminum-silicon alloy with a thin aluminum layer chemically etched away from the bores to leave silicon crystals as the pistons' working surface. The design had the advantage of providing microscopic "valleys" that ensured constant surface oiling. For strength, the pistons were forged aluminum, and the con rods were forged steel.

The rest of the 911 drivetrain was fairly familiar. A Fichtel & Sachs single dry-plate clutch sent power to a fully synchronized Porsche transaxle, initially with five forward ratios and a racing-style shift pattern with first to the left and down (below reverse), out of the basic "H." Initial rolling stock comprised 4.5-inch-wide, 15-inch-diameter steel disc wheels shod with surprisingly modest 165-15 radial tires.

As with every 356 evolution, the 911 garnered mixed initial reactions from confirmed Porschephiles, though most soon grew to accept it and, inevitably, respect it. Press response was enthusiastic. *Car and Driver* gushed: "Race breeding and engineering development ooze from the 911's every pore. The whole package, especially the powertrain, is designed to be more reliable and less difficult to service. . . . Although the 911 costs a lot less than the Carrera [about $6500 in 1965]—and a lot less than the current [356] C and SC—it's worth the price of all the old Porsches put together. More importantly, the 911's appeal should be considerably wider than the earlier models. . . ."

A bigger surprise was the glowing February 1966 assessment by Denis Jenkinson in Britain's *Motor Sport*. A veteran Porsche driver, but never one to mince words (even at the expense of advertising revenue), "Jenks" declared the 911 "the best car Porsche have yet built for normal road use [and] one of the best cars I have ever driven."

Like so many after him, Jenks faced a dashboard dominated by an elliptical binnacle housing five circular gauges, the largest of which was a tachometer mounted dead-center. To its left were dials for fuel/oil levels and oil pressure/temperature; the speedo and electric clock sat to the tach's right. Below this cluster, a strip of genuine teak presented various knobs and switches. A molded crash pad stretched across the dash top, and the usual shapely bucket seats offered Reutter's "stepless" backrest recliner adjustment. Yet all this left Jenkinson unmoved: "Driving quietly away, [the] lack of character was even more noticeable, so that seasoned Porsche owners commented that it was all right, but hardly a Porsche. . . ."

Jenks found the car's "character" when he flogged it: "Out into the open country, the whole car immediately became alive. . . . The more I drove it and the harder I made it work, the more Porsche-like it became. . . ." Helping to solidify his impression—literally—was the usual "all-of-a-piece" Porsche feel regardless of surface or speed. "The whole car [seems] indestructible, coupled with suspension, ride, road-holding, steering, braking and general good manners that are truly modern, and the nearest to perfection that production cars have yet reached. . . . Why don't all manufacturers make cars like this?"

Supply was Porsche's biggest early problem with the 911, as demand was strong from day one. A mid-1963 purchase of Reutter assured better quality but did nothing to increase production capacity. Accordingly, Porsche soon contracted with the Wilhelm Karmann works for additional bodies.

But that effectively ended production of the 356C (in September 1965, by which time it was being sold only in the United States), so Porsche decided to fill the gap with a four-cylinder 911, the 912 (again, the project number was 10 digits below the type designation in actual order). Both 911 and 912 bowed "officially" in late 1964, when a Porsche representative said he feared that new-model announcements were becoming a habit at Zuffenhausen: "We just had one 15 years ago."

The 911s went on sale in the United States in early 1965, for model-year '66; the first 912s arrived in June, two months behind initial European deliveries.

Inevitably, the 912 carried the 1600SC engine from the last of the 356s, though slightly detuned to 102 bhp (SAE) at 5800 rpm and 91 pounds/feet of peak torque at 3500 rpm. On paper, it should have been slower than the SC because the 911 bodyshell added some 100 pounds to curb weight. But the five-speed gearbox (a $75 extra) and aerodynamics were superior, so the 912 was actually faster all-out. Porsche's top-speed figure was a conservative 116 mph. *Car and Driver* reached 115, and *Road & Track* managed 119, both with five-speed. The typical 0-60 run was 11.5-12 seconds, the standing quarter-mile an 18-second affair at 77-78 mph. Predictably, the 912 was much thriftier than the 911, averaging 25 miles per gallon versus 16-20 mpg.

R&T said the 912 "isn't a car in which one can amble around town in high gear with abandon. It's necessary to make full use of the five speeds, and there seem to always be more wrong gears than right ones," a snipe at the racing-style shift pattern. Britain's *Autocar* found it possible to go from first

Design differences between the 356 and the '63 Type 901 seen here were subtle. On balance, the 901 did not share the "hippy" aspect of the 356, and appeared trimmer. "Butzi" Porsche designed the 901 with 2+2 proportions that carried on the already familiar sharply sloped "hood," ovoid rear side windows, and high fenderline. Wheelbase was a trim 2211mm (87 inches), just a bit longer than the 2200mm limit set down by Ferry Porsche.

to fourth, missing second gear, but that shifting became "subconscious" with practice. Conversely, said *R&T*, the 912 engine "runs without fuss at low speeds and idles smoothly at 1000 rpm, [though] it's anything but quiet. It never sounds overworked, mind you, but it seems that all the clatter comes right through the bulkhead." The 911 also wasn't particularly quiet inside, so Porsche still had some work to do in that area.

Speed aside, the 912 drove much like its six-cylinder sister. Both had strong, virtually fade-free brakes; light, accurate, well-damped steering; and German Dunlop SP radials that worked perfectly with the suspension to deliver strong cornering with a good ride. "Oversteer is a thing of the past," *R&T* concluded, "and one no longer need be an expert to keep from losing it—even in the wet. The 912 is a car that is very responsive to small steering inputs . . . but not at all likely to wag its tail in vigorous cornering."

R&T judged the ride as firm "but most definitely not a harsh one. There's very little tendency to pitch or roll and, true to Porsche tradition, the body itself adds to the impression of a good ride by being absolutely rigid and rattle-squeak-free. . . ."

Reflecting its lower price ($4700 U.S. POE), the 912 was more "stripped" than a 911: For example, the dash was trimmed with plastic instead of teak, a clock and oil-pressure/temp dial were lacking, and the optional gas heater was initially unavailable. But *R&T* noted that "nothing is left out that is really necessary. If you want to order a Porsche with no extras, be assured it will be a 'fully equipped' car." In both 911 and 912, full equipment included three-speed wipers, a rear-window defroster, and backup lamps.

The 901 Series saw few changes through 1966. July '65 brought revised gear ratios to both models and a standard four-speed for the 911, so Porsche could advertise a lower starting price. Complaints of carburetion flat spots and fouled plugs were addressed the following February by a switch to Weber 40 IDA 3C carburetors. Gripes about front-end float and abrupt understeer/oversteer transitions brought a very un-Porsche solution: an 11-kilogram (24.2-pound) cast-iron weight bolted and glued to each inner outboard end of the front bumper.

A more sophisticated idea appeared at Frankfurt in 1965: an open 901 with a clever yet practical lift-off roof panel above the front seats and a fixed rear "hoop" for rollover protection. The new body style was called *Targa*, after one of Porsche's most successful competition venues, the gruelling Targa Florio road race in Sicily. Available in both 911 and 912 form, the Targa began export sales in 1967.

Butzi Porsche had objected to retaining the coupe's rear sheetmetal for the Targa, saying a "trunkback" (as on the T-7) was the only proper shape for a cabriolet. Nevertheless, shared bodywork was a must given the modest sales projections. The plus side was that this decision "forced" Butzi to design in the strong rollbar. Initially, the Targa had a zip-out plastic rear window and a folding roof panel of rubberized fabric. The rollbar was trimmed in brushed stainless steel—chosen, Butzi said, to emphasize its functionality.

As it turned out, the public wanted far more Targas than Porsche had planned (originally 12.7 percent of total series production). Porsche also found that the 912 sold much better than the 911, though that wasn't too surprising given the price difference. Of the nearly 13,000 Porsches built in 1966, more than 9000 had four cylinders.

But these were problems of success that everyone in Zuffenhausen was happy to endure. The new-generation Porsche was a solid hit. All that now remained was to apply the same sort of carefully considered honing that had been lavished on the 356.

And indeed, the 901 had ample scope for development, though perhaps only the Porsche organization could see it. The first major advance came in late 1966, and it was an exciting one: the hot 911S—"S" for Super. With this, Porsche returned to its old three-tier lineup of Normal, Super, and Carrera, respectively represented by the 912, standard 911, and the new S.

The S boasted modifications typical of a higher-performance Porsche: reprofiled cam, larger valves, better porting, loftier compression (9.8:1 vs. 9.0), larger jets for the Weber carbs (which were otherwise much like those given the base 911 from early '66). The result was 30 more horsepower for a total 160 DIN (180 SAE). Torque improved fractionally, to 127 pounds/feet but peaked fully 1000 rpm higher. Unlike other models, the S lacked a choke, but pumping the accelerator was usually enough for starting. On the other hand, merely blipping the throttle on the freer-breathing S would send the tach needle zinging to its 7300-rpm redline. Porsche thus wisely fitted an ignition cutout that interrupted spark to the plugs near maximum revs, thus protecting the valvetrain from overly enthusiastic drivers.

Naturally, the S also had chassis upgrades to match its extra power. These included a rear anti-roll bar (augmenting the one in front), Koni shocks,

Porsche introduced the four-cylinder Type 912 in Germany in April 1965, offering it as a less-expensive alternative to the 911. Although the 912 had plainer looks and less oomph than the six-cylinder 911, it won raves for its ride, handling, and thriftiness. Power came from the 1600SC engine used by the last of the 356s, detuned to 102 bhp. A five-speed gearbox was a $75 option. Top speed came in at a hair below 120 mph and the 0-60 mph sprint could be managed in 11.5 to 12 seconds. Interestingly, the five-speed's shift pattern placed second above third on the central plane, and first on the dogleg down and to the left— race-car style instead of in the usual H- pattern arrangement.

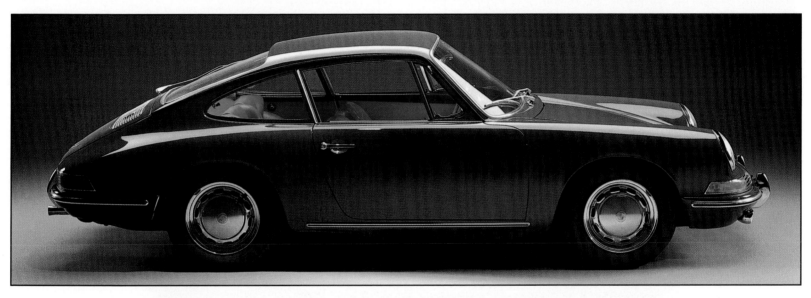

ventilated instead of solid-rotor disc brakes all-round and—soon to be a 911 hallmark—pretty, five-spoke Fuchs alloy wheels that cut five pounds from unsprung weight at each hub. Curiously, the S had the same skinny tires as the normal 911, at least for the moment.

S gear ratios were evenly spaced except for the five-speed transmission's overdrive top, which was purposely very "high." It gave 100 mph at only 4200 rpm, hardly a strain for the free-revving flat-six. Pulling max rpm in the lower gears netted 0-60 in eight seconds or less and ran a standing quarter-mile of under 16 seconds at 90-plus mph.

Interestingly, the torque curve had two distinct steps. As *Autocar* reported: "The catalogue peak comes at 5200 rpm, but before that, at about 3000, the engine takes a deep breath and literally surges up to the next step, where the extra punch feels like an additional pair of cylinders being switched in. This kick in the back leaves passengers unaccustomed to it slightly winded, and it is sudden enough to cause momentary wheelspin on wet surfaces, even in third."

As for road manners, the S earned mixed reviews. "Oversteer is back—and Porsche's got it!" screamed *Car and Driver*. "At low lateral accelerations it understeers mildly. . . . By 0.70g, it's in a full-blooded four-wheel drift. . . . Beyond the limit of . . . adhesion, the 911S reacts like any car with a rearward weight bias, and spins, or, if you're quick enough to catch it, power-slides like an old dirt-track roadster." *Road & Track* found "less of the [low-speed] understeer that so surprised us in the 911, [though above 40 mph] we were hard-pressed to detect any difference. . . . Certainly it's easier to hang out the tail if you're in the right gear, simply because of the increased power. But the simple application of steering to the 911S at highway speeds gets the same results as in the 911, which means stick-stick-stick-oversteer! And you'd better know what you're doing in that last phase."

In a calmer vein, *C/D* declared that "Porsche's admonition, 'not for the novice,' is a bit gratuitous. Within normal driving limits and with reasonable caution, the 911S handles predictably, controllably, and head and shoulders above anything else on the road." As proof, the magazine reported lateral acceleration of 0.93g in right turns, 0.89g in lefts, and a calculated 0.81g overall. These figures, good even today, came despite the modest rubber.

Both U.S. magazines were disappointed in 911S braking, blaming the skinny tires for unchanged stopping distances despite the model's new vented rotors. *C/D* also found some minor lapses in work-

manship, though its test car was admittedly "right off the boat" and had not been dealer-prepped.

The engines in both test cars evidently weren't up to scratch either. Though *C/D* cut a full second off Porsche's claimed 7.5-second 0-60 time, *R&T* managed only 8.1. But there was no disputing that the engine itself was beautifully smooth and fantastically willing.

Autocar applauded "the superb lightness of all the controls" and "excellent seating. . . . The Porsche 911S is a car one never likes to leave parked when one could be driving it. . . ." *Road & Track* was more critical, saying that in American conditions the 911S "offers no real gain over the 911 and perhaps even a slight loss. It is a bit less flexible at ordinary speeds; deceleration below about 1800 rpm brings on bucking and considerable clatter from the drivetrain, demanding an immediate downshift." But even *R&T*'s hard-nosed editors weren't immune to that intoxicating powerplant: "For the driver who really wants to get on with it, the 911S is bound to be more fun than the 911."

The fun suddenly stopped when the 911S left the American market for 1968 (though it continued in Europe). While the ostensible reason was that year's new federal emission standards and the engine retuning needed to meet them, some say it was the persistent plug-fouling, which had become a tremendous service problem. But the S would return, for 1969.

Meantime, three new variations appeared: two for Europe, one for the United States, and both part of what was called the 911 "A-Series." America's model was the 911L, replacing the standard issue just after the start of the model year. The L stood for *Luxus* (luxury) and denoted what was basically an S with the normal-tune engine. An upmarket move, it sold for $600 more than the previous year's 911, some of the increase reflecting modifications to meet the aforementioned federal safety and emissions standards.

Europe also got an L-model (from August 1967) as well as a low-priced 911T (Touring). The latter, trimmed to 912 standards, carried a detuned 110-bhp (DIN) six with reduced compression (8.6:1), cast-iron rocker arms and cylinders, milder cams, no crankshaft counterweights, steel wheels, and a lighter front anti-roll bar.

Make no mistake: Even these 911s weren't perfect. Plug-fouling afflicted even the base model (though not as severely as the S), and a switch to Weber carbs didn't completely cure the jetting and adjustment bothers of the old Solexes. Bosch WG

Given that the German autobahn has no speed limit, it's not completely surprising that the polizei selected Porsche 911s as pursuit vehicles (above). German taxpayers may have wondered, however, just why these officers were piloting the pricey Targa model. Production-line images (opposite, left and top right) from 1966 make clear that Porsche, although a "volume" carmaker, ran an operation that was very much committed to careful hand work. Note the line's order and cleanliness. By the time the peck 'o Porsches photo (top row, bottom right) was snapped in 1966, annual production was up to about 13,000 units, with four-cylinder 912s (bottom) accounting for about two-thirds of the total.

The '67 912 was the match of the more powerful 911 in handling, braking, and other dynamic aspects. Brakes were strong and fade-resistant, and steering was light and accurate. German Dunlop SP radials contributed to good cornering. Although the four-cylinder engine wasn't exactly quiet, it idled smoothly and was happy in city traffic. Inside, the 912 gained a five-dial instrument cluster for '67. Front seats were functional and comfortable.

Porsche introduced the Targa in 1965. Besides offering the pleasure of open-air motoring, the Targa was a potent performer capable of surprising the unwary or inexperienced driver with squirrely rear-end behavior in the wet or during aggressive cornering. In the photo above left, a Targa driver eyes Porsche's 906 Carrera 6 Coupe, a purpose-built racer.

265 T2SP sparkplugs helped some, but the '68 L met emission limits with an air-injection pump at the exhaust manifold that produced rough running and backfiring on deceleration. It was a makeshift solution for Porsche, and another one that would not last. In fact, the factory later made amends with a retrofit kit comprising revised jets and readjusted accelerator rods.

Outside, all '68 U.S. Porsches were distinguished—if that's the word—by add-on side marker lights, again per Washington edict. Why Porsche didn't simply integrate them within the wrapped taillight and parking-lamp clusters isn't known, though this would be done later.

Announced in Europe during 1967 was a surprising new 911 option that went to America for '68. It was Sportomatic, Porsche's first automatic transmission. Devised by Fichtel & Sachs expressly for the United States, it was, said *Car and Driver*, a throwback to "Detroit's bizarre efforts at clutchless shifting that died a merciful death in the middle Fifties." That was true, which made the Sportomatic a semi-automatic transmission. Specifically, the system combined a three-element hydraulic torque converter with a single dry-plate clutch and Porsche's own four-speed manual gearbox.

Road & Track described it this way: "The converter is a 'loose' one, with a stall speed of 2600 rpm and stall torque ratio of 2.15:1; its oil supply is common with the engine's, adding 2.5 qt. to that reservoir. The clutch is disengaged by a vacuum servo unit that gets its signal from a microswitch on the shift linkage; thus, a touch on the shift lever disengages the clutch. The gearbox is the usual all-synchro 4-speed unit but with a parking pawl added."

Gear ratios differed considerably, though. The Sportomatic's first through third were all numerically lower than the manual four-speed's, while its fourth was slightly higher. Its final drive was numerically lower too. With that, a Sportomatic L was slower off the line than its manual counterpart but almost as fast all-out. Helping performance was a very high converter efficiency of 96.5 percent.

Driving with Sportomatic took some practice. As *R&T* explained: "For all normal acceleration from rest, D (2nd gear) is used. The converter lets the engine run up to 2600 rpm immediately and . . . gets the car moving briskly, but noisily. . . . A direct shift to 4th at some casual speed will be the usual upshift. For . . . vigorous driving, the Sportomatic is just like the manual 4-speed except that one shifts without the clutch. . . . We found that the best technique was to engage 1st gear, let the clutch in (by taking the hand off the stick), 'jack up' the engine against the converter while holding the brakes, and release the brakes to start."

The technique was a little hard on the transmission but good for 0-60 in 10.3 seconds and a standing quarter-mile of 17.3 seconds at 80 mph. *Car and Driver* did better: 9.3 seconds to 60 mph and 16.8 seconds at 82 mph in the quarter. "There's absolutely no trouble in shifting," the magazine asserted. "Just grab the lever and move it. No matter how fast you do it, it's impossible to beat the clutch or the synchronizers."

In effect, Sportomatic was a compromise answer to the penchant of U.S. drivers for lugging along in high gear at low revs, thus fouling plugs and otherwise loading up engines. It was also perhaps a nod to American preference for easier driveability than previous Porsches offered. Where the 911's high torque peak meant lots of manual shifting, *R&T* found that Sportomatic allowed one to stay "in 4th gear down to ridiculous speeds like 20 mph and still accelerate smartly away with traffic. The 911 engine likes revs, and the converter lets it rev." Unhappily, it also made for more engine noise, which *R&T* likened to "a GM city bus."

Viewed objectively, Sportomatic was a typically well-judged Porsche response to a perceived need, and it didn't much hurt performance or mileage. Yes, declutching by mere touch *was* disconcerting (one wag suggested putting burrs on the shifter, to be removed after 500 miles), but drivers grew accustomed to it. Still, it wasn't the sort of thing most real Porsche fans could endorse, and by the early Seventies, demand for Sportomatic in the United States was practically nil. Regardless, the option would be available to special order all the way through May 1979.

Though "unhappy" with Sportomatic in its March 1968 road test, *Car and Driver* was pleased to note the adoption of 5.5-inch-wide wheels for all 911s. "Racing seems to have improved the breed here, and Porsche, which stormed off with the under 2-liter championship in the '67 [Sports Car Club of America] Trans-Am series, has obviously paid attention to how they accomplished that. Ride harshness suffers, but what the hell." Though *C/D* liked 911 handling more than ever, it warned first-time pilots to "approach [the car] with great respect."

For 1969, the 911 line was sorted out on both sides of the Atlantic with a three-model B-Series that entered production in August 1968. The 912, to be replaced in 1970 by the "Volks-Porsche" 914, continued to evolve in parallel, though its engine

The Targa rollbar (above) was strong, and thus functional as well as handsome. Brushed stainless steel enhanced its appearance. Good looks and high performance told just part of the 911 story in the late Sixties, the Targa included. Spark plug fouling was an ongoing problem, and fit and finish were not always up to the standards set by the earlier Type 356. Some models were prone to a rough idle and backfiring. Still, the 911 was a considerably more polished—and dependable—machine than most other performance sports cars.

was unchanged. The new 911 trio would continue for three model years. The initial U.S. versions were as follows:

911T - 110 bhp DIN (125 SAE) at 5800 rpm, 8.6:1 CR, 110 mph official top speed; base price (coupe): $5995.
911E - 140 bhp (160) at 6500; 9.0:1; 134 mph; $7195.
911S - 170 bhp (190) at 6800; 9.8:1; 140 mph; $7895.

Only the T used carburetors (twin Weber 40 IDTs). The new E (replacing the L) and the revived S both sported fuel injection, the modern way to reconcile high performance with low emissions. Transmission choices comprised Sportomatic and four- or five-speed manuals for T and E; the S was now five-speed only.

Developed by Porsche and Bosch, the new fuel injection was a mechanical system similar to the one used by Mercedes, with a squirter at each cylinder (making it a multi-point design in today's jargon) and a double-row, six-plunger pump driven by toothed belt from the left camshaft; tubes delivered fuel to the ports just below. An electric fuel pump fed the injection pump; check valves in the injectors opened at a set pressure from the injection-pump plungers. The ram tubes and a richer mixture improved power at higher crank speeds while reducing pollutants at lower rpm. To combat the old plug-fouling problem, a capacitive-discharge (CD) ignition was installed.

Fuel injection permitted other power-boosting changes. The E reverted to the original 911 cam profile, which was wilder than the L's. The S had slightly higher compression and reshaped inlet passages, plus an extra oil cooler for greater reliabilty with the higher power. Crankcases switched from aluminum to cast magnesium construction.

The one obvious visual change for '69 was slightly flared wheel openings, necessitated by wider brakes that expanded E and S track width by 0.4-inch. The S also got six-inch-wide wheels. Less apparent was a 2.25-inch (57-mm) wheelbase increase (to 89.3 inches/2268mm) via longer rear semi-trailing arms. Despite an unchanged drivetrain position, fore/aft weight distribution ended up more even, going from 41.5/58.5 percent to 43/57. At the same time, the previous Nadella axle shafts gave way to Lobro assemblies with Rzeppa constant-velocity joints; the shafts were also re-angled slightly rearward from the inner joints.

Another new chassis wrinkle for '69 was Boge self-adjusting hydropneumatic front struts, which came standard with the E and early S models, and as an option with the T and later S's. Replacing the normal front struts, torsion bars, and shocks, they kept the nose at a specified height regardless of passenger or cargo load. Unlike Citroen's oleopneumatic system, their pump was not engine-driven but pressurized by suspension movement. Though the longer '69 wheelbase shifted static weight distribution forward about 1.5 percent, this was balanced on Boge-equipped cars by deleting the front sway bar. Still, final oversteer remained the dominant handling trait in any 911, but it was never a surprise to the skilled, knowledgeable driver.

The Boge struts were part of a new 911E Comfort Package that was optional in Europe and standard in the United States. Also included were 14-inch wheels and tires, aluminum brake calipers, a more strident "highway" horn, bumper rub strips, bright-metal rocker-panel trim, gold deck script, velour carpeting, a leather-covered steering wheel, and an oil pressure/level gauge.

Fuel injection and the CD ignition wrought terrific improvements in 911 driveability. The E, for example, could lug down to 35-40 mph and then pull smoothly away, yet it was almost as fast as a '67 S. *Road & Track*'s example ran 0-60 in 8.4 seconds, the standing quarter in 16 seconds, and hit 130 mph while averaging near 20 mpg overall.

Completing 1969 refinements were a new three-speed heater fan, flat-black wiper arms, and an electric rear-window defroster. The last was also standard for Targas, as Porsche abandoned the model's leaky and noisy zip-out rear window for fixed wraparound glass that made things less open but more comfy and solid. In all, the '69s were the most tractable and pleasurable Porsches since the 356C.

All 911s became incrementally quicker with the 1970 C-Series, thanks to a 4-mm larger bore that upped displacement to 2165cc (132.1 cid). Compression ratios stayed put, but the T switched to Zenith carbs (40 TIN). Because horsepower and torque were higher across the board, clutch diameter was increased 10mm (to 225mm). On the chassis, the front-strut upper attachment points were moved 0.55-inch (14mm) forward, which reduced steering effort and kickback. Model-year 1970 also marked the first-time availability of an optional limited-slip differential. The 1970 U.S. lineup was as follows:

911T - 125 bhp DIN (145 SAE) at 5800 rpm, 128 mph official top speed; base price

Model-year 1969 was the last for the Type 912 (top and opposite, bottom row). Garage space at the home of Ferry Porsche (above) at Feuerbacher Weg, Stuttgart, was sufficient for a 912 and one or two other Porsches, as well. Meanwhile, the 911 Coupe (opposite, top) carried on, by now with an optional Sportomatic four-speed semi-automatic transmission.

(coupe): $6430.
911E - 155 bhp (175) at 6200; 137 mph; $7895.
911S - 180 bhp (200) at 6500; 144 mph; $8675.

Porsche used the extra cc's to make the S engine a trifle more composed, with still better low-end flexibility and cleaner exhaust. "As impressive as the fact that it meets smog laws is the way the 911S runs," said one tester. "It idles smoothly at 800-1000 rpm and runs without any of the common symptoms of mixture leanness found in today's emission-control high-output engines at moderate speeds." Even so, the S remained too much car for speed-limited U.S. driving, displaying "very little torque until about 4500 rpm. . . . But going up through the gears. . .brings out noises that will warm hearts even of those accustomed to exotic V-12s. Glorious noises!"

While the S was in the same performance league as the Jaguar E-Type and Chevy Corvette, it was far better built and achieved its exciting ends through finesse, not brute force. But it was also becoming quite costly now, rarely delivering for under $9000—though even that had a certain appeal. As *Road & Track* quipped, the S offered "performance on the order of an American Supercar but without the stigma of low cost."

By contrast, the bottom-line T was relatively affordable in 1970-71 at around $6500. True, that was more than a Jaguar E-Type or a Corvette but $1000 less than a Mercedes 280SL—fortunate, as the prospective T buyer was quite likely to consider the Merc.

After a little-changed group of 1971 D-Series models came the E-Series 911s for 1972, again showing increases in both displacement and wheelbase. A longer stroke (to 70.4mm, up 4.4mm) on an unchanged bore took the flat-six to 142.9 cid/2341cc, though engine-lid badges optimistically stated "2.4" liters. Wheelbase lengthened a mere 3mm to 89.4 inches (2271mm), a change that has never been explained.

The extra displacement stemmed from Porsche's desire to maintain performance against the fast-stiffening U.S. emission standards. California, still requiring lower pollutant levels than other states, mandated that all cars be operable on low-lead 91-octane gasoline beginning with model-year 1972. Detroit responded by simply reducing compression—and thus performance—while most European producers went to different pistons and heads. Thus began the disappointing era of "federalized" imports marked by an ever-widening performance/economy gap with Porsches designed for the German market.

Porsche also lowered compression for '72, but the greater displacement more than offset it. In fact, all three engines showed useful output gains, so 911 performance scarcely suffered. The specifics:

911T - 130 bhpDIN (157 SAE) at 5600 rpm, 7.5:1
911E - 165 bhp DIN (185 SAE) at 6200 rpm, 8.1:1
911S - 190 bhp DIN (210 SAE) at 6500 rpm, 8.5:1

These figures weren't all that different from those of 911s sold in Europe (which would soon enact emission standards of its own), reflecting a corporate philosophy that Porsche publicly declared a decade later: namely, one engine spec and one performance level for all markets. As if to signal this, Bosch fuel injection was applied to the 1972 U.S.-market T.

Car and Driver compared all three 911s in a 1972 test, and the results bear scrutiny:

	911T	911E	911S
0-60 mph (sec.)	6.9	5.8	6.0
0-¼ mile (sec.)	15.1	14.3	14.4
¼-mile mph	91.7	96.9	96.8
Top speed (mph)	125	135	140
80 mph braking(ft)	271	234	280
Curb wt. (lbs)	2425	2475	2455
Base price	$8804	$10,506	$10,749

Two things emerge here: the T's continuing status as a remarkable buy in Porsche performance, and the close similarity between E and S, even though *C/D*'s E was the heavier Targa (the others were coupes). Evidently, the E was improving at a faster rate.

But then, that could be said for all 911s in '72. For starters, the oil tank was now made of stainless steel and relocated from the right-rear wheelarch to a position between it and the right door. Even better, it gained an external flap, like the one for the gas filler on the left front fender. But the arrangement was axed after this one year because people tended to put fuel in the oil tank by mistake—with disastrous results. The fuel tank was expanded to 21.1 gallons when its upper half was stamped around a new space-saver spare tire (an arrangement that was prohibited in Britain).

Aiding high-speed stability as well as appearance was a small under-bumper "chin" spoiler. The result of aerodynamic work by Porsche engineers, it reduced front-end lift from 183 to 102 pounds at 140 mph—though that was purely academic to Americans heading for a 55-mph national

Horsepower on the 1969 911S Coupe (top) came in at 170 at 6800 rpm. With 9.8:1 compression and Bosch mechanical fuel injection, the S summoned potent performance. Larger brakes necessitated flared wheelarches. The 911E Coupe (left) ran with 140 horses at 6600 rpm, good enough for a 134 mph top speed, just six mph less than the S. The '69 912 Coupe (right), in contrast, summoned 102 horsepower from its 96.5-cid flat-four. As with earlier 912s, the '69's forte was finesse rather than brute power.

speed limit. The spoiler was optional for the T and E, standard on the S, but became so popular that it was included on all models after 1973.

Among chassis changes for '72 were larger-diameter anti-roll bars for the S (now 15mm front and rear), and cancellation of the Boge struts, which had garnered few orders. The S reverted to a standard four-speed gearbox. The optional five-speed was strengthened, made easier to shift, and—a welcome change—given a conventional gate with fifth on a dogleg to the right and first at the top left of the "H."

Car and Driver's comparison test reported that the T "has exactly the same acceleration in the quarter-mile as the 2.0-liter 911S of 1969 and is a whole lot less fussy about the way it's driven. . . . The E is easy to get along with too. . . . It's smooth at low speeds, feels strong at 3000 rpm, and climbs up to its 6800-rpm redline with determination." By contrast, the '72 S was "a top-speed car more than anything else. The engine doesn't feel capable until about 5000, and you usually end up shifting there even in routine traffic. . . . It is rough at low speeds and wants to buck in traffic. The torque band is narrow, so much so that even though all of the 5-speed 911s have the same transmission ratios, they feel too wide only in the S."

After track testing at California's Riverside Raceway, the least costly 911 emerged as *C/D*'s favorite "because it was the most predictable. The E, whose Targa roof probably give it a fractionally higher center of gravity, had slightly more steady-state understeer and more vigorous tail-wag in transients. Its most conspicuous trick, however, was its three-legged dog stance in turns. Typically, 911s lift the inside front wheel, but few to the dizzying heights of this Targa . . . ."

Car and Driver went on to say, "The S was much like the E. Perhaps a little less understeer and an extra increment of twitch. Like the T, the S was a coupe, but its electric sunroof alters its weight distribution somewhat. There were extra pounds in the roof and the electric motor was back in the engine compartment. If handling is your goal, it's best to stick with the plain coupe."

The 911 continued its winning ways for 1973. Changes for that year's F-Series models began with big black-rubber bumper guards and steel reinforcing door beams per federal mandate, plus distinctive "cookie-cutter" alloy wheels on the E. Engines stayed the same through mid-model year, when the T gained Bosch's new K-Jetronic fuel injection (a.k.a. CIS—Continuous Injection System), good for an extra 10 DIN horses (seven SAE).

The 911 was now a decade old yet seemed to have aged hardly at all. Of course, it was getting progressively better—and not a moment too soon, given the upheavals that rocked the American auto industry in 1974. The toughest U.S. emissions standards ever made most engines less efficient than ever. A new federal edict for 5-mph bumpers brought power-sapping weight and ugly looks to too many cars. Inflation was still pushing prices up and sales down, even as soaring insurance rates continued devastating the ranks of performance machines.

But the real shocker came in late 1973 from a heretofore little-known cartel called OPEC (Organization of Petroleum Exporting Countries), which decided to make "black gold" as precious as real gold by shutting off Middle East pipelines. Long waiting lines began to form at gas pumps across the United States, and prices for all petroleum-based products went out of sight. That winter was longer and colder than usual for the world's industrial nations as rationing and other energy-conserving measures threatened to become a way of life.

Against this bleak backdrop stood refurbished 911s that remained uncompromising high performers in utter defiance of the day's news. Naturally they had "crash" bumpers but so skillfully integrated as to look like they'd been there all along. And while many automakers resorted to smaller engines, the 911s got a larger one that met all the latest "smog regs" while sacrificing little in performance or fuel efficiency.

Of course, these changes were pure coincidence, for no one could have predicted the events of model-year '74. Still, the 911 entered its eleventh year as unassailable proof that when the going got tough, Porsche knew how to get going.

Much of the groundwork for the '74s was laid in 1973 with a very special European 911: the Carrera RS. The initials meant *Rennsport* ("racing sport"), signifying a competition Porsche—here, a 911 trimmed and tuned for the Group 4 GT class. Rules specified a minimum 500 be built, and Porsche deliberately held the price to the equivalent of about $10,000 in Germany to ensure they sold. Happily, demand proved so strong that 1636 were ultimately produced. With that, the RS was reclassified as a Group 3 series-production GT, a class it stood to dominate because of minimal allowable modifications. Porsche raised the car's price by several thousand dollars to more closely reflect true worth. The late Dean Batchelor recorded that some 600 RS models were trimmed *a la* the 911S for road use in

The static but neatly organized Porsche engine assembly line (above), snapped in 1970. The '70 911E Coupe (opposite, top left) developed 155 horsepower in U.S. trim; top speed was 137 mph. The same year's 911S (bottom left and bottom right) was considerably more robust at 180 bhp and had better off-the-line performance. Top speed was 144. The 911T of 1971 (remaining photos) was the "bottom-of-the-line" Porsche—an oxymoron if ever there was one. Although it cost more than a Jaguar E-Type or a Corvette, at $6500 it was nevertheless a bargain-priced exotic. Horsepower was 125 at 5800 rpm. Versatile gearing allowed the T to lug down to 30-40 mph in fourth and still accelerate away smartly. 911 body styles for '71 were restricted to Coupe or Targa; buyers cold choose from three transmissions: four- or five-speed manual or the seldom-selected semi-automatic Sportomatic.

The 911's wheelbase was stretched to 89.4 inches for 1972. Engine displacement was bumped up to 2341cc—a tad shy of the "2.4" badge the 911 now carried. The 911T (all photos left and above) managed 157 SAE horsepower at 5600 rpm. At 6.9 seconds in the 0-60 run, the T was less than one second slower than the 911S— which cost some $2000 more. The '72 911 Carrera RS (below) was a no-no for street running, but was a fearsome track competitor. Only 500 were built that year, for purposes of Group 4 homologation. The street 911 (opposite page) saw few changes for 1973. Engine manufacture continued to be as meticulous as before; at mid-year the T-type received Bosch's new CIS fuel injection. The S (top right) and E Targa (bottom) summoned 180 and 165 bhp, respectively.

Europe. None came to America, though: "dirty" engine, you know.

Dirty or not, the engine was indisputably powerful. Designated Type 911/93, it was a new 2.7-liter version of the now legendary flat-six, achieved by boring out the 2.4 from 84 to 90mm. This required deletion of the Biral cylinder liners and a coating of the bores with Nikasil, a nickel/silicon carbide alloy that brought a happy bonus in reduced internal friction. The 2.4's valves, timing, compression, and fuel injection were all retained, but the extra cc's added 20 horses for a total of 200 DIN/230 SAE at 6300 rpm in roadgoing trim.

As a homologation special, the RS 2.7 was much lightened (thin-gauge body steel, for instance) and thus tipped the scales at less than a ton—about 300 pounds under a stock S. The chassis was beefed up with gas-pressurized Bilstein shocks, super-stiff sway bars, and aluminum wheels measuring an inch wider at the rear than on a roadgoing S (six inches as opposed to five).

Outside, RS 2.7s were unmistakable. All were finished in white, and Zuffenhausen designers played up the return of a production-based Carrera by putting an outsize version of the traditional name script (in blue) above the rocker panels. Rear fenders were further flared to suit the wider wheels (also blue), and a small "bib" spoiler sprouted beneath the front bumper. But the visual keynote was a prominent rear spoiler molded into the engine cover. Aptly nicknamed "ducktail," it kept the rear firmly planted at speed by reducing lift from 320 to just 93 pounds. It also improved airflow through the engine-cover grille and moved the effective center of pressure about six inches rearward as another aid to stability.

The Carrera RS was greeted with high enthusiasm, and the full-fledged RSR track version wrote a brilliant record in Group 4 competition (detailed in Chapter 7). Porsche upped the ante for '74 with the RS/RSR 3.0, needing to build only 100 for homologation as a 2.7 "evolution."

Despite similar weight-reducing mods, the 3.0 was some 400 pounds heavier than the 2.7. But that was more than offset by another 5-mm bore stretch that gave 2993cc and net roadgoing horsepower of 220 (DIN) at 6200 rpm. Also featured were a wider, horizontal rear spoiler, quickly dubbed the "whale tail"; a bulkier front spoiler with large, rectangular air intake; even wider wheels (8-inch front, 9-inch aft) and tires (215/60VR15 front, 235/60VR15 rear); die-cast aluminum crankcase; and huge cross-drilled disc brakes from Porsche's mighty turbocharged 917 Can-Am racer. The 2.7 had needed

a special road permit in Germany because the ducktail was deemed hazardous to pedestrians. Porsche got around this on the 3.0 by supplying two engine covers: one with a large racing spoiler, the other with a smaller whale tail edged in protective black rubber. Several wild colors were added, and black replaced chrome on most body trim.

In testing a 3.0 for *Road & Track,* journalist/race driver Paul Frere *averaged* 124 mph over 78 miles of Italian *autostrada.* What's more, "60 mph is reached in a staggering 5.2 seconds with the help of superlative rear-wheel grip, and the ¼-mile mark comes in 14 seconds. . . . The car understeers, though lifting off at the limit of adhesion will swing the tail out sharply. On the Casale track, near Torino, I found that fast bends must still be approached with some power on and that getting the car around fast *and* safely still calls for a certain amount of delicacy."

Like the 2.7, the "street" 3.0 wasn't sold in America, though Roger Penske gave the RSR lots of publicity by using 15 in his inaugural International Race of Champions series of driver showdowns. Another 49 were built and continued to dominate the likes of SCCA Trans-Am and the IMSA Camel GT series. A final 60 were finished as roadgoing RS models.

But it scarcely mattered that these race-and-ride 911s didn't ply U.S. streets, for their influence was evident in a new top-line '74 model looking much like the 3.0 RS—whale tail, bulged fenders, big graphics, and all. It, too, was called *Carrera,* returning the name to American showrooms for the first time since the last 356 Carrera 2s. Inevitably, it was slower than its European cousin but somewhat more civilized.

At the other end of the scale, the base '74 was just plain 911 again, and much like the previous. T. With the new Carrera, the S became the middle model and equivalent to the former E in trim and performance. All used the new 2.7 engine but much more mildly tuned than in the 2.7 RS. The American-version Carrera and S packed 167 bhp (SAE net) at 5800 rpm, the base 911 "only" 143 bhp. The extra displacement was yet another timely Porsche response to tightening emissions limits, complemented by linewide adoption of Bosch's more modern CIS injection. This same model group was also sold in other markets, though with freer breathing and commensurately more horsepower: 150 bhp (DIN) at 5700 rpm (911), 175 at 5800 rpm (911S), and 210 bhp at 6300 rpm (Carrera 2.7).

Regardless of tuning, all '74-model 911s wore the new front and rear bumpers mandated by Am-

The '73 911S (top left) was twitchier on the street than the E (other photos); this was partly due to the weight of the electric sunroof and accompanying electric motor sited at the back of the engine compartment. S and E models ran with the same rubber, 185/70VR-15. Porsche took pains to show the 911's considerable luggage capacity (top right) in the front boot.

erican law. After all, why have different bumpers for just one market? *Road & Track* noted (in customary overkill fashion), "Porsche went beyond 1974 requirements for sports cars and did a major redesign to put the bumpers' effective heights at the 16- and 20-in. level already required for sedans and to be [required] for sports cars next year." This involved pulling the bumpers out and putting them on aluminum-alloy tubes that collapsed when struck at 5 mph or above—and thus had to be replaced. Still, they did protect the body much better, and the bumpers were now aluminum, too, which saved weight. Hydraulic shock-absorber attachments that didn't need replacing were standard for the United Kingdom and extra cost elsewhere—in the United States, a $135 "mandatory option." Accordian-pleat rubber boots neatly filled the gaps between body and bumpers, which were overlaid in color-keyed plastic with black rubber inserts.

Here was yet another thoroughly Porsche solution, and one that made most other "crash" bumpers seem clumsy. Not that Zuffenhausen didn't have reason to do it right: The United States was now taking over 50 percent of its total yearly production. (By contrast, the United States accounted for well under 20 percent of annual BMW and Mercedes volume.)

Other changes for '74 included a full-width taillight lens bearing the Porsche name, black-finish engine grille with a "2.7" legend in chrome, highback bucket seats, tiny fresh-air vents at each end of the dash, and new steering wheels. Targas lost their fold-up roof panel for a more convenient one-piece affair.

Chassis-wise, forged aluminum replaced welded steel for rear semi-trailing arms in all '74s, and sway bars and wheel/tire packages were tailored to each model. The base 911 had the usual 5.5 X 15 alloy rims and 165HR15 tires; the 911S rolled on forged 15 X 6 wheels with 185/70VR15 rubber (optional on the base car). Both sported a 16mm-diameter front anti-roll bar and could be ordered with an 18mm rear bar. The Carrera used the S wheel/tire combo in front and 215/60 tires on 15 X 7 rims at the rear. It also came with the rear bar, plus a larger 20mm front bar.

Road & Track sampled all three '74s, and its results were about what you'd expect despite non-stock tires on base and S examples that made handling comparisons tricky. The Carrera had more stick and less understeer on the track, but equal-size tires made the base 911 quicker and more agile through the slalom. *Car and Driver* also found the "plain Jane" model had more cornering power than the Carrera: 0.83g versus 0.80. Of course, neither figure was exactly shabby. In fact, they still pass muster today.

As for go-power, *R&T* observed that "all our '74s would beat [a '73] 911S soundly in the ¼ mi despite having taller gearing. The basic 911 is plenty quick, getting to 60 mph in 7.9 sec and covering the ¼ mi in 15.5 sec; its top speed is limited by power to 130 mph. The 911S and Carrera accelerate identically to 100 mph and beat the 911 to 60 or the ¼ mi by 0.4 sec; the margin widens to 2.6 sec by 100 mph. There's quite a difference to be felt by the driver, too: whereas the less powerful 911 pulls evenly toward its rev limit (all three [stop] at 6400 because of their rev limiters) the S/Carrera unit comes 'onto the cam' strongly at about 3500 rpm and shoots toward 6400 at a dizzying rate. All our test cars, by the way, had the optional 5-speed gearbox—which we think you can jolly well do without, so strong is the low-speed response of either engine."

Unfortunately, the high-power engine still suffered "a good old-fashioned case of temperament" at low speeds, "bucking just like the more highly tuned older S unit." At least fuel economy was "still reasonably good. At 17.5 mpg overall, the 911 is a bit more thirsty than last year's 911E and the S/Carrera does another 1.5 mph less but remains more economical than the old S."

R&T carped about prices, which were up some 20 percent from '73 to a minimum $10,000 and close to 14 grand for the Carrera. "The Porsche people also have the nerve to charge you extra for opening rear-quarter windows in all but . . . the Carrera, and the air conditioner costs $1125!" At least the Carrera came with power front windows. Still, as *R&T* grudgingly concluded, "they've got you over a barrel: a Porsche is like no other car, and if you want one there's no substitute."

In the meantime, comfort and performance options had proliferated greatly. The five-speed was still reasonable at $250 in '74, a new two-stage electric rear window defroster cost $70, and buyers could now order Koni shocks, a deluxe steering wheel, and contrast-color 911S road wheels. Also on the list were paint and upholstery "to sample," meaning any hue or trim material the buyer wanted. By default, Zuffenhausen was becoming a "boutique" automaker in the face of soaring prices fueled by rampant inflation.

For 1975, the Carrera gained a deeper front spoiler and IROC-style rear spoiler. The 911S was visually unchanged, but the base 911 disappeared. Perhaps

1974 was a watershed year for Porsche, as the 911 entered its second decade with Coupe and Targa body styles, and new iterations: base, S, and RS Carrera. Note the well-integrated "crash bumpers," to comply with new American standards. The 911 engine was enlarged to 2687cc and developed 143 horsepower at 5700 rpm—an impressive feat given emissions restrictions decreed for the U.S. market. Overall length grew by .5 inch, to 168.9.

responding to *Road & Track*'s griping, Porsche expanded standard features to include the aforementioned push-out rear windows, plus intermittent wipers, a rear anti-roll bar and, for the Carrera, a leather interior. Having bowed in Europe during 1974, high-pressure headlight washers (developed with Hella) arrived as a new option for buyers in the United States. The heating system gained separate left/right controls, and a higher-capacity alternator was fitted along with a single battery (ousting the two smaller cells used since '66).

Engine news was less heartening, as both Carrera and 911S lost 10 horses (15 in California) to detuning for lower emission levels. The Carrera's 0-60 time was up a second (to 8.4), and its official top speed fell 10 mph (to 132), yet fuel consumption was no worse than before—though no better, either. Still, Porsche had avoided the worst maladies of the "desmogging" era by offering exhaust-gas recirculation on 49-state cars and twin thermal reactors for smog-beset California. And in city driving, the '75s were better behaved than the '74s.

The Carrera now cost $1700 more than the S but made up for it with standard bodyside graphics in special colors, a three-spoke steering wheel, and the items mentioned above. Interiors were becoming funereal, with matte black or silver replacing the shiny stuff now banned by the feds. Overall, though, the 911 remained "one of the world's best sports cars," in *R&T*'s widely shared view. "If an automotive bargain still remains in our inflation-ridden world, the Carrera, or any 1975 911, is it."

Honoring 25 years of Stuttgart production, Porsche issued a limited-edition Silver Anniversary 911S in 1975. Only 1500 were built, with half going Stateside. Each wore diamond-silver metallic paint, custom interior trim of woven silver-and-black tweed, and a numbered dash plaque with Ferry Porsche's facsimile signature. Ever looking ahead, the good doctor confirmed that the old warrior was far from finished: "With all the regulations that are known to us now, we think the 911 can keep going for the next six years." As usual, he was being modest.

America celebrated its bicentennial in 1976, and Porsche joined in by unleashing the mightiest 911 yet: the Turbo Carrera. This was yet another creation of the prolific Ernst Fuhrmann, who became Porsche chairman in 1972 (after the Porsche and Piech families relinquished control and the company became a joint-stock corporation with a board of directors—today's Dr. Ing. h.c. F. Porsche AG). Fuhrmann, you'll recall, had designed the original quadcam 356 Carrera engine; he also

directed development of the 1972-73 European Carrera RS/RSR.

Fuhrmann appreciated good engineers (he hired many himself) and shared Ferdinand and Ferry's belief that racing really does improve the breed. He also knew a good deal about turbochargers from work on the racing 917's tremendous hyperaspirated flat-12. What could a turbo do for the 911? Soon after taking the helm, Fuhrmann set up a program to find out.

One of the first fruits of the program was a "911 Turbo" displayed at several 1973 European shows—without comment on possible production. The following year, the Martini & Rossi team had mixed results with a turbo 2.1-liter Carrera RSR packing 333 bhp (one was doing 189 mph on the Mulsanne Straight at Le Mans when it threw a rod and retired). Nevertheless, Fuhrmann and company were sufficiently encouraged to proceed with a production turbocar: a smooth, quiet, very fast 911 coupe with a blown version of the 2993-cc Carrera 3.0 RS engine.

It bowed at the 1974 Paris Show as a prototype called *911 Turbo*, a name later changed to simply *Porsche Turbo*. So extensive were the modifications that it bore a new type number: 930. Motive power was a terrific 260 bhp (DIN) at 5500 rpm and 245 pounds/feet of torque peaking at 4000 rpm. An American version, emissions-tuned to 234 SAE net horsepower (245 DIN), arrived for model-year 1976 as the Turbo Carrera.

The ultimate 911 to date, the 930 packed most every luxury the factory could squeeze in. Air-conditioning, AM/FM stereo (U.S. version), electric antenna and windows, leather interior, tinted glass, headlamp washers, rear-window wiper, oil cooler, and Bilstein shocks were all included in the initial East Coast base price of $25,880—a bundle of bucks in those days. The U.S. options list was short: electric sliding sunroof ($675), limited-slip differential ($345), heavy-duty starter ($50), "Turbo" graphics ($120), and custom paint ($250). The 930 came only as a coupe and was never sold with Sportomatic (though several factory test cars were so equipped and worked well).

The 930 engine (produced in /50, /51, and /52 variations) testified anew to the amazing adaptability of the 911 flat-six. The 3.0-liter size was chosen for good off-boost performance with the lower compression then deemed necessary for turbocharging (6.5:1 for all markets). The blower itself sat on a cast-aluminum manifold studded to the heads, and the Bosch injection was upgraded with Ultramid plastic tubing. Maximum boost was set

Besides the integrated bumpers that were new for 1974, the model year brought flared rear wheelarches and a new chin spoiler. The 911S (top) had the look of a serious street machine, while the Targa had an even more fun-loving aspect. Of course, 911 prices that had increased 20 percent over 1973 tended to temper the fun. Even rear-quarter windows that opened cost extra (except on the high-buck Carrera).

at 11.5 pounds per square inch. Even in emissions-legal U.S. form the 930 had a prodigious 246 pounds/feet of torque (SAE net) at 4500 rpm, which Porsche thought sufficient to pull a wide-ratio four-speed transaxle instead of the close-ratio five-speed.

If the 930 was predictably less torquey than a 911 below 3000 rpm, things started happening quickly above that. Yet there was "no sudden surge of power as there is with the cammy S," said *Road & Track.* "Rather, the buildup is . . . strong and silent as the turbocharger muffles the usual raucous-sounding Porsche exhaust to a dull roar. It takes the driver a moment or two to realize [that] some awesome, unseen force is pushing him back into his seat and thrusting the Carrera forward at an incredible rate. And another brief moment to realize that the engine is starting to stumble because it's reached its 6950-rpm rev limit. Then it's shift into the next gear and prepare for the same heavy loads and fireworks to start all over again."

R&T allowed that a slipping clutch made its test car a bit slow, so it's interesting to compare the magazine's results with *Car and Driver*'s 1976 Turbo test:

	C/D	R&T
0-50 mph (sec.)	3.7	5.2
0-60 mph (sec.)	4.9	6.7
0-80 mph (sec.)	7.9	9.9
0-100 mph (sec.)	12.9	15.3
0-1/4 mi. (sec.)	13.5	15.2
top speed (mph)	156	156

Though dynamic behavior was basically routine 911, *R&T* judged the Turbo more stable at speed because of its larger rear tires and wider track. Not everyone agreed. NASCAR ace Bobby Allison, after testing the similar '75 Carrera for *C/D*, termed handling "almost squirrely." But *R&T* insisted that the Turbo was "far and away the easiest Porsche to drive near the limit that we have ever tested." Its 62.8 mph through the slalom broke a record held by a Ferrari Berlinetta Boxer by 2.4 mph. And the driver Sam Posey, who happened by while *R&T* was testing at Lime Rock, hopped in and unofficially broke the track record for production cars!

The 930 had stiffer springs and shocks in addition to its wider rear boots, so it didn't ride as well as a normal 911. Its steering was heavier, too, and tire noise was considerable. There were no complaints about the brakes, however, for they were fade-free, impossible to lock, and capable of 60-mph halts in less than 160 feet—excellent for the fairly hefty 2825 pounds of curb weight.

In all, the 930 was a remarkably civilized and undemanding ultra-performance car. "It can be pottered around town all day in top gear and a bit of second without bother," said Britain's *Autocar.* "And when the town limits are past, there is all that ocean of surging performance under your right foot, immediately, with not the slightest need for tiresome plug-clearing first."

Today, of course, we take street-legal turbocars for granted, but they were big news in '76—as was the 930's shattering performance. Like so many technical breakthroughs, Porsche had pioneered this one. And it was only the beginning.

Though ousted by the Turbo from the '76 U.S lineup, the normally aspirated Carrera continued in Europe, along with a base 911. Both offered 200 bhp (DIN) at 6000 rpm—still pretty impressive—and sold in Germany starting at dm44,950.

The 1976 American-market S was little changed aside from a $1000 higher base price that included most of the '75 Carrera's standard features, plus remote-adjustable body-color door mirrors and a still-further improved climate system with optional automatic temperature control (also available on the Turbo). Another new extra for both '76 models was Porsche's first cruise control. Sold under the catchy name "Tempostat," it was devised mainly for long-distance driving conditions in the United States.

Responding to buyer concerns about durability in the face of rapidly rising prices, Porsche began galvanizing all 901-series bodyshells on both sides, and backed it with a six-year no-rust warranty. It was only fair. If Porsches had to cost the earth, they should at least outlast the loan payments.

A new 912 was far more down to earth—and not entirely unexpected. The mid-engine 914, the "people's Porsche" developed with Volkswagen to replace the original 912, had failed to make much headway in the popular-price sports-car market since its 1970 debut (as related in the following chapter). A substitute was coming, the radical 924 (chronicled in Chapter 5). But it wasn't quite ready yet, so the 912 was brought back to anchor the bottom of the '76 line while the last 914s quietly exited showrooms.

Yet this new 912 was again typically Porsche in being no mere rerun. For one thing, it was now called 912E—E for *einspritzung.* And it carried not a Porsche engine but the injected 2.0-liter VW four available in 914s after 1972. While that change was dubious, the 912E did benefit from most all the body and chassis improvements accorded the 911 since '69, and its U.S. East Coast price of just under

Road & Track asserted that the 911 remained "one of the world's best sports cars" for 1975 (top), this despite a 10-horsepower loss on the 911S and Carrera (the base 911 having been dropped), to satisfy increasingly stringent U.S. emissions controls. The Turbo Carrera (other photos) that appeared in Germany in 1975 became available in America a year later. It was the most potent 911 yet, cranking out 260 bhp (DIN) at 500 rpm, with 245 pounds/feet of torque. Horsepower of the American version was 245 (DIN). So special was the Turbo 911 that it picked up its own internal designation: 930.

$11,000 was considerably lower, though more than charged for late 914s. But then, this was a "real" Porsche to most eyes, not a half-breed like the mid-engine "Vo-Po."

"The 912E will obviously find favor with those who prefer a slightly more practical and tractable Porsche," predicted *Road & Track*. "It's a car with almost all the sporting virtues of the more expensive 911S, yet its simpler pushrod 4-cyl. engine should make for better fuel economy and less expensive maintenance than the 911's six" (though the injection tended to misbehave in cold weather). SAE net hosepower was just 86 at 4900 rpm, torque a more useful 98 pounds/feet at 4000. Curb weight was 2395 pounds, which meant the 912 had somehow picked up 400 extra pounds since '69. Still, *R&T*'s 11.3-second 0-60 mph time and 115-mph top speed looked good against the observed 23.0-mpg economy.

As a stopgap, the 912E was the single instance of "planned obsolescence" in Porsche history. Only 2092 were built, but this plus year-only status and the desirable qualities inherited from contemporary 911s have since made the 912E one of the more collectible four-cylinder Porsches.

A busy 1977 saw Porsche introduce its "heretical" new water-cooled front-engine models: the V-8-powered 928 in Europe (see Chapter 6) and the four-cylinder 924 in America. As a result, the 911S and Turbo were little changed. An extra pair of air vents appeared in the middle of instrument panels, heater controls were altered again, interior door locks were reworked to better foil thieves, and carpeting was run up onto the lower door panels. A bit depressing were a special speedometer and speed governor on U.S. models. These limited maximum velocity to 130 mph, the speed rating for the tires now specified. Sportomatic 911s (except with right-hand drive) and the U.S. 911S received an ATE vacuum brake booster, and softer tires and shocks were optional in a $495 U.S.-market Comfort Group that also included electric windows.

Like most everything in these years, Porsche prices kept going nowhere but up. The Turbo stood pat for '77, but the 911S that had been under $12,000 three years before was now nudging $15,000. Even so, the 911 remained an outstanding premium sports-car buy. Through one of the most troubled periods in automotive history, when most designers and engineers bowed to the wishes of politicians and bureaucrats, Porsche kept the 911 within the law—and as exciting as it had ever been.

On June 3, 1977, Porsche built its 250,000th car.

Fittingly, it was 911, a European 2.7-liter S. Yet many still wondered just how long such an "old-fashioned" car could go on. After all, except for Alpine-Renault in France and, soon, John Z. De-Lorean, nobody was building rear-engine cars anymore. Air cooling? Ancient history. But Porsche's pride wouldn't permit neglect, and though bean-counters have never ruled in Zuffenhausen, the 911 remained central to Porsche's image and, increasingly, to sales. This explains why it got a new lease on life with the 911SC of 1978.

Hewing to tradition, the SC bowed at the Frankfurt Auto Show in September '77 alongside a virtually unchanged 930. Essentially, it was the old Carrera 3.0 in everything but name, with the same basic specifications, appearance, and features. (*Autocar* called it "a Carrera with a broader market appeal.") Displacement and cylinder dimensions were unchanged, but 8.5:1 compression and other tuning differences took DIN horsepower down to 180 at 5500 rpm (172 bhp SAE net). But that was up slightly on the previous "cooking" 2.7, and a flatter, fuller torque curve with a peak 189 pounds/feet at 4200 rpm (SAE net) made the SC even easier to drive.

In line with Porsche's policy of a "world" specification and performance level, all 1978-model 911s, regardless of market, got a U.S.-style air pump and Bosch breakerless electronic ignition with rpm limiter. But the American SC used the more efficient catalytic converter instead of thermal reactors as its main emissions-control device, which also enhanced driveability. Other SC improvements included a stronger crank with larger bearings, and the return of an aluminum crankcase. Outside were the Turbo Carrera's wider rear wheels and tires and flared fenders to cradle them. A new Sport Group package option added the well-known whale tail and front air dam.

With the SC, the 911 could finally claim tractability as a virtue. In fact, *Road & Track* likened it to "a big V-8-powered Detroit car. There's lots of torque, so constant downshifting isn't necessary even in slow traffic. No Porsche owner is going to let the revs fall to 1000 rpm in 5th gear and then attempt to accelerate. But to prove a point, we did this with the SC and the engine accepted the treatment with never a judder of protest . . . just roll your foot off the clutch pedal and glide away." *Autocar* found that in fourth gear "there was scarcely more than half a second's difference between the times for every increment between 30-50 mph [6.5 seconds] and 80-100 mph [6.3 sec]. . . . Even in fifth gear the same pattern emerges."

Production of the mighty 930 Turbo (top row) continued in 1976. As before, it was powerful and luxurious (note the headlight washer, bottom right), and was constructed with a significant amount of hand work; likewise the "regular" 911s (bottom left). Factory testing included runs over "moonscaped" tracks peppered with deep craters (middle right).

The 911S was succeeded by the 911SC for 1978. As inflation continued, price moved up dramatically, from close to $15,000 in '77 to more than $22,000 the following year. The SC's engine displaced 2933cc (182.6 cid) with bore and stroke of 95 X 70.4mm. Former twitchiness was eliminated, making the 911 much easier to drive.

The '78 SC (top) picked up the wide rear tires of the Carrera, and the fender flares that went with them. The SC carried on for 1979 (left and above), adding standard servo-assisted brakes and a new clutch-disc hub that quieted low-speed gear chatter. Stateside base price now topped $25,500.

Some testers still griped about notchy shift action, though the tendency usually disappeared after a few thousand miles. The linkage was stiff on purpose (though less so starting with the '87 models, suggesting second thoughts). Spring loading was biased toward the middle plane (third/fourth), so selecting top gear demanded conscious effort, at least by neophytes.

Like previous 911s, the SC tended to final oversteer, but it was set up to maintain understeer through higher cornering speeds and forces. The bigger rear wheels and tires helped, and even bigger Pirelli P7 boots were available (205/55VR16 front, 225/50VR16 rear). Apply too much power through a hard bend and the pilot merely got more understeer; lift off mid-bend and the back end might try to catch up with the front. Still, it usually took a professional now to elicit tail-wag.

In all, the SC was widely judged the most forgiving 911 yet, though the "wide tyres [sic] have some demerits in wet weather," warned Autocar. "We suffered occasionally from front-end aquaplaning under braking on water-covered roads, and understeer is also far more noticeable on wet surfaces. In these . . . conditions the tail can sometimes be provoked out of line with the throttle, and understeer can also be killed by the traditional remedy of easing back on the throttle, being prepared to catch the resulting slide. Such intracacies of handling make the Porsche very much a driver's car; experience with it constantly teaches new skills."

The SC rolled into 1979 with standard power brakes and a new clutch-disc hub that minimized gear chatter at low speeds. The latter necessitated moving the engine back 30mm (about 1.2 inches), but no handling changes were noticeable except on the track. Porsche engineers also decreed higher rear tire pressures (from 34 to 43 psi). The Sportomatic option was finally dropped for lack of interest, and base prices jumped in the United States by some $3500.

Up at $34,000 sat the most powerful production Porsche yet, a fortified 930 simply called Porsche Turbo. Widening bore by 2mm upped displacement to 3299cc (201.3 cid), and a new air-to-air intercooler squeezed more air into every intake stroke to extract more energy from every power stroke. The intercooler was a squeeze itself. Shoehorned into the engine bay, it pushed the A/C condenser to the right side of the whale-tail's air intake.

Compression was higher, if still mild at 7.0:1, and combined with the intercooler and extra cc's for 300 bhp (DIN) at 5500 rpm (253 SAE net) and 303 pounds/feet of torque at 4000 rpm.

Even so, Turbo performance improved little. Again, Porsche fitted a larger engine mainly to keep pace with U.S. emissions limits—and new European standards that had started to creep in, as well. For the record, Car and Driver timed 0-60 at 4.9 seconds and 0-100 at 12.1, still quite colossal. Braking? C/D reported that the huge, cross-drilled four-piston discs delivered 70-0 mph in just 168 feet. Skidpad performance was as impressive as ever at 0.81g.

As always, though, numbers weren't the whole story. As C/D's Don Sherman related: "Steep first-gear acceleration will jerk one wheel right off the ground if you light the booster exiting a slow turn. The shift linkage occasionally binds up to add a little extra excitement. . . . Speed lightens front wheel loading dramatically, so understeer goes up with velocity. This would be a marvelous safety device were it not for the Turbo's lift-throttle antics. Aerodynamic understeer tricks you into lifting off the throttle when the nose starts drifting wide in a high-speed turn. It's not the thing to do . . . because this reverses longitudinal forces in the rear suspension. The back wheels toe out, the tail swings wide. . . . The Turbo won't spin easily, but things can get very scary if you don't hang in there with some throttle and lots of steering."

All this may have prompted Sherman's conclusion that the Turbo wasn't so much a car anymore as a "valuable piece of auto-art"—understandable given its high price and the high skills demanded of its driver.

It would be hard for any American to buy a Turbo for the next few years. Although the 3.3-liter 930 would continue in Europe through 1986, it was temporarily withdrawn from the States as a public-relations response to a second energy crunch that began late in 1979. Of course, there are always those with extra will, and the notorious "gray market" provided the way for a few European models to reach determined, wealthy U.S. buyers.

With inflation still galloping, the base U.S. 911SC coupe jumped $5000 for 1980, though the hike partly reflected former options now made standard: electric front windows, A/C, leather-rim steering wheel, under-dash console, and matte-black exterior trim. The Targa remained about $1500 upstream. Federal law now required that speedometers be calibrated no higher than 85 mph—absurd for a car with capabilities like this one's—with visual emphasis at the 55-mph mark to remind drivers of the national limit. But like the starter interlock of 1974, this silliness wouldn't last, and realistic speedometer markings

Trivial yet controversial: That describes the op-art upholstery (above) offered on 911 Turbos in 1978. It caused many Porsche purists to shudder, but some buyers loved it. The '79 Porsche Turbo (opposite), formerly called the 930, was the most brutish production Porsche yet. The engine, bored out by 2mm, displaced 3299cc and had 253 SAE horsepower. Sixty mph came up from rest in a neck-snapping 4.9 seconds, and if that didn't shake you up, the price—$34,000—surely would. But after one look at the Turbo's distinctive "whale-tail" spoiler, many shoppers became owners.

would again be legal after 1984.

The "double-nickel" occasioned an even odder change for 1980: an accelerator placed considerably below the brake, Detroit-style, because the factory thought it would be more comfortable at 55 mph! Throttle travel was unaffected, though, and an adjustment was built in so that with an hour of wrench work the pedals could be properly set for the sort of heel-and-toe shifting favored by enthusiasts.

Road testers had long since called the 911 flat-six "venerable," but the 1980 SC's 3.0-liter felt quite youthful thanks to a more efficient three-way catalytic converter that allowed higher 9.3:1 compression for better driveability and mileage. Rated power and torque were unchanged, but there were no peaks, valleys, or flat spots in acceleration, and the car could still drop down to ridiculously low revs in the upper gears without protest.

As with the V-8-powered 928, Porsche issued a special Weissach Edition 911 coupe during model-year 1980, named for Porsche's then-new development center near Stuttgart. Only 400 were built, all for the American market. Priced at $32,000, the WE 911 was perfect for those who felt the $27,770 standard coupe lacked status, being nothing so much as a Turbo *sans* blower and wide-body tail. Features included stiffer shocks, power-remote door mirrors, a power antenna, sealed-beam halogen headlamps, leather cockpit trim, wider wheels, and special paint. Porsche press blurbs said the model represented a 15-percent savings to the buyer over the cost of those items ordered individually, but the hype was unnecessary, for there were never enough cars to go around.

Further SC upgrades appeared for 1981: halogen headlamps and rear seatbelts, plus an anti-rust warranty extended to seven years (a palliative, perhaps, for "sticker shock"). Little else was changed. The story was much the same for '82, when Porsche added a heated right door mirror, an improved sound system, headlight washers, and leather-covered front seats. Vinyl remained in back—practical for the toddlers most likely to ride there.

Model-year 1982 brought a particularly welcome addition to the Porsche line, the long-rumored 911SC Cabriolet, which was unveiled to the public at the Geneva auto show in March. This was Porsche's first factory-built convertible since the 356. (Because of its fixed rollbar, the Targa was not generally considered a true convertible.) As with its fondly remembered predecessor, the body was built by Porsche's Reutter division.

The Cabrio met with a warm U.S. reception on its 1983-model debut despite a chilling $34,450 sticker. Though a manual top might seem needlessly cheap at that price, it kept curb weight the same as that of the SC coupe and 30 pounds less than the Targa's. Typical of Porsche, the top had three bows, spring-loaded self-adjusting steel cables, and a concealed steel panel in front to keep things taut and snug at high speed. Porsche said that the design also afforded minimal heat loss in winter (air-conditioning was available for summer) and milder wind noise.

Road & Track was divided on operating ease, but at least the top was compact enough to allow retaining the normal back seats. A conventional fabric boot covered the roof when stowed; a cockpit tonneau was optional. The rear window was plastic, broadly wrapped for good outward vision, and could be zipped out for copious top-up ventilation.

Oddly, Porsche claimed "the aerodynamic lines of the Cabriolet made it possible to match the 140-mph top speed of the 911SC coupe." In truth, the drop-top was nowhere near as slippery, topping out at 124 mph in *R&T*'s hands. Though it could stay with a coupe up to 60 or so, it fell back as air drag began to assert itself—and that was with the top up. But it mattered little. Where else could a driver enjoy a combination of open-air pleasure and 911 virtues?

Of course, the Cabriolet had several virtues of its own. For one, it was exceptionally solid for a convertible. The Auto Editors of Consumer Guide® found nary a rattle from body or top—this in a pre-production prototype, no less. It was a tribute to the literal integrity of the 911 hull. In fact, the coupe bodyshell was so rigid that little reinforcement was needed to restore torsional stiffness lost from slicing off the roof. The inherent soundness also testified to Zuffenhausen's painstaking workmanship. (A detachable Targa-type rollbar was optional but added nothing to rigidity.)

Another nice thing was that the Cabrio could be driven with the top down and windows up without the nasty wind buffeting that plagued so many convertibles. Testers from Consumer Guide® found this true even at modestly illegal speeds. But the best thing was that this was an open 911, with all that implied for excitement and prestige.

It also implied that the 911 was being given new emphasis in the scheme of things—as indeed it was. A major impetus was American-born Peter Schutz, who'd approved the Cabriolet for production shortly after he replaced Dr. Ernst Fuhrmann as company chairman in 1981.

The 911 Turbo was officially withdrawn from the American market after 1979, so examples like the '81 model (top row) and '82 (bottom) seen here reached U.S. shores through the so-called "gray-market" reserved for Americans with connections and money to burn. Meanwhile, the 1982 SC Targa and Coupe (middle) added a heated right door mirror, headlight washers, and leather front seats. Horsepower came in at 172 SAE at 5500 rpm; torque was 175 pounds/feet at 4200 rpm.

Unlike those who'd long written off the rear-engine Porsche, Schutz felt it should be "back on the front burner," as *R&T* reported. His reasoning was sound. Despite ups and downs in sales of 928 and 924 models, the 911 was still good for a steady 9000 units or so a year and had a vast and loyal following. Under Schutz, the 911 would continue to be upgraded but more aggressively—and more often. The Cabriolet was a first step. A new Carrera would be the second.

Alas, that 1984 model looked little different from the superseded SC—added were i.d. script on the engine lid and standard foglights in the front spoiler. But different it was. Reflecting both the times and Porsche philosophy, the 3.0-liter was enlarged to 3164cc (193 cid) by combining the Turbo's 74.4-mm stroke with the SC's 95-mm bore. With that, the flat-six was now 50 percent larger than it was in the first 911. Fuel injection was switched to Bosch's sophisticated new Digital Motor Electronics (DME) or "Motronic" system, a computer-controlled multipoint setup with integrated electronic ignition.

Together with slightly higher (9.5:1 compression (via reshaped pistons and combustion chambers), SAE net horsepower returned to 200 at 5900 rpm, a gain of 28 bhp over the last SC. "More useful," noted *Road & Track*, "are a 12 lb-ft increase in torque [to 185 at 4800], sharply improved flexibility and no less than a 4-mpg increase in EPA fuel economy." Brakes received thicker rotors (by 3.5mm), larger vent passages, and 928 proportioning control to match the higher potential performance.

That potential was fully realized. "Like every major 911 engine that has gone before, this one produces tangible improvements," *R&T* enthused. "At lower speeds the Carrera isn't a quantum leap ahead of its predecessor, nor does it need to be. But as momentum gathers, so does steam. With fewer than 400 miles on its odometer, the test car's 6.2 seconds for the 0-60 sprint beat the 1983 car by 0.7 sec; by the quarter-mile mark it had gained 0.9 sec . . . and was fully 8 mph faster [14.6 at 96 mph]."

A fully run-in Carrera gave *Car and Driver* even better numbers: 5.3 seconds to 60 mph and 13.9 seconds at 100 mph in the standing quarter-mile. Top speed? A heady 146 mph. Tester Larry Griffin enthused: "The growling, thrumming flat-six remains in the forefront of the world's grunt-and-git, instant forward rushers."

"Just as impressive," replied *R&T*, "is the Carrera's newfound flexibility. With each enlargement the 911 engine has won low-speed torque, but this time it has reached the point where it can be driven 'like other cars.' It tugs lustily on the tires from 1000 rpm in 4th, and even at 40 mph in 5th—wonder of wonders!—there's enough acceleration for virtually any traffic situation on level ground." How odd, then, that Porsche fitted a warning light, located in the tachometer face and hooked to the DME system, that advised when to upshift for best mileage. Of course, no 911 was an econocar, but the Carrera proved surprisingly frugal. Though *C/D* got just 17 mpg, *R&T* obtained 24.5 mpg on a gentle highway run and 20.5 overall.

So the 911 had become better once more, no mean feat for any high-performance car in the mid-Eighties. "Not so long ago," mused *C/D*'s Griffin, "911s were beginning to feel like a bad joke that had run much too long in the telling. Over the past five years, Porsche has turned the tables. . . ."

Not that there wasn't room for improvement; poor ventilation and a still-balky shifter topped the list, and ergonomics had become clearly outmoded. Then there was the issue of price, the minimum by now up to a hefty $31,950. Options cost a bundle more: Cruise control added $320, 16-inch tires no less than $1580, AM/FM/cassette stereo another $600, electric sunroof $940, and the whale tail with deeper front airdam cost $1325. Porsche even charged $70 for a black headliner and $40 for a closer-set (extended-hub) steering wheel. Those who missed the 930 could order their Carrera coupes with a new "Turbo Look" option. This had similar sheetmetal, plus the 930's beefier chassis, for a frightening $12,000 extra. If Porsche hadn't bled buyers before, it certainly seemed to be doing so now, and for the first time the public grumbled with discontent.

But press and public alike still seemed willing to grin and bear it. "The Carrera is a car to get down and wrestle with," said Griffin. "In exchange you will come away winded, exhilarated, and probably laughing out loud, sure of why it was that you first came to love the evil weevil, and sure that you still do."

"Evil" was an apt term for the SC/RS, another race-ready 911 offshoot, of which only 70 were built for Europe in 1984. Price was a hellish $70,000 or so, but that bought an interesting melange of recent semi-competition components: lightweight Turbo-style bodywork, 930 brakes and special 3.0-liter blown engine, chassis bits from the RS/RSR of the early Seventies, and so on. Porsche sold the SC/RS in 255-bhp street form and as a 280-bhp rally car (inspired by the gruelling Paris-Dakar

(Opposite, top row and left, top to bottom): Porsche's first factory-built convertible was the 1983 911SC Cabriolet, which was introduced in America in 1983. U.S. buyers responded well, despite a scary price of nearly $34,500. And for that sum, buyers got Porsche craftsmanship and performance—and a manual top. But this was a successful weight-saving gambit, and anyway, the top folded easily and allowed use of the rear seats. Although quick off the line, the Cabrio's aerodynamics were less than sterling, and it could not stay with a 911 Coupe above 60 mph. The flat-six displaced 2944cc (183 cid) and produced 172 horsepower. For '84, Porsche enlarged the venerable flat-six to 3164cc (193 cid); SAE horsepower rose to 200. The '84 Coupe (far right, bottom) seen here poses with a 1965 model. Together, the cars are eloquent testimony to the way in which Porsche allowed the 911 design to evolve without compromising the cues that had made the car so special in the first place. Horsepower had risen dramatically in the intervening years (from 130 to 200), but then so had price (from $6500 to nearly $32,000).

enduro that Porsche had begun contesting). Both were stark and stunningly fast, with a claimed 5.5 seconds to 60 and 160 mph all out.

But they were also very mean devils. *Car and Driver* correspondent Georg Kacher reported that on massive Pirelli P7 tires the "street" SC/RS "understeers mildly toward its ambitious limit; once the borderline is reached, either feathering or standing on the throttle will kick the tail out without a moment's hesitation. . . . [This] unforgiving chassis, the thundering high-torque engine and the total absence of creature comforts make this *wunderwagen* extremely tiring to drive fast. [Yet] at the end of a day in Porsche's most potent rear-engine weapon, you will surely feel the satisfaction of a job well done."

There was more satisfaction in regular 911s for 1985. The Turbo Look option was extended to the Targa and Cabriolet, power front seats arrived (the driver's as standard, the passenger's at extra cost), shift linkage was revised (though to no real effect), a "safety" windshield was added, and central locking became optional. Also new was an expanded warranty: two years/unlimited miles on the entire car (up from one year), 10 years on rust, 5 years/ 50,000 miles on the powertrain.

During 1984, Porsche AG had taken over its U.S. operation from VW of America, creating Porsche Cars North America (PCNA), headquartered in Reno, Nevada. Zuffenhausen also kept moving toward a "world" 911 specification to simplify production and certification, as well as to reduce pesky gray-market doings, particularly in America. Thus, all non-U.S. 1985 models received the American catalytic converter and exhaust-gas oxygen sensor for emissions control.

Coinciding with the new distribution arrangement was Porsche's decision to reintroduce the storied 930 to the United States for 1986. Labeled 911 Turbo and base-priced at $48,000, it was all but identical to the European version. Unfortunately, performance was all but identical to that of the last '79 U.S. model despite an extra 29 horsepower— now 282 total at 5500 rpm—achieved via a three-way catalyst, oxygen sensor, and computer control for the fuel injection (mechanical Bosch KE-Jetronic). At least the beast was more predictable in really fast work thanks to wider-than-ever nine-inch wheels mounting 225/50VR16 tires in front and 245/45VR16s rear.

A genuine 930 stood to be a lot better than a Turbo Look Carrera, but *Car and Driver* wasn't so sure. Admittedly, said the editors, "it's obviously been taught some manners. Antics that would

have spun you out [in a 930] hardly faze [the 911 Turbo]. [But] back in 1979, there really wasn't any other car in America that offered anywhere near the 930's kind of speed. [Now] we're in the middle of a horsepower boom [and] the march of technology has produced a whole flock of turbo cars with much better manners. . . .Taking a cold, hard look at the 911 Turbo's vexing return, we get the feeling that fond memory may have been better left undisturbed."

Minor refinements attended '86 Carreras. Front seats were lowered for extra head room, and a heavy-duty windshield cleaning system became optional. Porsche again fiddled with climate controls and the shifter, though many testers felt neither was still quite right even after all this time. Wind leaks and minor rattles also persisted, which were downright curious for a car that had been around over 20 years, let alone a Porsche. More damning, these problems were big letdowns in light of towering prices that in part reflected a fair degree of handcrafting—which, come to think of it, may have caused the problems in the first place.

More encouraging was the extra power given the 1987 Carreras. Thanks mainly to recalibrated DME electronics, horsepower increased by 14, to 214 (SAE net) at 5900 rpm, and torque by 10 pounds/feet to 195 (still at 4800 rpm). A separate thermostatic electric fan was added for the secondary oil cooler in the right front fender, and the clutch switched from mechanical to hydraulic.

But the most welcome change for '87 was a new five-speed transaxle with cone synchronizers, and not the familiar Porsche ring type. More positive shifting was again claimed, but this time, testers agreed. After driving a Cabrio, *Road & Track* declared, the "new 911 gearbox shifts smoothly, has a well-defined gate and exhibits little of the old tranny's balkiness when cold. . . . Because the brake is part of the same pedal cluster as the redesigned clutch, its position is improved and it's now possible to heel and toe the 911 without contorting your right foot or resorting to wearing snowshoes." Victory at last.

The Turbo was mostly a carryover for '87 but could again be ordered as a Targa or Cabriolet. The latter cost $78,415 without options—a price virtually unreachable by mere mortals. Both the Carrera and Turbo gained electric front-seat height and cushion-angle adjusters. "Full" power seats, with electric fore/aft and backrest-angle movement, were standard for Turbos, optional on Carreras. Height-adjustable power lumbar support was another new separate option, borrowed from

The "hippy" Turbo look was extended to the Cabrio (top row) and Targa for 1985. A power driver's seat was standard, and optional for the passenger seat. Porsche was by this time no longer marketed in the U.S. by Volkswagen of America, but by a new entity, Porsche Cars North America (PCNA). Targa bodyshells and 911 engines await further work on the factory floor, 1984-85 (bottom row).

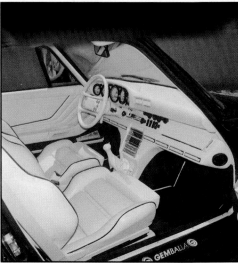

Among the more prestigious Porsche-conversion companies is Gemballa International, located near Stuttgart. 911s handled by Gemballa are modified inside and out, as on this 1985 model. The conversion seen here is called the Avalanche, and has a sculpted, functional tail, extra-wide flares, a slant nose, aerodynamic side-mirror housings, and heat-reflective windows. The engine, turbocharged by Ruf Automobiles, can propel the Gemballa to better than 180 mph. Inside, leather is the dominant theme.

Engineering of the 911SC remained above reproach for 1986, but a few complaints persisted: wind noise, rattles, a sometimes-obstinate climate system. Critics wondered why, but drivers were having too much fun to care. The short-travel gearshift that arrived for the model year helped, and a 149-mph top speed and 0-60 time of 6.1 seconds were nothing if not invigorating.

the 928S4.

By this point, the Turbo's styling had been widely copied in aftermarket body kits for ordinary 911s; likewise, the hidden-headlamp "slant nose" devised for the racing 935 (see Chapter 7). Porsche's decision to end those ripoffs had prompted the Turbo Look option. Now came a new package, the "Turbo slant-nose modification option," stupefyingly priced at nearly $24,000.

Available for any Turbo or the Carrera coupe, it comprised the *Flachbau* ("flat profile") nose with flip-up headlamps surmounted by washboard louvers, plus wide 935-type back wheelarches with grilled, forward-facing rectangular air scoops and extended rocker panels reminiscent of running boards. It all came from Zuffenhausen's new *Sonderwunsch* ("special wish") department, a sort of in-house customizing operation.

Outspoken journalist Brock Yates drove a Slant Nose Turbo Cabriolet for *Car and Driver*. Its sticker read a breathtaking $106,254, though at least that included a newly optional power top (available for all Cabrios)—and $500 in gas-guzzler tax (a recent Washington invention). It was a record price for a recent Porsche, and yet the 911 remained enormously compelling. "We don't mean to imply that, in Turbo Cabriolet Slant Nose form, the 911 is any more reasonable than it ever was," Yates wrote. "Nor do we deny that it is a very old warhorse—and yet it never seems to age like a normal car. Annual refinements, visual tricks, and new permutations keep the 911 in a class of one. A hundred-grand window sticker by no means guarantees perfection, but it does assure you of the most potent dose ever of the Porsche essence: fearsome speed and thoroughbred sounds in a back-road dance partner that you will never forget."

A fairly quiet 1988 model year brought standard three-point rear seatbelts (replacing lap belts) to all 911s. A new "Soft Look" leather option arrived, and a few more extras became standard on Carreras: headlight washers, heavy-duty windshield cleaning, central locking, and cruise control, which was now electronic instead of pneumatic. The Slant Nose Modification was made a separate model called *930S*, available for all body styles.

But wait: There's more. The 911 was technically 25 years old in 1988, and Porsche celebrated the milestone by building 300 U.S. Carreras with a Silver Anniversary package. As a commemorative it was quite tame, comprised of diamond-blue metallic paint (with matching wheels) and a silver-blue leather interior with Ferry Porsche's facsimile signature writ large on the headrests. At least

prices weren't too bad: $45,000 as a coupe, about $47,500 for the Targa, and $52,000 in Cabrio form.

More intriguing was the new Club Sport option for Carrera coupes. Looking much like the early-Seventies RS/RSR, it made the 911 virtually ready to race in production-class events yet was completely street-legal. The normal Carrera's foglights, air-conditioning, sound insulation, undercoating, power seats, and even the back seats were exchanged for fortified shocks, front and rear spoilers, manual sports seats, and an engine with hollow-stem valves, reprogrammed electronics, and a correspondingly higher rev limit (6840 rpm). Apparently expecting Club Sports to be used and abused, Porsche didn't offer them with its normal 10-year rust warranty, but it didn't matter. Despite its "stripper" mien, the CS cost the same $45,895 as a standard Carrera coupe, which may explain why only 50 were sold worldwide.

Had the 911 finally lost its magic? Hardly. In fact, the evergreen Porsche was about to be rejuvenated for the Nineties, as already suggested by the most awesome 911 yet, the limited-production 959. Here was the "everything car" enthusiasts dream of—the one that can do it all. *Motor Trend* aptly termed it "the fastest, most technologically advanced sports car in history." *Car and Driver* said, "The 959 can accomplish almost any automotive mission so well that to call it perfect is the mildest of overstatements."

The 959 began with the fully finished and evidently producible "Gruppe B" prototype unveiled at Frankfurt 1983 as Porsche's entry in the new Group B racing series for factory-experimental cars. Two years later, also at Frankfurt, Porsche announced that 200 production versions, designated 959, would be sold to meet homologation requirements. All were spoken for within weeks despite a price of about 225,000 U.S. dollars. Still, Porsche lost a bundle on every one, as actual unit cost was estimated at a cool $530,000.

That was evident from even a cursory glance at the specs sheet. Though it used the 911 wheelbase and a similar inner structure, the 959 was strikingly different. Distinctions began with a lower body reshaped for good surface aerodynamics, and with a profusion of ducts and vents for controlled airflow *through* it. The distinctions continued beneath the car, too, as a bellypan covered the entire underside except for the engine. Dominating all was a muscular, ultra-wide tail topped by a large loop spoiler. The results: a drag coefficient of 0.31 (creditable, if not the lowest around) and—the real achievement—*zero* lift. To save weight, the

Typical of Porsche, the instrument panel of the '87 911 Carrera Cabrio was a model of functionality.

Opposite: 911 horsepower increased by 14, to 214, for model-year 1987. The Carrera (seen here) picked up a new five-speed transaxle with cone-type synchronizers. The clutch was now actuated hydraulically, instead of mechanically.

doors and front lid were made of aluminum, the nose cap of polyurethane, and the rest in fiberglass-reinforced Kevlar.

Five-spoke, 17-inch alloy wheels wore low-profile Bridgestone RE71 tires specially developed for the 959 (and chosen over a Dunlop design, which raised eyebrows, as Porsche had not previously sanctioned Japanese rubber). Though heroically sized at 235/45 fore and 255/40 aft, the tires were only V-rated, meaning safe for up to 149 mph—curious, as the 959's claimed maximum was nearly 40 mph more. Hollow wheel spokes (first used on Porsche's 1980 Le Mans racers) provided extra air for the tires and a smoother ride. There was no spare because the tires were designed to run flat for 50 miles after a blowout. Another innovation was electronic sensors within the wheels to warn of pressure loss.

The 959 engine was masterful even for a roadgoing Porsche: a short-stroke version of the 3.3-liter Turbo unit with twin overhead cams per bank, four valves per cylinder, water-cooled heads (air cooling continued for the block), low-mass titanium con rods, and twin KKK turbochargers. Crossover pipes and bypass valves afforded "sequential" turbocharging. Only the port blower was active below 4000 rpm; the starboard unit progressively phased in as exhaust-gas flow increased toward 4000, thus marrying low-speed tractability with top-end power. Despite modest 8.3:1 compression, DIN horsepower was a heady 450.

Putting all that power to the ground was a unique full-time four-wheel-drive system with a *six*-speed gearbox, basically the five-speed Carrera unit with an extra-low first, ostensibly for off-road use (and thus marked "G" for *Gelande*—terrain). Power was taken aft in the usual way. Drive forward was by a tube-encased shaft to a differential using a multi-plate clutch in an oil-filled chamber. Varying clutch oil pressure determined the amount of front torque delivered, so no center differential was needed, though a locking rear diff was provided.

Torque apportioning was selected from a steering-column stalk controlling four computer programs and a full-automatic mode. "Traction" locked the front clutch and rear diff for maximum pull in mud and snow. "Ice" split torque 50/50 front/rear, while "Wet" provided a 40/60 division that progressively increased to the rear on acceleration. "Dry" also offered a static 40/60 but could vary that up to 20/80 in all-out acceleration. All this was accomplished via the Bosch Motronic engine computer used in conjunction with the wheel-mounted speed sensors of the new anti-lock braking system (developed with WABCO-Westinghouse)—a first for a rear-engine Porsche. This apart, the brakes were 911 Turbo with larger front discs.

The suspension departed sharply from 911 practice by employing double wishbones all around, plus twin shocks and concentric coil springs at each wheel. The shocks in each pair had separate damping roles; both were computer-controlled according to vehicle speed, with a choice of "soft," "firm," and "automatic" settings. A computer chip also managed a novel, hydraulic ride-height system offering three degrees of ground clearance (4.7, 5.9, and 7.1 inches), plus automatic lowering as needed from about 95 mph up for improved fuel efficiency and aerodynamic stability.

The 959 was built in two forms: as a "Comfort" model with air-conditioning, electric seats and windows, 911-type rear seats and the ride-height feature; and as a "Sport" version that deleted these items but weighed 110-130 pounds less. Though the Sport was the one given most journalists to try—doubtless because it was just a little bit faster (carrying 6.1 lbs/bhp versus 7.1)—the differences in performance proved slight.

But no matter. "With rocket-sled acceleration and the highest top speed we've ever measured, the 959 stands alone at the pinnacle of production-car performance," said *Car and Driver.* "If that sounds like hyperbole, how does a 0-to-60-mph time of 3.6 seconds strike you? Or 100 mph from rest in just 8.8 seconds[?]. . . . The 959 devours the standing quarter-mile in twelve seconds flat [at] 116 mph." Top speed? With boring regularity, *C/D* and others matched the factory claim of no less than 195 mph.

Perhaps more impressive, the 959 was as docile in town as any 911, at least as quiet, and so stable on the highway that 100 mph felt more like 60, even in driving rain. In corners, it was a revelation. British writer Mel Nichols observed, "At different times, I lifted off when near maximum power, and all the car did was tighten its line neatly at the front. There was no way that tail—so deadly in these circumstances in a 911—was going to come around. . . . What I liked was the clarity and accessibility of the handling that went with it." A virtual absence of body roll helped mightily, as did the twin-turbo engine's smooth, seamless, relentless power delivery, though one scribe reported an "explosion" of thrust once the second blower cut in.

But life at the pinnacle can be difficult. Troubles with the drive system and brakes, and Porsche's insistence that this amazingly complex supercar be

Porsche headquarters at Zuffenhausen (above) looked impressive in 1988, particularly for what was in essence a low-volume automaker. The company's Weissach development center (opposite) located near Stuttgart opened in 1980, and allowed Porsche to put cars through their paces like few other automakers. Track configuration leaves no doubt as to Porsche's special interest in handling.

The mighty 959 was based on the 911, yet shared no exterior body panels with it. Production prototypes were introduced at the 1983 Frankfurt Auto Show and testing—including a run by driver Jacky Ickx at the '85 Paris-Dakar rally—continued for some years. The 959 seen here is a 1988 production model. The flat-six engine produced 450 horsepower at 6500 rpm, achieved via four-valve, water-cooled cylinder heads and twin, sequentially operating KKK turbochargers. Zero-to-60 could be managed in less than 4 seconds, and top speed was at least 195 mph. Prices started at about $230,000, but the car never was street-legal in the U.S.

absolutely right, delayed initial 959 deliveries by over a year. Dr. Wolfgang Porsche, Ferry's youngest son, got the first one, in April 1987, by which time it was clear that the run wouldn't be finished for another year still. One reason was agonizingly slow assembly. Because the 959's construction was too involved for even Porsche's usual methods, a small shop was set up to build the cars virtually by hand from numerous custom-fabricated components.

Meantime, rich-and-famous folks everywhere scrambled to be among the few chosen for 959 ownership. Tennis star Boris Becker was refused (too young and inexperienced, Porsche said), but not tennis player Martina Navratilova, Indy 500 winner Danny Sullivan, actor Don Johnson, and conductor Herbert von Karajan. However, money alone wasn't enough. To qualify you had to be a Porsche owner and promise not to sell your 959 for at least six months. You also had to be willing to travel: Sales and service were handled only from the Stuttgart factory.

You were out of luck entirely if you lived in America and drove on public roads. Porsche reneged on a promise to certify 959s to U.S. standards, and a later plan to sell 26 as "racers" through driver/dealer Al Holbert was stymied by Holbert's death in 1988. So even the wealthiest and most influential Americans could only dream of owning this engineering marvel, the car that had won the gruelling Paris-Dakar rally not once but twice (1984 and '86, in competition 961 trim).

Although the exact total number of 959s is hazy, assemblies ended at only about 230, including development prototypes and racing 961s. But the 959 had blazed a trail. As Nichols noted, "[T]he good news is that . . . other Porsches will gain the 959's technology and degrees of its prowess."

Sure enough, the first of its progeny appeared in late 1988. Called *Carrera 4*—"4" for four-wheel drive—except for smoother bumpers and side sills, it looked like most every 911 ever built. But the "C4" was nothing less than the vanguard for what amounted to a second 911 generation. Indeed, it was developed under a new program, Project 964, and was said to be 85 percent new.

That it was, starting with a new floorpan shaped to smooth airflow beneath the car, plus 959-inspired all-round coil springs with integrated tube shocks (single units in each case). Rear semi-trailing arms and front struts on lower wishbones continued. A bore and stroke job—to 100mm/3.94 inches X 76.5mm/3.01 inches—took the flat-six to 3.6 liters, and there were reshaped combustion

chambers, revised intake manifolds, twin-plug ignition, and ultra-high 11.3:1 compression. In Stateside trim the Carrera 4 produced 247 bhp at 6100 rpm—a gain of 34, and less than 40 shy of the vaunted Turbo—plus 228 pounds/feet of torque at 4800 rpm. Rolling stock was upsized to suit: 16-inch Bridgestone RE71s, like the 959's, but 205/55 fore and 225/50 aft, and with the higher Z speed rating (good for 150 mph and up).

But the big attraction was the all-wheel drive that made the Carrera 4 a "people's 959." To be sure, it was drastically simpler than the 959 system, and thus helped hold initial retail price to "just" $69,500.

This time there were center and rear differentials, each with an electro-hydraulic multi-plate clutch. Power went forward from the engine to the center differential, then back to the rear wheels via a driveshaft housed within the countershaft of the five-speed manual gearbox; a second shaft sent power to a normal front diff and halfshafts. Both clutches were computer-controlled in response to signals from the four wheel-speed sensors of the first antilock braking system ever offered on a "volume" 911.

Though the center diff normally divided torque 31/69 percent front/rear, the computer could vary that through selective use of the clutches whenever wheel sensors signaled tire slippage. Response time was reported at less than a tenth of a second—three times faster than the 959 system. Additional sensors for straight and lateral acceleration allowed the computer to engage the rear differential on lifting the throttle in a corner, thus increasing understeer and stability. For safety as well as longevity, both clutches disengaged under braking. A dashboard switch could be flicked to lock the diffs for maximum grip on slippery surfaces below 25 mph; above that speed, the clutches automatically released.

Here was yet another inventive Porsche answer to a customer request—a more controllable 911—and the company was right to term this drive system "intelligent." Further aiding stability were a front suspension modified for zero-scrub radius, and new rear suspension mounts designed to vary toe angle with cornering load (like the vaunted "Weissach axle" in the 928). For straighter high-speed running, the C4's engine grille automatically flipped out and up above 50 mph to become a spoiler that increased rear downforce; below 6 mph, it snugged neatly back into the lid. Porsche also claimed the appearance changes gave the C4 a 15 percent lower drag coefficient than previous

Variations on the 911 seemed endless in 1989. The Speedster (top) was joined by the Anniversary Edition (middle row) and the perennially popular Targa (bottom). Of this group, the limited-run Speedster was the most impressive, producing 214 horsepower with its air-cooled flat-six. In profile, the 911 Speedster was reminiscent of its earlier namesake, the 356 Speedster of the late Fifties. Price on the '89 Speedster started above $65,000, and within three years examples were being bid up as high as $90,000.

911s, plus "zero-lift characteristics at highway speeds."

Some doubted the Carrera 4's ability. "The new suspension and driveline banish the 911's penchant for tail-out antics," said *Car and Driver*. "Throw the car into a corner while braking or suddenly lift the throttle at the limit and the Carrera 4 barely rotates; its tail stays solidly planted at all times." *Motor Trend* judged real-world cornering "incredible, although the Carrera 4's ultimate . . . 0.84g is not as high as the Corvette's or even a Pontiac Firebird Formula. What this shows is that lateral g numbers are just one indication of handling ability. Perhaps a better indication is slalom speed, in which the Carrera 4 [is stellar]."

Though the C4 was no 959 in acceleration, *Road & Track* got a zippy 5.8 seconds to 60 and 14.4 seconds at 96.5 mph in the standing quarter-mile—close to the level of racing 911s from not too many years before. *C/D*, as usual, did better—a quick 5.1 seconds to 60 and 13.6 at 102 mph in the quarter. But the real point was this: "[Porsche has] gained so much balance with the Carrera 4 that we no longer consider its discontinued cousin, the antsy 911 Turbo, a class contender among high-dollar sports cars."

Positive reaction to the Carrera 4 prompted Porsche to again drop the Turbo but only for a while. The company was battling some fierce fires now, including management dissension and a sudden drop in U.S. sales. From a 1986 high of over 30,000 cars, Porsche sent over just 9479 in calendar-year 1989 and 9139 in 1990. What was happening? The main culprit was a never-ending increase in prices that was making all Porsches too expensive except for the ultra-rich. There was also the waning appeal of the 928 and 944, which evidently weren't changing fast enough to suit the market. The advent of a U.S. luxury tax and a sharp recession in late 1989 didn't help, either.

What to do? Well, if a 356 Speedster had helped old Max Hoffman move more Porsches, perhaps a 911 Speedster would help Porsche U.S. win back customers. Actually, Porsche had built such a car back in 1982, a prototype based on the then-new Cabriolet. But "chop shop" converters had quickly stolen the Cabrio's thunder, and Porsche feared the same would happen to a new Speedster, so the company kept mum about the idea until 1987, when 911 sales began easing.

When it bowed at Frankfurt, the reborn Speedster was an instant hit. Unlike the Spartan prototype, this new-yet-nostalgic 911 catered to comfort with roll-up windows (instead of side curtains)

and a slightly taller, more conventional windshield (for some semblance of top-up head room). Most usual 911 options were available, but ordering too many would quickly swell the $65,480 base price to nearly $75,000. Perhaps as a showroom lure, Porsche announced production of only 2100, then delayed building any Speedsters until the summer of 1989. As it turned out, all but 159 wore the Turbo Look package, but every one got the Turbo's beefier chassis and heavy-duty four-piston cross-drilled disc brakes.

Recalling its 356 forebear, the 911 Speedster used a simpler manual top than the normal Cabriolet. Unlined, it folded beneath a flip-up fiberglass cover behind a seatless rear package shelf. The cover's double-hump design didn't please everyone—least of all Butzi Porsche—and top operation required some fiddling. Otherwise, the Speedster was pure 911. But because it was designed pre-Carrera 4, it was not a 911 of the future. In fact, the '89 Speedster would be the last 911 model built at the old Stuttgart factory; with the 964 program, Porsche shifted 911 production to a modern new plant near its Stuttgart headquarters.

Undeniably, the Speedster had "collectible" written all over it, and all 2100—of which just 800 came to America—were quickly snapped up by would-be profiteers. And profit they did, but only for a time. Though asking prices soared above $90,000 within three years, according to *Road & Track*, Porsche would have another last laugh by reviving the Speedster after five years.

Ferry Porsche turned a vigorous 80 on September 19, 1989, and his workers gave him a splendid birthday present in the Panamericana, a Carrera 4 with chunky, futuristic bodywork rendered in fiberglass and carbon fiber. The name, of course, honored the great Mexican road races of the Fifties, the *Carreras Panamericana*, where the Type 550 Spyder and 718 RSK had so conclusively proven themselves.

The Panamericana's unique feature was a roof-line tapered sharply down from windshield to rear deck as a frame for slim doors and rear-side windows. A canvas cover allowed the entire cockpit to be opened to the sun. It was a striking machine that was destined to remain Dr. Porsche's alone—a pity, for a production version could have been wondrous.

The Carrera 4 implied that an updated rear-drive 911 was just around the corner, and it duly arrived for U.S. sale as a 1990 model. Logically badged Carrera 2, it boasted most of the improvements wrought for project 964, including the 247-

A glorious one-shot was created in 1989 to celebrate the 80th birthday of Ferry Porsche: the Panamericana (top two rows and bottom right), a Carrera 4 modified with sleek, aggressive bodywork rendered in carbon fiber and fiberglass. The car's most noticeable feature was a dramatically sloped roofline supported by thin, graceful pillars. The name was a fond reference to the challenging Mexican road races of the Fifties, the Carreras Panamerica. In the meantime, work continued on production Porsches, as witness this dynamic rendering of an '89 Speedster (bottom left).

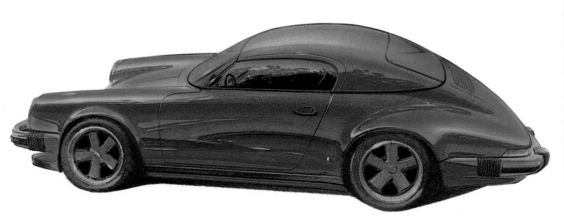

bhp 3.6-liter engine. It also came with dual airbags, the result of Porsche's commitment to standardize those passive restraints for all of its U.S. models—the first company to do so.

As expected, the C2 tipped the scales at some 220 pounds less than the C4 and was thus slightly faster to 60 mph. While Porsche modestly claimed 5.5 seconds vs. 5.7 for the lightest of its coupe models, *Road & Track* managed 5.4 seconds with a heavier C2 in Targa trim, and *Car and Driver*'s coupe needed a mere 4.8 seconds.

Those times were achieved with the usual five-speed manual gearbox, but there was something else new for the Carrera 2: Tiptronic, the 911's first fully automatic transmission. Evolved from the "PDK" gearbox of the championship-winning 962 Group C GT racer (PDK for Porsche *Doppelkupplung*—"double clutch"), Tiptronic was a four-speed torque-converter transmission with electronic controls linked to those of the Motronic engine-management system. What set it apart from ordinary automatics were sensors utilized to monitor wheel slip (again shared with standard ABS), as well as throttle angle, vehicle speed, engine revs, and longitudinal and lateral acceleration. The gear selector was equally unique: a two-plane affair with a conventional P-R-N-D-3-2-1 quadrant to the left and a separate "M" (manual) gate to the right, accessible from Drive by slapping the lever over into "tip" mode. There, the driver nudged the stick forward toward "+" to upshift, as on a motorcycle; move back toward "-" and the transmission kicked down.

Well, it worked that way *most* of the time. With all its sensors, Tiptronic might upshift early to maintain stability under power in, say, a slippery corner. In other situations, such as a tight turn taken on light throttle, it might delay a change for the same reason. That was in full-automatic mode, where five "program maps" constantly adjusted shift points to match driving style (from leisurely to sporty, Porsche said). Of course, like other automatics, this one wouldn't select a lower gear if it meant overrevving the engine.

For economy, Tiptronic was programmed to start in second gear—no sweat with the torquey 3.6 engine—unless the driver tromped on the gas; it would also "default" to second in "tip" mode if the driver forgot to change down after coming to a stop. A pair of indicators in the speedometer face showed which gear was active in either shift mode.

Road & Track found Tiptronic quite efficient in several ways, largely because "Porsche's torque converter locks up above 40 mph and barely unlocks during shifts. . . . This is reflected in [our ob-

served] fuel economy, 17.5 mpg, just a sip more than our 5-speed Carrera's 18.0 mpg. It's also borne out by top speed (159 versus 162 mph). Perhaps the only significant difference is in acceleration (0-60 in 6.9 sec. versus the stickshift's 5.4)."

So was Tiptronic "the best of all worlds? Not to a Porsche purist," concluded *R&T*. "But to an urban dweller who spends a lot of time in traffic, or to an enthusiast/non-enthusiast couple that prefer to share the car, Porsche's [new] automatic may be just what Dr. Porsche ordered." It was certainly light years ahead of the old Sportomatic.

The big news for 1991 was yet another return of the fabled 911 Turbo. Mixing old and new, it combined the 964 body with the trademark 930 whale tail, ultra-wide back wheelarches, and 3.3-liter engine. Wheels were now 17-inch Speedline alloys spreading seven inches wide up front and nine inches in back. All wore purpose-designed Z-rated Bridgestone Expedia S-1 tires, jumbo-sized at 205/50 fore and 255/40 aft. As usual, springs, shocks, anti-roll bars, and rear semi-trailing arms were all beefed-up from Carrera specs. Best of all, ABS was finally standard for this super-fast car that needed it more than ever.

The 1991 Turbo out-powered its '89 predecessor thanks to a 50-percent larger intercooler, a bigger blower with lower-mass turbine wheel, cleaner and smoother intake passages, and a new low-restriction exhaust system with three-way catalytic converter and a separate catalyst for the turbo's bypass valve. All this added 23 horses for a thumping 315 total in U.S. form; torque improved some 14 percent to 332 pounds/feet, though it peaked 500 rpm higher, at 4500. Even better, given the world's rising environmental consciousness, this Turbo was cleaner at the tailpipe and easier on the ears. Though five-speed manual remained the lone transmission, stouter and wider ring and pinion gears enhanced durability. An optional limited-slip differential, another new feature, provided 20 percent lock with throttle on and up to 100 percent with throttle off.

Final drive was unchanged, but the '91 Turbo had a 0.36 drag coefficient (down from 0.39), reflecting the smoother 964 styling, so official top speed was up 11 mph to 168. Claimed acceleration improved, too, with 0-60 available in 4.8 seconds instead of 5.3. Typically, *Road & Track* bettered Porsche's numbers with 4.6 seconds to 60 and a 12.9-second quarter-mile. "Suffice to say that the ['91] Turbo . . . is the quickest factory Porsche we've ever tested."

The '91 Turbo was one of the priciest 911 ever, with a startling U.S. base list of $95,000. Regular

The Carrera 4 was introduced in Germany in 1988, and although 911-based, it was sufficiently different to warrant its own development code, Project 964. Coil springs and intregrated, single-unit tube shocks, and center and rear differentials improved ride quality and stability: at last enthusiasts had a 911 with a tail that would stay planted during hard maneuvers. The "4" indicated four-wheel drive, and the flat-six was bored and stroked to an impressive 3.6 liters, good for 247 bhp.

models were still escalating as well. A Carrera 2 coupe now began at $60,700, a C4 Cabrio at $80,600. Tiptronic added a steep $2750 and the usual plethora of options could run up final tabs faster than a Turbo peeling off the line.

Porsche was only too aware of the problem and had begun looking for ways to build its cars at lower cost without compromising quality. But for the time being, the company could only watch helplessly as calendar-1991 U.S. sales dropped over 50 percent to just 4388, of which the 911 family accounted for nearly three-fourths. The story was the same worldwide, as Zuffenhausen's total production declined from just over 32,000 to about 27,500, again the vast majority 911s.

All the more curious, then, that an even costlier Carrera 2 Cabrio bowed in the United States for 1992. It bore the name "America," and press releases struggled to paint a link to Max Hoffman's like-named 356 of 40 years before. And at $87,900 to start, the new America "Roadster," as it was euphemistically labeled, was just as expensive, relatively speaking. But it was no "stripper," delivering Turbo-style body, suspension, brakes, and tires, plus all the Carrera's comforts and conveniences—even a power top. Still, a $15,000 premium over the regular Cabrio struck even Porsche's well-heeled customers as gouging, and although no production or sales breakouts are now available, this new America was surely one of the scarcer modern roadgoing 911s.

But perhaps not so exclusive as the Turbo S (a.k.a. *Turbo S2*), of which just 80 were built in 1992, all coupes. Where the America convertible was allegedly inspired by the near-stock 911s running in the European "Carrera 2 Cup" series (inaugurated in 1990), the impetus for this more powerful Turbo was the American IMSA Supercar Series, where blown 911s piloted by Hurley Haywood claimed the championship in 1991 and again in '92. IMSA mandated that certain critical racing components be offered for the street. The Turbo S was built to satisfy the rule, but ironically the model wasn't street-legal in the United States and thus wasn't exported here.

Frankly, at a towering $180,000 it was none too affordable *anywhere*. But for those who could see their way, the Turbo S had plenty of will. The factory's deletion of non-essentials saved over 400 pounds in curb weight, while a larger and more efficient intercooler, freer-breathing turbo, and wilder cams provided a modest horsepower increase from 315 to 322 at a higher 6200 rpm; torque also improved, going from 332 at 4500 to

354 at 4800. To cope with the extra low-end grunt, Porsche specified wider wheels of 18-inch diameter wrapped with massive 235/40 tires fore and 265/35s aft—Z-rated, of course. Other upgrades included the chassis modifications implied by a claimed 180-mph top speed—up 12 mph from the normal Turbo—plus twin oil coolers and a long-distance 24.5-gallon fuel tank.

The '92 Turbo S was something of a handful even for the likes of Paul Frere, the astute Le Mans-winning race driver and engineer turned journalist. As he wrote in *Road & Track*: "Most of the time, the car corners as if on the proverbial rails. . . . It is, of course, possible to induce power oversteer, but to achieve that, you must be not only very brave, but also very accurate in your anticipation of full turbo boost. Let the boost come in too late, and you fail; let it come in too soon, and you are in trouble. On less than smooth surfaces, driving really fast requires a lot of attention as the combination of very hard suspension and wide, ultralow-profile tires . . . tends to make the car deviate from its course." In short, a 911 Turbo could still be a very unruly beast.

There was good news and bad news as the 911 entered its 30th year. The bad news was mostly from the sales staff, as deliveries to America eased again, this time to 4115, with 911s accounting for over half. Worldwide production also continued its slide, from over 22,000 for model-year '92 to 15,082—again, the vast majority 911s. And, sad to say, the Targa was no more, dropped as a money-saving measure after years of losing sales to the Cabriolet.

But there was very good news in a new 911 RS America coupe, which hit U.S. showrooms in April 1992 at $10,000 less than a standard $64,000 Carrera 2. *Car and Driver* aptly termed it "a frill-less 911, one that sheds 70 pounds of fluff and looks pure and ready for some serious fun."

That "fluff" stuff involved the standard air-conditioning (made optional at $2940), power steering (no option there), stereo, the token rear seats, even the armrests (replaced by simple pull handles). But buyers did get a whale tail instead of the smaller auto-extending spoiler, plus the inch-wider wheels and tires that cost $1352 extra on a C2.

Owners also enjoyed the best performance yet in a non-turbo 911. *C/D*'s example rushed through the 0-60 sprint in 4.6 seconds and scaled the standing quarter-mile in 13.3 seconds at 105 mph. With that, the magazine labeled the RS a "foolproof way to convert almost anyone into a full-lather Porsche-phile. . . ." *Road & Track*'s numbers were only a bit

The Carrera 4 was followed in 1990 by the Carrera 2 (opposite, top), a lighter, somewhat faster variation that ran with the 4's 247-bhp flat-six (bottom right). A skillful driver could take the 2 from 0-60 mph in a shade less than 5 seconds. The familiar 5-speed manual continued to be available, and a new transmission—the Tiptronic—was available, as well. Simply put, it was a "brainy," interactive automatic trans that relieved city drivers of the tedium of constant manual shifts with little loss of power or performance. At Weissach in 1990 (bottom left) development of future Porsches continued.

less stunning: 5.3 seconds to 60 and 13.8 at 102.5 mph in the quarter.

Alas, the RS America appealed scarcely more than the old 1988 Club Sport, and only some 300 were built in 1993. Although it looked another "instant" 911 collectible, *R&T* concluded that a "mothballed classic is not what the RS America is meant to be. Spirited, even frisky, this 911 is a thoroughbred designed to do one thing really well: run like a Preakness winner." So full credit is due to Porsche for what it was able to achieve. Despite having to grapple with a myriad of business problems, Zuffenhausen was still willing to deliver a *pur sang* GT, even though only a few might want one. Most other automakers wouldn't have bothered.

The 911's most exciting 30th Anniversary developments didn't appear in Europe until late 1993, which means Americans didn't see them until the 1994 models were available. But they were worth waiting for. The Speedster was back, and after another year-long absence from the U.S. lineup, so was the Turbo.

Actually, the Turbo came back twice. First up was a revised "standard" model badged Turbo 3.6, with 355 emissions-legal horsepower in U.S. trim. *Road & Track* described its powerplant as a Carrera 2 unit "modified to accept heftier cylinder barrels and lower-compression pistons [7.5:1], new camshafts, plus the old Turbo's single-plug heads (Porsche says there's no room for dual-plug heads). Also, the same induction system with Bosch K-Jetronic fuel injection . . . the same KKK turbocharger and intercooler and the same exhaust system." But the result was "an engine that produces not only more horsepower but considerably more torque at low rpm (2500) . . . while delivering plenty of low-end performance and all-round smoothness. In short, a turbocharged powerplant with the instantaneous response and linear power delivery of an aspro [normally aspirated]."

The rest of the Turbo 3.6 was much like the last regular 3.3-liter model, but again, Porsche prudently upgraded rolling stock to sticky Yokohama A-008P tires—225/40ZR18 front and 265/35ZR18 rear—wrapped around handsome new three-piece Speedline wheels. This plus more considered chassis tuning made all the difference. Said *R&T*'s Joe Rusz: "Nearly two decades ago, or even as recently as 1988, trailing throttle in a corner was a no-no. . . . But with nearly a foot of rubber on the road at each wheel, the Turbo 3.6 is very forgiving even when I . . . overcooked it going into a turn . . . [I]t's still possible to get oversteer—on loose pavement or by punching the throttle to break loose the rear

wheels. But [it] takes some doing. . . ."

R&T measured astounding lateral acceleration of 0.91g—real race-car stuff. Forward acceleration was similarly eye-opening. "There's a horrendous amount of driveline judder as tires cling to the pavement (and visions of driveline repairs dance in our heads)," said Rusz. "But a bit of fancy footwork nets a 4.5-second 0-to-60-mph time. . . ." He demurred on top speed, but typical of Porsche, the official 174-mph claim was probably conservative.

"Better to enjoy the new Turbo's other strong points," Rusz added; these included excellent drivability in heavy traffic, a smoother ride than the old Turbo, and the traditional 911 virtues of great long-haul comfort and solid construction. Even fuel economy wasn't bad: about 25 mpg on American highways, though just 8 mpg in heavy flogging. One thing not to like was price: $99,000 to start and nearly $110,000 with guzzler and luxury taxes. "The Turbo has come a long way," Rusz concluded, "shedding a lot of nasty habits. Except one: It's still an E-ticket ride. . . ."

This fact made the revived Turbo S the key to the whole park. This one *was* U.S.-legal, hence its simultaneous premiere at the Los Angeles and Detroit shows in early 1994. Built to honor the Turbo's third consecutive IMSA Supercar crown, won in '93, it carried a racing-inspired 3.6 engine with a unique four-branch exhaust system that helped boost rated horsepower to no less than 380, making it the latest "most powerful production Porsche" yet sold in the States. Of the approximately 100 built, most did come Stateside. One hundred was a tiny run indeed, and the car's pricing assured further exclusivity, as it came in at $119,121 minimum; with the slant-nose and matching front spoiler, the tab flexed its way to an intimidating $159,179.

The reincarnated 911 Speedster was a different ride entirely, but just as thrilling in its way. *Road & Track* said drivers should think of it "as a cross between the Carrera 2 Cabriolet and the 911 RS America"—and as "the antidote to the 1989 car."

Being based on the C2 platform made all the difference here, abetted by the same wheel/tire package and a judicious "de-frilling" accorded the RS America. But being a Porsche, the '94 Speedster benefited from considered changes that included a stengthened windshield frame, a smoother-looking fiberglass top cover, and easier top operation. Paint colors were limited to red, white, or black, and the mostly black cockpit was dressed up with liberal swatches of red on the gauge cluster, seat shells, and gear lever. The seats themselves were nor-

Porsche prices had escalated steadily since the Seventies, but few fans were prepared for the $180,000 needed to purchase the limited-run edition of the 1992 Turbo S (top), which was never street legal in the U.S. This super 911 was a lightweight, 322-bhp wonder that practically flew. And when the turbo boost kicked in, even experienced drivers had their hands full. Somewhat less wild (and more reasonably priced) was the '92 911 Carrera RS (bottom left), which retailed for $53,900 and could run from 0-60 in less than 4.5 seconds. And then there was the '92 Carrera 2 Targa (bottom right), available for $65,500.

CHAPTER THREE

119

All-wheel drive naturally continued for the '92 911 Carrera 4 (above, near right, and below). The 247-horse flat-six was a model of efficiency, particularly when mated to the mandatory five-speed manual (the Tiptronic semi-automatic trans was optional on the rear-wheel-drive Carrera 2, including the Cabriolet model (far right).

Not every Porsche that looked like a Turbo model was the real thing. This 1993 Carrera Cabriolet (above) has "Turbo Look" fender flares and other add-ons, but ran with a normally aspirated engine. Although performance was not up to Turbo standards, this imposter was nevertheless a swift car, and with great looks, to boot. Other models in Porsche's lineup for '93 included the 911 America Roadster (far left) and 911 Carrera 2 (left).

mally one-piece racing-type buckets that were a tad snug for heftier occupants. However, less restrictive sports seats and power Carrera-style seats were both available.

Other extras included air, stereo, and cruise control; power windows and central locking were standard, as was modern 911 performance: By *R&T*'s clock, 60 mph came up from rest in 5.7 seconds to 60, and the standing quarter was conquered in 14.1 seconds at 103 mph. Handling? Try 0.90g.

But best of all, the '94 Speedster was more affordable than in the past. Of course, "affordable" is always a relative term, but at $66,400 base, the '94 listed at $1000 less than the '89 and managed to be better in most every way. Maxie Hoffman would surely have approved. And as *Motor Trend* advised: "Pay the money, drop the top and take off down the road. You'll forget all the about the price after 10 minutes."

In a late 1993 interview with Georg Kacher, Dr. Ferry Porsche confirmed what most everyone already knew: a third 911 generation was on the way. "We once believed that it would be a good idea to replace the 911 with the 928," he said. "But to do that would have been a dreadful mistake. . . . It is possible to modify, hone, and improve [the 911], but we must never alter its character and its unmistakable visual appeal."

Though he had long since ceased running Porsche day-to-day, Ferry was sanguine about its future, especially the company's ability to remain independent even after other small specialist producers had been gobbled up by giants. As he told Kacher: "Back in the mid-Eighties, at the height of our success, we let excessive windfall profits obscure the true earnings. Instead of investing in fresh products and more efficient production techniques, we hoped the golden years would continue forever. But they didn't, and we had to learn how to play this game the hard way. . . . Believe me—this company will prosper again even without outside support, and we will owe the lion's share of that comeback to a car that is as unique today as it was thirty years ago."

As if to fulfill his prophecy, Porsche's U.S. sales finally saw an upturn in 1994, rising modestly to 5838 from a modern low of just 3729 in calendar '93. Not surprisingly, this reversal was mostly the 911's doing, and that year's U.S. lineup was the strongest in years, what with the Speedster, Turbo 3.6, RS America, and Carreras 2 and 4 (the curious America Roadster was deservedly dropped). But at last it was time to pass the torch. The 964 had done

its job. All hail the 993.

The product of a $300 million makeover, the 993 was the most sweepingly changed 911 ever. Visually, it echoed the late 959 in a more fulsome lower body with wider, reshaped rear fenders. Front fenders were lowered to accommodate 959-style lay-back headlamps above prominent wrapped turn signal/foglight units and two thin, full-width air slots below. Also new were a slimmer, full-width taillight lens; a wider auto-extending rear spoiler; and new 17-inch wheels that nevertheless had a classic 911 look.

This classicism was appropriate, for the timeless basic shape penned by Butzi Porsche so long before was still clear and intact. So, too, was the traditional 911 cockpit, though there were now new seats, an attractive new four-spoke airbag steering wheel with full-hub horn press (no more little tabs to search for), minor controls redesigned to be handier and more intuitive, and a new ventilation filter to trap pollen and other impurities.

Despite a 3.3-inch gain in overall width, the 993 boasted the same 0.33 drag coefficient as the 964. The smoother lower-body contours helped but so did a newly flush windshield, side glass pulled out 7mm to be near-flush, and new, so-called "air relief" vents in the front wheel arches ahead of the wheels. Other dimensions changed little, if any, and even curb weight was nearly the same as before. In rear-drive Carrera form (the "2" was now left off), the 993 was just 23/33 pounds heavier than a manual/Tiptronic 964. Also unseen, but greatly noticed in driving, was a 20-percent increase in torsional stiffness. Other body improvements included resited center-pivot wipers that gave full coverage to 80 percent of windshield area, beefier door beams to meet Washington's new 1997 standards for side-impact protection, and trunk room that was increased by 20 percent despite the lower new front hood (though that wasn't so difficult, as there'd been precious little space before).

Chassis revisions were just as extensive. The 3.6-liter engine was treated to a lower-mass valvetrain; hydraulic lifters that required no periodic lash adjustment; lighter pistons and con rods; a stiffer crankshaft (still with eight main bearings) that eliminated the need for a weighty harmonic damper; a quieter new low-pressure exhaust system with twin catalysts and mufflers; and Bosch's latest Motronic 2.10 engine-management system with a hot-film air-mass sensor (replacing a less precise hot-wire type). All this lifted horsepower to 270 at 6100 rpm and peak torque to 243

The '93 911 Carrera 2 platform (top left) was used as the basis for the revived 911 Speedster (bottom row), available as a 1994 model. Priced at $66,400 base, the Speedster lived up to its name, zipping from zero to 60 in less than 6 seconds and dashing through the quarter mile for Road & Track *in 14.1 seconds at 103 mph. Body colors were restricted to red, white, and black. The pricier ($78,450) '94 Carrera 4 (top right) carried on, but the biggest news for the model year was the 3.6-liter Turbo (center), a performance powerhouse that cranked out 355 horses and generated more low-end torque than before. Porsche's claimed top speed of 174 mph was probably conservative, but the Turbo's price—$99,000—surely wasn't.*

pounds/feet at 5000. Valve covers, timing-chain cover, and intake manifold were now made of plastic-like composites, which didn't add muscle but did save weight and help reduce noise.

To take advantage of its extra power, the 993 employed a new Porsche-designed six-speed manual transaxle with closer intermediate ratios and dual-cone synchros for first and second gears. Despite its extra cog, the six-speed was no heavier and not much larger than the old five-speed and was complemented by a lower-effort clutch. Buyers who favored automatic transmission could order improved Tiptronic S, with shift maps optimized for the retuned engine, plus programming that allowed downshifts to be triggered by braking. A real Detroit touch was the new pair of rocker switches in the upper steering-wheel spokes for changing gears in "tip" mode without taking one's hands off the wheel. The regular floor quadrant was unchanged.

Perhaps the biggest single improvement in the 993 was its new rear suspension. Largely rendered in lovely aluminum castings, it replaced the feared semi-trailing arms of old with what amounted to double-wishbone geometry. Porsche called the arrangement "LSA," for "Lightweight-Stable-Agile," but it was really like Detroit's hallowed "long-/short-arm" setup. Here, a solid A-arm sat below a triangulated two-piece upper member with bushings that gave stabilizing toe-in under braking—the famous "Weissach" effect. Better yet, the whole assembly was mounted on a cast-aluminum subframe—a first for a rear-engine car—which was rubber isolated to dampen noise and soften ride. The new rear end was also claimed to reduce unsprung weight and be easier to build. Front suspension was much as before, but an inch wider track and increased caster improved stability and on-center steering feel. The steering itself remained power rack-and-pinion, but a quicker ratio cut nearly half a turn lock-to-lock, to 2.47. Turn diameter was also tightened a useful two feet to 38.5.

Porsche never adds engine power without increased braking ability, so the 993's four-wheel discs grew about 0.2-inches, to nearly a foot in diameter. The rotors were also thicker, newly cross-drilled as standard, and treated to Bosch's latest "ABS 5," a three-channel antilock system with reduced pedal "kickback" and better ability to cope with uneven surfaces.

Speaking of traction, the 993 featured a new wrinkle called ABD—Automatic Brake Differential. An extension of the ABS system, it used the same wheel-speed sensors and computer-managed hydraulic actuator to apply braking force to restore grip at any wheel at which slip was detected. While manual-shift 993s came with the usual limited-slip rear differential, ABD was optional for Carreras and standard on the Carrera 4.

And so far, everything we've said of the rear-drive 993 Carrera applied to its C4 sister except that Tiptronic still wasn't available, though buyers did get "titanium-colored" engine-lid script, brake calipers, and shift-knob insert. However, the all-wheel drive system was further simplified from the 964 design for increased effectiveness.

Instead of electro-hydraulic differentials, the 993 C4 used mechanical units comprised of the aforementioned locking rear differential and a center diff with a viscous coupling—basically a multi-disc clutch running in a silicone goo, not unlike that used in newer sport-utility vehicles like the Jeep Grand Cherokee. A driveshaft ran from the center differential to a small front diff with associated halfshafts. Unlike the previous C4 system, this new one diverted power to the front only when signaled by sensors monitoring rpm, temperature, and wheel speed (shared with the ABD and ABS), regulated by the rear differential. Thus, if both rear wheels began spinning, as on ice, up to 39 percent of available power was sent forward; in most other conditions the front/rear torque split could be varied between 5/95 and 25/75 percent.

The real beauty of the new system was that it weighed just 111 pounds, which trimmed curb weight by a substantial 165 pounds, and suffered 50 percent lower frictional losses. Even so, the new C4 ended up a bit thirstier than the rear-drive Carrera and landed in the "guzzler" category, though only by one mpg.

Testers agreed that these rejuvenated 911s performed brilliantly. Let's start with the rear-driver, piloted for *Car and Driver* by Briton Peter Robinson. He noted that "no 911 has ever handled as well nor been as easy to drive. But do not think for a moment that this more friendly temperament has compromised driver pleasure. . . . The [steering] wheel still transmits useful messages with typical 911 clarity as it writhes gently in your fingers, so that you feel there's almost no hydraulic help. Yet any artificial messages are eliminated, and so is kickback.

"The result combines razor-sharp turn-in response and sensitivity with staggering high-speed stability and a newfound sense of security. The contrived understeer engineered into the old Carrera 2 and 4 models has been replaced by a new agility . . . the greater roadholding and reduced

Redesigned and called 993 internally, the rear-drive '95 911 Carrera had the familiar low stance of earlier 911s, now mated to an aggressive, pleasingly rounded look dominated by newly enlarged fender flares. Controls were simple and practical; storage space beneath the front boot was modest but not absurdly so. The 3.6-liter flat-six generated 270 horsepower at 6100 rpm, and the manual shift now had six forward speeds instead of five. All this, plus increased stability made this new 911 ferocious yet tractable.

understeer requiring far less steering effort. . . . At its limit, the 911's not quite as serene as an Acura NSX, but it is far more predictable than a Ferrari 348"—high praise considering the pure mid-engine configurations of the Acura and Ferrari.

As for the Carrera 4, *Road & Track's* Joe Rusz tested it back-to-back with the rear-driver at Southern California's demanding Willow Springs Raceway, and his comments are interesting: "Without a doubt, the Carrera 4 is quicker, getting off the line with a fair amount of wheelspin but without the severe axle judder that seems to dog the Carrera 2. . . . In fast sweepers the Carrera 4 feels more stable, its excellent awd enabling it to toe the line perfectly. The Carrera 2, on the other hand, gets very nervous and tends to oversteer at the slightest hint of throttle lift-off."

But Rusz found that "in slow, 90-degree corners, the C4 . . . understeers, so much so that power-on exits often found the steering wheel reaching full lock. What's more, throttle liftoff only slightly reduces understeer—in contrast to the C2 in which a reduction of power brings the tail out slightly and allows the front tires to bite. Why does the Carrera 4 understeer? Because when the front wheels are driven, less of their tires' grip is available for lateral traction. And with the rear tires getting such excellent traction, they propel the car forward, causing the lightly loaded fronts to lose their grip."

Of course, a racetrack isn't the real world, and the fact was that both new 911s were admirably suited for the kind of driving most people do. As Robinson declared, "[I]t seems Porsche's engineers have finally purged [the] flaws . . . and what's left is the sharpest 911 yet. And the most friendly." Rusz had a more precise take: "If I were a Porsche purist who knows how to drive . . . and who fully understands the meaning of rear-engine weight bias, the Carrera would get my vote. It's lively, responsive, challenging. . . . But if I were the same fella and realized that there's a lot to be said for all-wheel-drive stability and all-weather traction, the new Carrera 4 would get my nod."

So as ever with the rear-engine Porsche, "you pays your money and takes your choice"—only now buyers didn't pay so much. At just $100 shy of $60,000, the '95 U.S. Carrera coupe was $5000 less expensive than its '94 counterpart, while the $65,900 C4 was fully $12,000 more affordable. Corresponding Cabriolet prices were $65,900 and $74,200. (Tiptronic S added $3150 to either Carrera.) In convincing fashion, Porsche had made good on its promise of a better 911 for less money.

We're not forgetting performance, but gains here over the 964 were relatively less impressive. *R&T's* rear-drive coupe matched the factory's 5.2-second 0-60 claim, which was a tick quicker than the departed RS America. The magazine's Carrera 4 clocked 5.7 seconds 0-60, 0.3-second off the official time, though about what you'd expect given a 111-pound weight penalty. *Car and Driver* got 4.9 seconds with a C4 coupe in the same sprint, which seems a shade optimistic even for that magazine.

As for skidpad cornering, *R&T's* Carrera 4 turned 0.85g versus 0.90 for *C/D's* car—a wide disparity that's probably explained by different test sites. Porsche itself claimed "in excess of 1.0g on high-traction surfaces" for both 993s, rear- and all-drive alike, which sounds uncharacteristically boastful in view of the above.

Regardless, enthusiasts again have new 911s to argue about and marvel at, including an exciting new rear-engine Porsche that we'll save for our final chapter.

For now, let's raise a glass to the latest 911s for preserving the essence of Porsche in thoroughly modern cars that are even more accomplished than their many forebears, yet no less memorable. In a faddish world where too much is discarded simply for being "old," Porsche's fabulous 911s are reassuring signs that good things do endure.

Porsche owners daydream about running their cars on the flat, open highways of the American west. Little doubt that the '95 911 Carrera Coupe and Cabriolet (top) would be right at home in such a setting. Likewise the '95 Carrera 4, (bottom left). And as for future 911s, one direction is suggested by this computer-enhanced spy shot (bottom right) of the upcoming 996 variant; note the separate taillamps. Whatever the car's final configuration, it's likely to be a 1998 model. Another new direction for the 911 is suggested by this rendering (bottom right) of what may ultimately be called the Panorama, and which will feature a tinted glass top that can be slid open or lifted. A powered roller blind will protect passengers from the sun. The Panorama is based not on the 911 Coupe but on the Cabriolet.

The 914 Chronicle: Back to Basics, Part I

Don't cry for the 914. Though chided during its five-year life as an ersatz Porsche, it has lately been recognized as an interesting car that just happens to be the cheapest modern Porsche one can buy. And that's ironic, for few would have predicted *any* enthusiasm for the 914 when it was abandoned in 1975 like the star-crossed child it was.

Hopes were high when the 914 was unveiled at the Frankfurt Automobile Show in September 1969. It was very much a back-to-basics car—a return to Porsche's roots, much as the 356 Speedster had been some 15 years before. Of course, the 914 was quite different because of the way it came about and particularly because of its mid-engine configuration (though Porsche was hardly a stranger to "middies" by then). Yet like the Speedster, the 914 was a more affordable Volkswagen-based sports car, conceived to bring the pride and pleasures of Porsche ownership to a much wider audience in the face of steadily escalating prices for the 911 and 912.

The 912 was the car the 914 replaced, and with good reason. As the late Dean Batchelor explained: "The least expensive 912 cost more than $5000 by 1969 and could top $6000 if all the available options were ordered. This seems like a tremendous bargain today. . . . But there were problems related to the reduced horsepower in a car that looked faster than it was and had a reputation for performance that many 912 drivers seemed to feel obligated to maintain. . . . [They] had to push [their cars] harder yet couldn't begin to achieve the performance of a 911. And, if [they] tried it often enough, the engine suffered abuse that drastically shortened its life.

"Also, too many mechanics, and some owners, thought the 912 engine was 'just another Volkswagen' and this muddled thinking could prove fatal. . . . It was a Porsche design through and through, and needed good care and maintenance by a qualified Porsche mechanic or a knowledgeable owner."

Aware of this situation, Porsche had begun planning in 1966 for a new four-cylinder model to sell for less than the 912. The need to keep price to a reasonable level, coupled with production constraints at Zuffenhausen (owing to strong 911 sales), made it inevitable "that Porsche should seek a partner in the building of such a car," as Karl Ludvigsen recorded. A mid-engine design was almost as inevitable because it would "put Porsche in the position of being able to draw direct marketing parallels between the successes of its mid-engined racing cars . . . and the attributes of [its] production cars."

Perhaps no less important, mid-engine design was beginning to look like the wave of the future for production sports cars. All the buff magazines said so, and Lotus unveiled a roadgoing middie in 1966, the Renault-powered Europa. But though others would follow—Fiat's X1/9 in the Seventies, Toyota's MR2 and Pontiac's Fiero in the Eighties, plus assorted Italian exotics—the mid-engine layout is still far from universal.

The reasons are well known. Though perfect for the track, the mid-engine layout is less desirable in a road car. Putting the drivetrain right behind the occupants puts noise, vibration, and heat that much closer, requiring more heroic insulation than in a front- or rear-engine design. Few production middies have succeeded in overcoming these problems, not to mention limited over-the-shoulder vision, difficult service access, and challenging shift quality, all of which tend to be compromised too. Further, a midships package is more difficult and expensive to engineer and build than a conventional one. While it eliminates the need for a driveshaft, it mandates a costly independent rear suspension and convoluted shift linkage.

But none of this seemed very important in the mid-Sixties. Midships cars were dominating the tracks, and the more adventuresome automakers expected their competition auras to work sales wonders for showroom models. Porsche was no exception, but the 914 wasn't destined to bring buyers beating down the doors.

In Ferry Porsche's words, the 914 sprang "from the realization that we needed to broaden our [model] program at a less costly level [and] that we couldn't do it alone." Accordingly, the chief of Zuffenhausen contacted the chief of Wolfsburg, Heinz Nordhoff, who had brought VW to the peak of success by decisively making it America's top-

Even as Porsche was launching the 914, it was thinking about faster, more powerful versions, hence this "914/8," of which two were built in 1969. As the designation suggested, both were fitted with eight-cylinder engines— nothing less than the 3.0-liter unit from the 908 world GT racing car. This is the first 914/8, which was used for a time by Ferdinand Piech, then Porsche chief engineer. With full-race tuning and about 300 horsepower, it was clocked at a smashing 250 km/h (155 mph). The car resides today at the Porsche Museum in Stuttgart.

selling import car.

Together, they hit on an early example of what we'd now call a "joint venture." And in this case, it was a natural. VW and Porsche had worked together for years. Both firms were German, with all the clarity of understanding that that implied. VW's expertise in volume production was as obvious as Porsche's talent in engineering sports cars. And as luck would have it, Nordhoff wanted a sportier model to replace the slow-selling Type 3 Karmann-Ghia, not the winsome Beetle-based original but a later, square-rigged coupe never sold in the United States (though closely related to the late-Sixties Fastback and Squareback "sedans"). A mid-engine two-seater designed around VW components by the folks at Porsche might just fill both companies' needs.

In due course, Nordhoff and Ferry hatched an intriguing plan. Porsche would design a car to accept the powertrain from VW's forthcoming upscale rear-engine sedan, the 411, in which form it would be sold by Volkswagen as a "VW-Porsche"; in return, Zuffenhausen could buy bodies for installing its own engines and sale through its own dealers. An incidental benefit was to give the Wilhelm Karmann works something to build in lieu of the Type 3 Ghia, thus avoiding employee layoffs.

Porsche was more than willing. Its dealers were clamoring for a less costly offering now that 911 and 912 prices were way above 356 levels. Even better, Porsche had recent mid-engine experience in a near-roadgoing car, the sports-racing Type 904 GTS (see Chapter 7).

Styling was deemed critical. Nordhoff didn't want the new sportster to look like a VW, and Porsche didn't want it to resemble a 911/912. Again, luck was with them. Gugelot Design GmbH in Neu-Elm, located about 50 miles from Stuttgart, had been working on a front-engine prototype to demonstrate a new body material: a foam core within layers of bonded fiberglass. This "sandwich" construction interested Porsche, VW, and Karmann, as well as BMW and Daimler-Benz, despite tests suggesting it was unsuitable for mass production. But the prototype's distinctive styling was just what Nordhoff and Ferry Porsche were seeking. A team directed by Ferry's son Butzi, who'd created the template for the 911, suitably revised it for a mid-mounted drivetrain and the desired image. The 914 was born.

The result was unorthodox, though that was, perhaps, inevitable given the midships layout. To lend Teutonic rigidity to the open, all-steel monocoque, a Targa-type rollbar (which some journalists dubbed the "basket handle") was made part of the design; between this and the windshield header sat a removable fiberglass panel. The body was devoid of ornamentation, but the bumpers, designed to meet pending U.S. impact standards, were less than beautiful. They were normally finished in body color but looked better in extra-cost chrome. Because the nose was so low, pop-up headlamps were used to meet minimum-height regulations.

The headlight design was a typical piece of *Porschearbeit*, with every contingency anticipated. For example, each unit had an electric motor and provision for manual operation in case of power loss. Both methods were designed so that either could easily break the thickest coat of ice the engineers could conjure in cold-weather tests. To prevent catching unwary fingers as the lamps closed, Porsche provided a safety panel that would give way before one's digits did.

Reflecting economic constraints, the cockpit had all the essentials but little warmth. Instruments recalled those of the rear-engine 901 Series, with an upright binnacle presenting a large central tachometer flanked by a speedometer on the right and a fuel gauge and warning lights in a matching circle to the left. Heat/vent controls came from the 901; door and dash hardware were cribbed from VW.

The cockpit was roomy enough for the largest occupants, although the bucket seats were criticized for being too flat. *Road & Track* noted the hunkered-down seating position (the 914 stood four inches lower overall than a 911) but said "vision to the rear is the best of any mid-engine car (except roadsters) we've driven—the blind spot made by the basket handle is so far forward that it can't obstruct anything that needs seeing."

One of the more unusual touches was a pull-up handbrake mounted outboard of the driver's seat. Ordinarily, this would have made entry/exit difficult, but Porsche thoughtfully gave it a double-jointed handle that could be folded down, out of the way, once the ratchet engaged. It was a predictive feature: Later Corvettes and Porsche's own 928 would have one too.

Car and Driver observed that "since the [914's] structure is concentrated in the flat, platform floor . . . the door sills are low and the tunnel is no higher than what is required to house the shift linkage and a few electrical wires [so] almost the entire width of the car becomes available for seating. The designers like to think that, if you drop a cushion between the seats, there is a place for a third person and they've included an extra set of seat belts for just that eventuality."

Two more views of the first 914/8 (top right and bottom) reveal how closely it resembled the stock four-cylinder 914. Indeed, surprisingly few changes were deemed necessary to accommodate the larger flat-eight racing engine: just stiffer shock absorbers, titanium coil springs (replacing steel items), and minor body changes like wider headlight doors and an oil-cooler air intake in the front bumper (both visible in the photo on pg. 129). A factory cutway illustration (top left) shows the more economically feasible approach taken to improved 914 performance that resulted in the 914/6. Introduced in late 1970, this model carried the 2.0-liter 110-horsepower flat-six from the contemporary 911T.

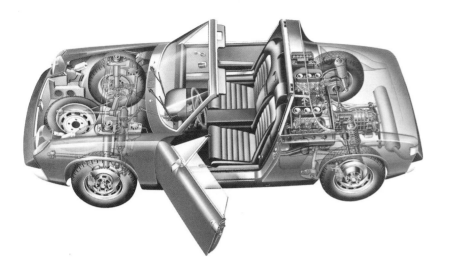

However, only the driver's seat had fore/aft adjustment (and generous at that), another cost-cutting measure. The passenger made do with a movable footrest anchored to the right kick panel by a plastic strap. *C/D* derisively described this as "a chunk of what feels like wood, shaped like a concrete brick, covered with mouse-fuzz grey carpet. . . . If you're tall enough so that your feet will reach the front bulkhead, the strap can be unhooked and the block stored in one of the trunks. Or heaved over the side."

Was that "trunks," plural? Yes, like some other mid-engine designs, the 914 had two. Up front was a deep main hold with a horizontally stored spare tire; behind the engine was a wide but shallow compartment with its own forward-hinged lid and clips for carrying the roof panel. The engine was reached, if none too easily, through a narrow lift-up hatch just behind the rear window.

Production economics naturally dictated shared chassis components, so front suspension—MacPherson struts, lower A-arms and longitudinal torsion bars—was lifted almost intact from the rear-engine line. Out back were 901-type geometry but new pieces: semi-trailing arms and coil springs, the latter a first for Porsche. So little body roll occurred that anti-roll bars were deemed unnecessary at first. But springing was very stiff, so ride quality was quite hard. As a result, early 914s developed squeaks and rattles literally unheard of in a 911 or 356. The lift-off roof was mostly to blame. It also generated a lot of wind noise. Steering was rack-and-pinion, brakes solid-rotor discs all-round. VW also provided the wheels, skinny four-lug 4.5 X 15 rims from the 411. Boge telescopic shocks were standard, but gas-pressurized Bilsteins were optional.

The 914 engine was a 1679-cubic-centimeter (102.4-cubic-inch) fuel-injected overhead-valve flat four, unchanged from its 411 application, though it soon would be. The injection system, devised by Bosch under Bendix patents, allowed clearing U.S. emission limits without an air pump. Mild 8.2:1 compression yielded modest initial outputs of 85 SAE horsepower at 4900 rpm and 103 pounds/feet of torque peaking at 2800 rpm. The standard and only transaxle was the 901's five-speed manual, complete with its awkward racing-style shift gate. Sportomatic was advertised as an option but apparently was never fitted.

On the road, the 914 was initially both more and less than enthusiasts expected. In acceleration it was comparable to the antediluvian MGB, according to *R&T*, able to do 0-60 mph in about 14 seconds and the standing quarter-mile in a tick over 19 seconds at 70 mph. *Car and Driver* got somewhat better numbers: 11.3 seconds and 18.1 seconds at 75 mph. Top speed was quite good at 105-110 mph, though at nearly 2100 pounds, the 914 wasn't exactly light for its 96.4-inch wheelbase and an overall length two inches shorter than a VW Beetle's. Weight distribution front/rear was a reasonably good 46/54 percent.

Through the twisty bits, *R&T* reported that for a middie, the 914 didn't have "great absolute cornering power—at least not yet," this despite inch-wider wheels fitted by the West Coast distributor. By contrast, transient behavior was judged "excellent. Initial response to steering input is utterly without delay. . . . And what happens when the driver lifts his foot off the throttle in a hard corner—this is the trickiest thing about rear-heavy cars—is simply a mild tuck-in of the front or, at the extreme, a smooth breakaway of the rear."

C/D had a slightly different view: "It understeers . . . a lot. While you are making the transition from straight to curve, there is no real problem unless you have to slow down abruptly. . . . Here the 914 has the same trailing-throttle oversteer characteristics [of] the 911E. . . . Lift your foot off the gas as you enter a hard bend and the tail tries to come around. An expert driver can use this to set up for a corner, but a novice will probably never try it twice."

Bearing VW-Porsche badges (on steering wheel and tail), the 914 went on sale in Europe in February 1970. But when it reached U.S. dealers a month later, it wore only the Porsche name (in block letters on the engine cover), plus a Zuffenhausen crest on its steering wheel (but never on nose or road wheels). This badging was deliberate—and about all that remained of the verbal agreement between Nordhoff and Ferry Porsche.

What had happened was this: Nordhoff had passed away in April 1968, and his successor, Kurt Lotz, had changed some terms of the deal. The results were three. First, a new company called VG (*Vertriebsgesellchaft* "Motors Inc."), owned 50/50 by the partners, was formed to handle European sales and marketing for VW, Porsche, and Audi (the last by now part of VW), as well as the new Volks-Porsche. For the United States, Porsche and Audi would be combined as a division of Volkswagen of America and the new middie sold as a Porsche through the separate "Porsche + Audi" dealer network.

Second, Karmann (also a VW subsidiary by this time) was to build four-cylinder 914s on a "turn-

A trio of contemporary factory photos shows the second "914/8" that was built in 1969 to investigate a super-performance version of the mid-engine VW-Porsche sports car. Aside from wearing a Porsche crest on its nose (something no production 914 ever did), this second "/8" differed from the first primarily in using a milder 260-horsepower version of Porsche's GT racing flat-eight, complete with four carburetors and air cleaners. Registered for the street, the car was given to Dr. Ferry Porsche for his 60th birthday. In the profile shot (top) it poses with a pair of contemporary 911 Targas.

key" basis for VG in Europe and Porsche/Audi in America. And third, Porsche could still buy 914 bodies but at a much higher price than originally agreed.

Initial U.S. advertising for the 914 emphasized the advantages of its mid-engine design—lower center of gravity, better handling and braking, increased tire life—as proven in competition Porsches. "If there's one thing we've learned from racing," said one ad, "it's where to put the engine. . . . So if you're thinking about a true two-seat sports car, think about this: When you don't get a back seat, you should at least get an engine in its place."

Yet neither press nor public were much impressed. A big reason was price. Though announced in Germany for the equivalent of $3015, the 914 came to the States just five bucks short of $3500. At that, it competed not against the MGB (to which it was clearly superior) but the Triumph TR6 (cruder but quite a bit faster), the Fiat 124 Spider (a prettier, full convertible) and—most worrisome for Porsche—the new Datsun 240Z from Japan, a conventional but modern closed GT bargain-priced at $175 *less*.

Against these rivals, the 914 seemed a so-so buy. *Road & Track* tested them all in June 1970—except the 240Z, then in a class of one and really better than the rest—and the results were telling. Though the 914 was slowest off the line, it was marginally fastest all-out. It also equaled the Italian car and handily beat the two Brits in braking, and outdid all three in fuel economy. But its blocky styling was the most controversial of the group, and neither workmanship nor materials seemed worthy of the Porsche name—or the price.

On considering the latter, *Car and Driver* dismissed the 914 as "an altogether underwhelming car. It offers less performance and less comfort than its competitors and has tricky handling in the bargain. It does have a midship engine (be the first on your block!) and it would allow you to tell everybody that you drive a Porsche [but] you'll have to make up your mind if it's worth it."

A lot of folks—over 100,000—would eventually conclude that the car *was* worth its price. But given its VW engine, some marque fans found it hard to accept the 914 as a "real" Porsche.

Zuffenhausen was uncomfortable with that, too, and thus decided to make the 914 a real Porsche in fact as well as name. The result appeared in late 1970 as the 914/6 (at which point the four-cylinder model informally became the 914/4). Powered by the 2.0-liter 110-bhp flat-six from the 1969-model 911T, with capacitive-discharge ignition and twin

triple-choke Weber carbs, it came with 5.5-inch-wide five-lug wheels (distinctive 10-spoke light-alloys were available), plus suitably fatter tires and ventilated front brakes. Amenities were also more generous: 911-style full instrumentation (with 150-mph speedo and 8000-rpm tach), three-speed wipers and electric washers (the latter replacing a foot-operated bulb type), dual-tone horn, and a vinyl covering for the basket handle.

Built entirely by Porsche and badged as such in all markets, the 914/6 sold for better than $2500 more than the four-cylinder job—about $6100 in the United States—and was thus even more difficult to sell. To no one's surprise, it was quietly canned after 1972 and only 3351 examples.

Still, the extra cylinders made a world of difference. It was hard to think of the 914/4 as anything but a VW; indeed, *C/D* conceded that it would have made a fine replacement for the original Karmann-Ghia, surely a case of damning with faint praise. But there was no escaping the flat-six engine's exciting wail or that seat-of-the-pants feeling, sufficient to make clear that the 914/6 was a genuine Porsche.

It certainly performed like one. *Road & Track* clocked 8.7 seconds 0-60, the standing quarter in 16.3 seconds at 83 mph, and 123 mph flat out, plus 21.3 miles per gallon—in all, typically balanced Porsche performance. Nevertheless, *R&T* said they'd "probably pay the extra $431 for a 4-speed 911T, with its handsomer body, better detailing, extra years of development, slightly better performance and +2 seating. For those who insist on open-air driving, the 911T in Targa form is $675 dearer or more than a grand above the 914/6. This differential, plus the technical novelty of the mid-engine package, will assure the new car plenty of buyers [obviously, it didn't]. What we all hoped for was a true Porsche nearer to $5000, but that's asking a lot."

One critical factor made any 914 less than a true Porsche: the lack of intensive yearly development accorded the 911. This might have been expected for a car that fell between corporate stools, but "it indirectly led to the demise of the 914," in Dean Batchelor's view.

Still, the four-cylinder cars would see a few changes over time. The '71s had virtually none, but the '72s gained a revised engine (designated EA-series, replacing the original W-series unit) with recalibrated fuel injection that let it run on 91-octane fuel, as required that year in California. Unusually, it delivered about 10-percent better mileage with no harm to performance.

Above: *Porsche developed the 914/6 GT for rallies and road racing in 1970, after which privateers took over in SCCA and other venues. The car's best showing was sixth overall and first in the GT class at the 1970 Le Mans 24 Hours.* Opposite page: *An extension of the 914/6 was the 916 (top left), conceived in mid-1971 as Porsche's reply to the Ferrari Dino. Besides a surprisingly lush cockpit (top right), it featured a fixed roof for structural strength, special lower body and chassis modifications, five-speed gearbox, and a 2.4-liter 911S engine with 190 DIN horsepower. However, a high $14,000 projected price implied minuscule demand, and Porsche abandoned the 916 after only 20 were built. Five-lug alloy wheels distinguished the "/6" from lesser 914s, but many examples wore 911-style Fuchs five-spoke rims (middle and bottom). Though sales hopes were high for the 914/6, its steep price (about $6100 in the U.S.) prompted Porsche to cancel the model after building just 3351 over less than three years.*

Also new were fresh-air vents at each end of the dash, a wiper/washer control incorporated with the turn-signal lever (as on the 914/6) and an adjustable passenger seat that eliminated the footrest. The most drastic—and unwelcome—change was a hike in the list price of nearly $700.

As before, buyers could pop for a $311 Appearance Group on top of that. This included the 914/6's vinyl rollbar trim and dual-tone horn, plus the aforesaid chrome bumpers, foglamps, upgraded carpeting, 165 X 15 radial tires on 5.5-inch rims, and a leather-rim steering wheel.

More ambitious tweaks followed for '73. The 1.7-liter engine was retained, with an even more anemic 69-bhp setup for smog-bound California, but Zuffenhausen added spice to the recipe with an optional 2.0-liter four. Rated at 91 SAE net horsepower, it was a simple bore-and-stroke job (from 90 X 66 to 94 X 71mm) that gave performance about midway between that of the original 1.7 and the 914/6. In fact, the 914 2.0, as it was badged, was effectively a replacement for the Porsche-powered model. Even better, base price was less lofty at $5599 (East Coast POE) and included the Appearance Group and alloy wheels plus a center console mounting clock, voltmeter, and oil temperature gauge. Still, the 914 remained a tough sell.

At least the 2.0-liter four offered better tractability along with its extra performance, being an easy starter and revving quickly to its 5600-rpm redline. With it, the 914/4 now roughly equaled TR6 performance. The five-speed gearbox was particularly useful here, allowing the driver to extract the most from the gutsier powerplant. Porsche had evidently changed its mind about anti-roll bars, for it fitted one at each end of the 2.0. This, in turn, permitted lower spring rates for a slightly softer ride.

As a result, the 2.0-liter seemed completely bereft of the dreaded Porsche oversteer. *Road & Track* had this to say: "The relative stiffness of the front and rear anti-roll bars seems to have been chosen to provide understeer at all times and under all conditions. When driven around a curve, the front end slides and the back end sticks. Apply full power and the front end pushes toward the outside of the turn. Let up on the throttle and the front end tucks toward the inside of the turn. This is very safe ... but the sporting driver may wish sometimes for the freedom of, say, a 911S, in which an occasional 'nasty' trait can be provoked and exploited with skill. Perhaps the not-quite-Porsche 914 isn't allowed to provide that sort of test and perhaps that's why the 914/2 [*R&T*'s term] isn't

allowed to be the 914S [the 2.0-liter's proposed designation, turned down by the factory]."

For 1974, American 914s received bulky front-bumper guards to meet the year's new five-mph impact rule. Standard power for all models was now the bigger-bore (93mm) 1.8-liter engine from the 411's upgraded 412 replacement. With modified rockers, combustion chambers and ports, plus larger valves, the 1.8 almost held the line against the drain of desmogging, delivering 72 bhp (SAE net) at 4800 rpm, four horsepower less than that generated by the 1.7.

The European version (with twin carburetors instead of fuel injection) was down a like number of DIN horses (76 versus 80). A jazzy U.S. version, prosaically called *Limited Edition*, was issued with front spoiler, side stripes, alloy wheels, a choice of black or white paint, and a special interior. It was supposed to perk up languishing sales, but nothing seemed able to turn that trick.

After grafting bigger bumpers onto American-market '75s, Porsche gave up on the 914. Production stopped at 118,947, including 914/6s—by no means a paltry total, but not what the partners had hoped for, either. Though a "people's Porsche" was a good idea, the car's half-breed image and the altered marketing arrangement defeated it. As Karl Ludvigsen wrote, the "VW-Porsche [marque] had neither image nor tradition. At the same time [the 914] was both VW and Porsche and neither VW *nor* Porsche."

Dean Batchelor noted that the 914 was also likely hurt in the United States by persistent hot-weather driveability woes, mainly vapor lock that made for hard—and sometimes no—starting and chronic overheating. These bothers were slow to be rectified. Indeed, Batchelor said "many 914 owners feel the demise of the car could partly have been Porsche's lack of a cure for vapor lock from 1970 to 1975, when the fuel pump was moved [from near the right heat exchanger] to a cooler position up front."

But mediocre value for money was always the 914's biggest problem. Because VW had directed Karmann to charge more per body than originally agreed, Porsche was never able to exploit the intended economies of scale that could have made for a less costly and more salable 914/6, and which would have helped the four-cylinder cars, too.

However, this shortcoming was not VW sabotage. Ludvigsen quoted Ferry Porsche as saying, "They calculate costs differently in a big firm. They couldn't consider the advantages of having a sports car in the line, the way it can attract people into the showroom." VW looked mainly at tooling

Above: *Pop-up headlamps gave all 914s a somewhat odd, "bugeye" appearance. Opposite page: An all-around look at a 1972 four-cylinder 914 that's been nicely optioned with vinyl rollbar trim (top and middle right) and foglamps (bottom left). Wheels appear to be borrowed from a 356B. Efficiency improved for '72 with adoption of a new EA-series 1.7-liter engine (bottom right) with recalibrated fuel injection that allowed running on low-lead 91-octane fuel.*

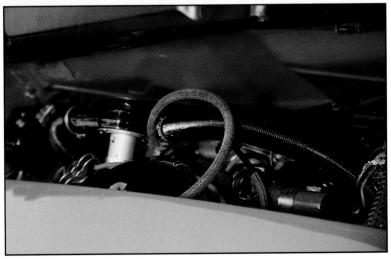

amortization, which meant a high per-body price at the 914's modest volume. Porsche, by contrast, never applied the true cost of an individual model to that model alone. "We put them all together and divide by our total volume," said Ferry.

There's no telling what the 914 might have become had it been better received or treated more seriously by Volkswagen; the potential was certainly there. Porsche demonstrated it by trying a flat-*eight*—the wonderful 3.0-liter unit from the Type 908 racer—in an experimental called *914/8*. Packing 310 DIN horses, it could do 0-60 in six seconds and reach 155 mph. *Road & Track* reported on a second "914/8," a conversion with 283 Chevy V-8 power conceived by Californian Ron Simpson. This "Porschev" hit 60 mph from rest in 6.3 seconds and the standing quarter-mile in 14 seconds flat at 90.5 mph.

Several other specials were based on the 914. Among them: a trio of GTs by Louis Heuliez in France, a study by Albrecht Goertz of BMW 507/Datsun 240Z fame, one by Frua, and the sensational gullwing Tapiro show car from master stylist Giorgio Giugiaro.

But the development that came closest to production was the factory's own 916, a swoopy 914 evolution powered by a 2.4-liter 190-bhp 911 engine. As Porsche's ultimate mid-engine road car, it would likely have sold at $15,000-$16,000, directly competitive with the Ferrari Dino 246GT. And with a curb weight of almost exactly a ton, its performance would have been *more* than competitive. Porsche claimed a 0-60 time of "less than seven seconds," and there was reason to believe that figure was conservative.

In appearance, the 916 differed considerably from the 914, sporting flared fenders and body-color bumpers front and rear, plus a fixed roof for extra structural strength required with the muscular engine. Inside were leather trim, 914/6 instruments, even a radio. The suspension employed heavy-duty Bilstein gas/oil shocks, stiffer anti-roll bars, 911S vented brakes, and 185/70R15 Michelin XVR tires on S-type alloy wheels. There was also a five-speed gearbox with the more conventional new gate arrangement Porsche was then giving its rear-engine models.

Sadly, the 916 was nipped in the bud just after the first press pictures were distributed. Only 20 were built (all prototypes); one escaped to America and Brumos Porsche in Jacksonville, Florida.

The 916's premature death was attributable to price. The factory had grave doubts about sales at $15,000, especially since the 914 had been roundly criticized as overpriced. In retrospect, Porsche was probably wise to cancel the 916, but it's a shame that a few more weren't built.

And what of the 914? Surely it was hurt by being more "Vee-Dub" than Porsche. Had it been Zuffenhausen's own, with a Porsche engine and looks to match, more people would likely have paid the admission price. One is compelled to recall that Ferry Porsche wisely insisted that the 911 look something like a 356. Granted, a mid-engine car has different requirements, but at least this one could have had more of a Porsche face. Then, too, four-cylinder U.S. 914s were supposed to have all the performance and quality implied by the Porsche name, and they didn't. One can't help thinking they would have sold better as Volkswagens. Yet VW, then suffering financial hard times, couldn't justify spending much on development of a niche car with modest sales potential.

With all this, the 914's dumpy styling was simply the final letdown. *Car and Driver* said the 914 had "all the fluidity of line of an Erector set"; *Sports Car Graphic* termed it "a pleasant eyesore." *Road & Track* suggested that maybe American eyes just weren't accustomed to mid-engine sports cars. Yet just a year later, *R&T* noted the unchanged 1972 styling and called that "a disappointment.... We were hoping for at least a mild reworking of the uncharming front end."

But let's not forget that for all its faults, the 914 paved the way for another Porsche/VW venture that would prove far more successful in both commercial and automotive terms. It was, of course, the 924, which would lead to the even better 944 and 968.

That story is told in the next chapter, but first, a final thought for this one. It's fitting that the 914 has something of a fan club now. A big reason for that is undoubtedly low asking prices, enabling thousands of folks to fulfill their dream of Porsche ownership without needing an enormous pile of cash. Of course, that may not always be true, and it doesn't make the cars more virtuous. But it does suggest that 914s are likely to be pursued and preserved well past the millenium—no bad fate for any car, even a "not-quite" Porsche.

An optional 2.0-liter four was the 914's main improvement for 1973. The alloy wheels shown on these European versions were standard on what was badged the "914 2.0." So was the Appearance Group (though it no longer included chrome bumpers), as well as center console, extra gauges, and front and rear anti-roll bars. Base-priced in the United States at $5599, the 2.0 stood to boost lagging 914 sales, but it didn't and Porsche gave up on its mid-engine sports car after model-year '75.

The 924/944/968 Chronicle: Back to Basics, Part II

As the 356 begat the 911 in the Sixties, so the 924 led to something better with the 944 of the Eighties and the 968 of the Nineties. Yet like the 914, the 924 has long been disputed as a "genuine" Porsche. Never mind that it echoed the 356 in using contemporary Volkswagen suspension, brakes, and steering. Somehow, like the 914, the 924 just didn't have the usual Porsche magic.

It certainly didn't have Porsche's usual format. Not only was the 924's engine water-cooled, it was located up front. At least the 914s had air-cooled rear engines like any "proper" Porsche should. So what if they sat ahead of the rear axle?

Even historical significance is denied the 924. Though it *was* the first front-engine, water-cooled Porsche to reach production, it was actually designed *after* the lusher, costlier, but similarly configured, 928 (see next chapter).

Something else made the 924 more 914 than 911. Where the latter was conceived as a Porsche, the 924 was designed by Porsche to be a Volkswagen.

The story begins in 1970 with two key happenings. The first was the arrival of Rudolf Leiding to succeed the controversial Kurt Lotz as VW general manager. Leiding was a sports-car advocate and racing-minded, but he was budget-minded too.

A very good thing, as he took over a financially troubled company. The Beetle, Wolfsburg's prime profit-maker, was waning in popularity and there was no replacement in sight, despite numerous attempts. VW's "big car," the 411/412, was proving a costly flop, and the in-between Type 3 range had never lived up to expectations. VW's 1969 acquisition of Audi/NSU from Daimler-Benz brought problems of its own and put a further drain on capital reserves. To ease the budget crunch, Leiding quickly handed over much of VW's developmental engineering work to Porsche, whose expertise was as obvious as VW's need for inspired new designs.

To that end, Leiding set VW on a new product-planning course: *Baukastenprinzip*—literally, "building-block principle." It was a General Motors-style approach, with cars of different sizes, shapes, and prices derived from a relative handful of components to reduce development costs and improve production economies of scale. This led to two spinoffs of newly planned front-drive VW models. The Audi 80/Fox spawned the VW Passat/Dasher to replace the 411/412, while the Golf/Rabbit, the Beetle's heir apparent, sired a Karmann-Ghia successor in the sporty Scirocco.

The second key event of 1970 occurred when VW-Porsche *Vertriebsgesellschaft*, the jointly owned marketing firm for Porsche-designed cars using VW components, realized that the 914 "was not going to become the lasting favorite that the 356 had been," as the late Dean Batchelor put it. "Management, therefore, began planning a new car to be designed by Porsche for VG to sell as a VW/Audi—no more 'VW-Porsche' in Europe and 'Porsche' elsewhere, as the 914 had been [marketed]." Coded EA425, this project was the conception of the 924.

The birth would not be easy. Batchelor recorded eight separate requirements for the new sports car: interior space comparable to the 911's, 2+2 seating, "useful" trunk volume (presumably more than a 914's), greater comfort than that offered by the 914, all-independent suspension, maximum use of high-volume VW components, and—most intriguing—a *front*-engine design with some technical and stylistic similarity to the luxury 928, then under development. "Once the parameters had been agreed to, components . . . were selected by a process of logical application. . . .

"It was understood that air-cooled engines were nearing the end of their production at both Porsche and Volkswagen [the 911 would prove otherwise], so one of the new water-cooled units under development would be used. The one selected was a Volkswagen design, built by Audi, used in carbureted form in the VW LT van..." It was also destined for the forthcoming Audi 100 and, of all things, the American Motors Gremlin.

Plans were well along in 1973 when VG was disbanded and EA425 became VW's own project. It was only fair. After all, VW had been footing the bills, which then totaled $70 million. But then Leiding announced that EA425 would be built *only* as a VW *or* as an Audi, mainly so it could be sold through VW's 2000 West German dealers instead of just the 200 VW-Porsche outlets handling the

One of the more interesting variations on Porsche's "front four-cylinder" theme was the 924S, which coupled the model's original styling (and interior) with the superior all-Porsche 2.5-liter engine of the 924's erstwhile successor, the 944. Debuting in U.S. form for 1987 (shown), the S was the first 924 sold in six years. Porsche revived this body as an economy measure so it could offer a lower-priced entry-level model in the face of a weakening dollar that was making even the standard 944 too costly for some buyers.

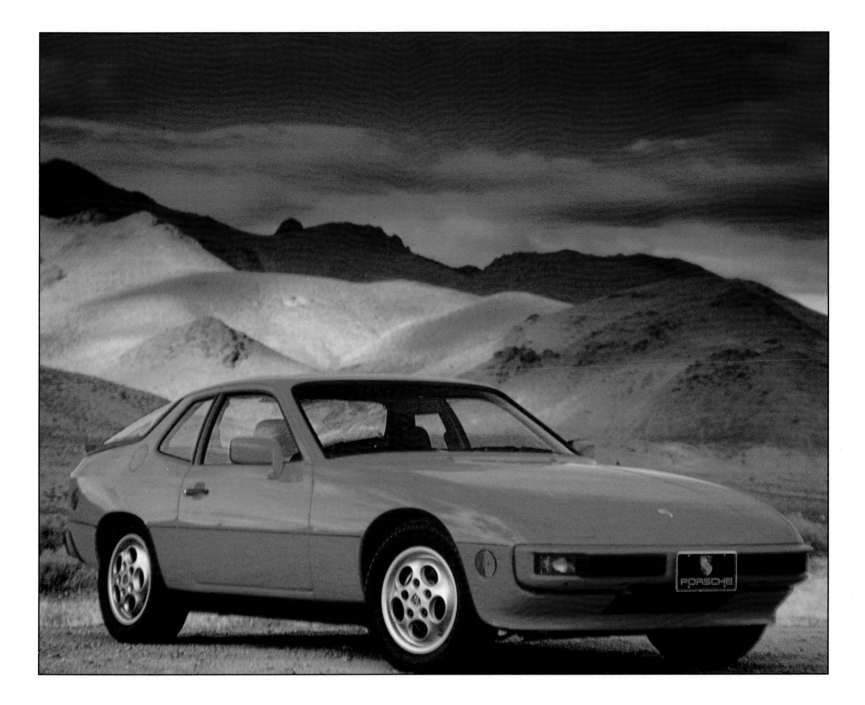

914. Zuffenhausen was stunned because the decision positioned EA425 as a potential competitor for its own four-cylinder 912.

The sticky situation seemed to have been resolved when Leiding suddenly departed in 1974, his expansion program having left VW/Audi more overextended than ever. But his replacement, former Ford Europe executive Tony Schmucker, promptly told Porsche there was now no need for EA425, given that the sports-car market was reeling in the wake of the OPEC oil embargo.

Porsche nevertheless had faith in the car and decided to save it by buying the production rights. The price was $60 million, and although that figure was a slight "discount" on VW's investment, Porsche would spend even more on further development.

The deal was sweetened for VW by Porsche's willingness to build the car as planned at the Audi/NSU plant in Neckarsulm, located a half-hour north of Stuttgart. This was more or less a necessity, as Porsche's Zuffenhausen facilities were completely absorbed in production of the 911 and in preparation for the 928.

The one matter left to settle was where to put the transmission. Despite what one might think, front-wheel drive was an option. Though admittedly a stranger to it in production cars, Porsche never wore technical blinders. Besides, the great Dr. Ferdinand's first car, the Lohner electric, had used it, so front drive wasn't exactly outside the realm of the company's heritage.

But with all the requirements, including VG's original notion that space be allowed for a larger powerplant from some future VW, the most appropriate setup seemed to be front-engine/rear-drive—and more specifically, a rear transaxle. Porsche's experience there was plentiful, and management thought the configuration "technically interesting." Even better, engineer Jochen Freund thought he could produce a good rear transaxle within EA425's cost constraints. Most important, the layout would provide near even fore/aft weight balance, thus minimizing the potentially dangerous oversteer of previous Porsches.

Thus did VW Project EA425 evolve into the Porsche Type 924, a designation chosen to signify a complete break with the 914. (Porsche never used project numbers between 917 and 924 except for 923, the internal code for the four-cylinder 912E engine.)

The front-engine/rear-transaxle concept wasn't new, having appeared on such diverse machines as Pontiac's "rope-drive" Tempest compact of 1961-63

and Ferrari's 275 GTB. But Freund's layout was carefully designed with *Baukastenprinzip* in mind. The driveshaft was a tiny, splined affair, 20mm in diameter, straight and without U-joints and encased in a tube to run in four bearings strategically placed at points of greatest torsional stress. At its ends were the gearbox and clutch, the latter bolted directly to the engine. Both engine and transmission were supported on a pair of rubber mounts. Another "clutch housing" was provided in back for the torque converter of Audi's forthcoming fully automatic three-speed transmission, which would be a 924 option and something new for Porsche. The manual transaxle initially offered had just four forward ratios (using non-Porsche baulk-ring synchronizers) driving through a single-plate clutch with diaphragm spring.

Conventional but contemporary described the engine: an overhead-cam inline four with aluminum head and cast-iron block. Slightly over-square bore/stroke dimensions of 86.5 X 84mm gave displacement of 1984 cubic centimeters (121.1 cubic inches). The cylinder head was a crossflow design with Heron-type combustion chambers (dished pistons, flat-face head). Unlike its VW applications, the 924 engine sipped fuel via Bosch's reliable K-Jetronic (CIS) injection (as did the Audi 100 version). Other features included toothed-belt cam drive, double valve springs, and, for reduced heat and wear, exhaust-valve rotators.

Installation was at a 40-degree tilt to starboard, making this a "slant four," technically speaking. It also made spark plugs hard to reach, as they sat on the right along with the alternator and exhaust manifold.

Though the 924 bowed in Europe with 125 DIN horsepower, it went to America with only 95 bhp (SAE net), the difference coming from lower compression—8.0 versus 9.3:1—and smaller valves. At least power was the same for all 50 states; California models used a catalytic converter to meet that state's stiffer emissions standards; "federal" cars relied on a simple air pump.

Chassis pieces also came from the corporate bins to satisfy *Baukastenprizip* but were carefully selected. The front suspension comprised lower A-arms from the Golf/Rabbit and coil-sprung MacPherson struts from the Super Beetle. Out back were torsion bars and Beetle semi-trailing arms; halfshafts came from VW's Type 181 utility vehicle (better known to consumers as "The Thing"). Bilstein shocks, cast-aluminum road wheels, and anti-roll bars would be optional. Steering was Golf/Rabbit rack-and-pinion with a slower ratio

Smooth styling gave little clue to the 924's front-engine/rear-transaxle layout. Other manufacturers would later borrow some of its appearance features, particularly the nose and upper rear-quarter treatments. All the photos show early 1976 European models; U.S. deliveries didn't commence until April 1977. Rear wiper (top left), alloy wheels (middle left), and foglights (upper right) were among several options on the initial list.

(19.2:1). Brakes were front discs from the Beetle and rear drums picked up from the VW K70 sedan that had been inherited from NSU.

These disparate elements worked together remarkably well; the 924 was certainly as much a "corporate kit car" as the 914, yet *Car and Driver* declared it was "still a non-conformist in the best Porsche tradition."

Fortunately, Porsche tradition was not in evidence on the price sticker. Thanks to high-volume engineering and the plethora of borrowed parts, Porsche achieved the production economies it had missed with the 914, and buyers reaped the reward. On its U.S. debut for 1977, the 924 carried a base price of just $9395, versus better than $15,000 for a 911.

As with the 914, styling of the 924 was deemed all-important but was more competently handled. Credit goes to Harm Lagaay, then working under the supervision of Porsche's American-born design chief Anatole "Tony" Lapine. Despite the order for a familial resemblance to the 928, the 924 was its own car, Lagaay reinterpreting familiar Porsche cues such as a grille-less nose and a strong increase in visual mass toward the rear. Emphasizing the latter was a large compound-curve rear window that doubled as a hatch that allowed access to the luggage compartment. All 924s wore color-matched bumpers; the five-mph aluminum units on American models were mounted farther out from the body on hydraulic struts.

Though the 924 was some 10 inches longer in wheelbase than a 911, its cockpit provided similarly close-coupled 2+2 accommodations. The driving stance was appropriately low and sporty, so outward vision wasn't the best, despite Porsche's claim that "at no point is more than 63° of the driver's full 360° obscured." As in the 914, furnishings were spare but functional, though there were obvious signs of cost-conscious borrowing: VW steering-column stalks, Beetle door handles, and Rabbit/Scirocco auxiliary gauges located above heat/vent controls in the vertical face of the tunnel console.

Though aerodynamics was not a major concern in the early Seventies, the 924's coefficient of drag (Cd) was a claimed 0.36, then among the lowest in the world for production cars.

Good points aside, the 924's design showed a few lapses. The steering wheel, for instance, was slightly oval to increase under-rim thigh clearance, but most testers thought it did just the opposite. Directly ahead of the driver were a large central speedometer, a tachometer on the right, and a fuel-

level/coolant-temperature dial on the left—which was fine, except that conical lenses distorted the gauge faces and picked up unwanted reflections.

Of course, as the "budget" Porsche, the 924 had fewer standard features and more options than the 911, but it could be made rather plush via options. Among U.S. extras were air-conditioning ($548), leather upholstery, the aforesaid automatic transmission (available in Europe in late 1976 and in America from March '77), stereo radio, metallic paint ($295), a removable sunroof panel ($330), front and rear anti-roll bars ($105), headlamp washers, rear-window wiper, tinted glass (a tinted backlight was standard), and a radio prep package (three speakers plus antenna, $105).

Two option groups were also offered. Touring Package I ($345) delivered 185/70HR14 tires and 6-inch-wide alloy wheels (versus 5.5-inchers with 165-14 rubber), the radio prep kit, and leather-rim steering wheel. Touring Package II ($240) added the headlamp washers, a right-door mirror, and the rear wiper.

In all, the 924 was distinctive and influential. Its nose, for instance, was aped by the Mazda RX-7 of 1978, and the new-for-'84 Chrysler Laser/Dodge Daytona coupes were unabashedly cut from the 924 pattern (as their G-24 project code suggested).

Early 924 road tests showed 0-60 mph times in the 11-12-second range, top speed of around 110 mph, and fuel economy of 20-22 miles per gallon. These weren't sensational figures, but they weren't bad for a well-tuned 2.0-liter four in a small, adequately equipped 2+2. In a comparison test with the rival Alfa Romeo Alfetta GT and Datsun 280Z, *Road & Track* gave the nod to the 924, even though the Z went for $3000 less in base trim. The editors loved the Porsche on the track and praised its balance, flat cornering, and light, fast steering. It's important to note, however, that the car driven by *R&T*'s editors had all the chassis options, and that the magazine did not think as highly of the standard-issue 924.

Road & Track had two big gripes: a rather buzzy engine and a jouncy ride with lots of thumping over rough surfaces. Over time, though, Porsche would apply its customary corrective balms.

European 924s were quicker and more flexible than American ones, particularly after the five-speed option, a Getrag unit, arrived for '78. By mid-1977, Porsche had partly attended to lackluster U.S. performance, bumping output to 110 bhp (SAE net) via a higher-lift cam, larger intake valves, modified pistons, advanced timing, and higher 8.5:1 compression (as used with automatic-

The initial 1977 U.S.-model 924 (top) looked much like its European sister. Add-on side marker lights, required by Washington, were the most obvious visual difference. Arriving with a $9395 base price, the 924 generated strong U.S. sales despite press criticism of its engine behavior, performance, and "mixed parentage." The 924 Turbo (other photos) addressed all these areas. "Spider web" alloy wheels were included in a $2045 Sport Group option. Initial U.S. base price was just under $21,000—quite a jump from that of the normally aspirated 924.

transmission models in the United States, Canada, and Japan). Of course, none of this affected running on 91-octane fuel.

Road & Track felt sure that the '78 924 could best the Alfetta and 280Z: "The Porsche's overall design, its interior layout and its handling are better. [It] looks great (especially with the optional alloy wheels), its seating is as comfortable as a well worn Gucci loafer and the car sticks to the road like chewing gum on the bottom of a theater seat."

Regrettably, the 924's engine still let loose with a fair amount of noise, and *R&T* repeated that this racket and the car's buzziness and Milquetoast performance were simply unacceptable for a $10,000 automobile—especially a Porsche. This was underscored in a later comparison test with the even more formidable Datsun 280ZX, Mazda RX-7, and Chevrolet Corvette. Here, the 924 finished third (ahead of the 'Vette), despite winning six "firsts" (braking, handling, visibility, exterior finish, and interior and exterior styling). "When it's good, it's very good, but when it's bad, watch out," the magazine warned.

"Very well," the Zuffenhausen folks likely said. "We will fix those problems—and we will give you a *turbocharged* 924 for good measure." So it was that a turbo 924 was introduced to Europe in 1979 and to America as a 1980 model.

This time, Porsche built both car and engine. The latter retained the basic 2.0-liter block (shipped from Neckarsulm) but hardly anything else. There was a new Porsche-designed cylinder head, still cast alumimum but boasting larger valves, modified hemispherical combustion chambers, and new water seals consisting of copper gasket and silicon rings. Spark plugs now had platinum tips and sat on the intake (left) side. So did the starter, displaced by the turbocharger mounted low on the right.

The blower itself, supplied by Germany's KKK (Kuhnle, Kopp & Kausch), fed a huge cast pipe that sent boost pressures of up to 10.15 psi (7 psi on U.S. models) up and over the head to the intake manifold, then down to the ports. Compression was suitably lowered, as was then necessary with turbocharging, set at 7.5:1 for all versions. The K-Jetronic injection was recalibrated to match, and there were two fuel pumps to assure full system pressure at all times. A standard oil cooler helped deal with the extra heat of pressurized power. As on the 930, a wastegate prevented boost from exceeding the specified maximum. Porsche also fitted a blow-off valve as "fail-safe" backup.

The result of all this in European tune was 125

bhp (DIN) at 5500 rpm and an abundant 181 pounds/feet of torque at 3500 rpm. American-model figures were 143 bhp (SAE net) at 5500 and 147 pounds/feet of torque at 3000 rpm, the latter figure still a worthy improvement. At 2780 pounds, the Turbo was considerably heavier than the normally aspirated 924 (and even most 911s), but its performance advantage was enormous: four seconds quicker in the 0-60 run—about 7-8 seconds—and almost 20 mph faster all-out. Similar gains were seen in Europe, where *Autocar*'s test car hit 60 from rest in 6.9 seconds and topped out at 144 mph.

To handle the Turbo's extra surge, Porsche took typical pains with the 924 chassis. The driveshaft was enlarged to 25mm to reduce chances of whipping, rear halfshafts were strengthened, and rolling stock was upgraded to 15 X 6-inch rims with 185/70 rubber. Gear ratios, spring/shock rates, and anti-roll bars were all revised, too, and a larger servo boosted the brakes, which were now ventilated four-wheel discs for Europe; American Turbos retained the previous disc/drum combo. The standard and only gearbox was the Getrag five-speed, complete with the awkward racing-style shift pattern that once plagued 911s.

Most early "turbo-era" cars were prone to poor low-rpm or "off-boost" performance, as well as turbo lag, the delay in response to throttle changes caused by turbocharger inertia. Both were apparent in the 924 Turbo but not irksome. Boost on the U.S. version began at a low 1600 rpm and peaked at just 2800 rpm. The larger, slower-revving European turbocharger began boosting at 1800 rpm.

Car and Driver observed, "As the turbo comes in, you can feel the zooming whee! of the crossover point and, with it, the character change in propulsion. . . . The boost is right there, coming aboard quickly with a firm punch that rushes you forward, picking off normal traffic and predictably defining the correct arc through every corner."

Internal gearbox ratios were altered to match this power and torque delivery, and were the same for all Turbos except fifth gear, which was somewhat taller for the United States—0.60:1 against Europe's 0.71:1—though that was offset by a shorter 4.71:1 final drive (versus 3.17:1). *Road & Track*'s John Dinkel observed, "Even though 5th is an over-overdrive (60 mph is only 2280 rpm), you can let the revs drop to below 2000 rpm in top gear, tromp the go-pedal and the engine pulls smoothly, albeit slowly. Try that with a stock 924 and you'll be greeted with a chorus of shakes, shudders,

Porsche built the 924 Carrera GT (top) to contest the 1981 running of the famed 24 Hours of Le Mans; racing versions were generally known as 924 Turbo Carrera. Appearance changes prefigured the facelifted 944, due the following year, but the large hood scoop was unique. So was the GT's engine (bottom right), good for 210 DIN horsepower, 150 mph all out, and just 6.5 seconds in the 0-60 mph sprint. A racing GT finished a creditable eighth overall at Le Mans '81. As expected of a Porsche, the 924 cockpit (standard Turbo model shown bottom left) was efficient and all-business, but few liked the low, slightly oval steering wheel (or its fixed position), or the conical lenses that tended to distort the gauge faces. Overleaf: Although it would last just two model years in the U.S., the 924 Turbo was treated to standard all-disc brakes for '81. New flat-face wheels were part of a limited-run U.S. special-edition package offered that year.

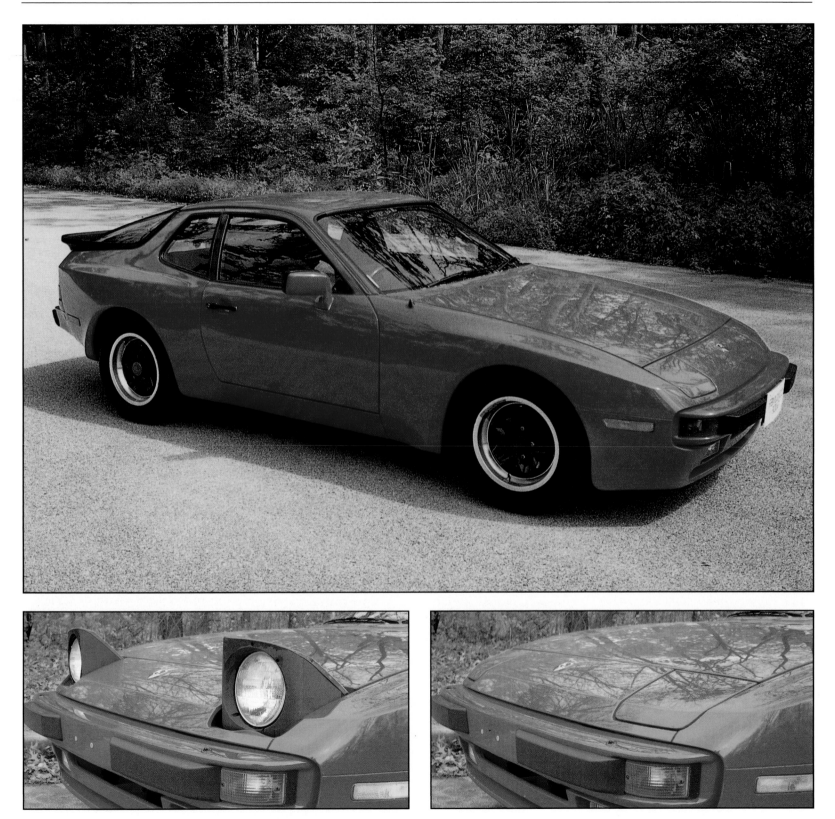

buzzes and groans of protest that won't stop until you downshift at least two gears."

So the 924 engine had been pleasingly transformed. Much of the old noise and harshness were gone, because the turbo helped quiet things somewhat—though its high-pitched whistle might make occupants think John Law was in hot pursuit. Porsche also added sound-deadening at strategic places in both 924s. That also helped, if not enough to satisfy *C/D*: "[It] does little to hide the thrumming, hissing, gurgling and sucking that come through the firewall like the sounds of plumbing in a cheap apartment. . . . " Still, those editors felt that "once you begin to associate the aural effects with the performance they accompany, you warm quickly to your little sound-effects symphony under the hood."

Visually, the Turbo differed just enough to be noticed: lovely "spider web" alloy wheels (optional on normal 924s), a functional NACA hood duct, four cooling slots on the nose, Turbo tail script, and a modest spoiler rimming the big back window. The last, Porsche said, reduced Cd to 0.35, which in America made this the best wind-cheater of 1980.

Differences were fewer inside. A leather-trimmed 911 Turbo-style steering wheel and shift boot were the most obvious (automatic transmission was not offered). Though the speedometer read to 160 mph (later to only 85 mph, per federal edict), a boost gauge was nowhere in sight. Porsche evidently had an abundance of confidence in the blown engine's strength and reliability.

Considering its performance, the 924 Turbo was remarkably frugal. Most early tests reported average mpg at about 25. But there was a price for all this: a little less than $21,000 in 1980 U.S. form. Yet as the sort of exciting evolution expected of Porsche, the Turbo was just the image boost the 911's baby brother so badly needed. "Here is another *real* Porsche," crowed *Autocar*, "a superb high performer. . . ."

Interim changes to the normally aspirated 924 were less dramatic but welcome nonetheless. The Getrag five-speed became standard for '79, along with a space-saver spare (except in Britain), pressure-cast alloy wheels, tinted glass, passenger's visor vanity mirror, and stereo speakers.

The 1980 models received a non-Getrag five-speed, basically the old four-speeder with an extra gear and—praise be—a conventional shift pattern. Emission control and driveability improved as three-way catalytic converters arrived during the year on both 924 and Turbo, making them 50-state

cars. Porsche also attended to the occasional severe judder and axle hop of previous 924s via tighter driveline tolerances, revised rear suspension mounts, and new hydraulic transaxle mounts. The result was a better, if still rather hard, ride. Finally, Stateside 924s gained a little performance thanks to an altered cam and revised ignition timing, plus lower final-drive ratios with manual shift (5.00:1 against the previous 4.11:1). Horsepower now stood at 115 SAE net and 0-60 mph acceleration at 10.5-11 seconds, yet mileage stayed the same.

Another new 1980 American item was the Sport Group, a package option priced at $2045 for the normal 924 and $1960 for the Turbo. These sums bought the ventilated all-disc brakes previously restricted to Europe, five-bolt "spider web" wheels wearing beefy 205/55VR15 Pirelli P7 high-performance tires (replacing four-lug rims and CN36 Pirellis), higher-rate shocks, and a 14-mm anti-roll bar to go with the stock 23-mm front stabilizer.

All 924s were little changed for '81—just standard halogen headlamps, rear seatbelts, and, belatedly, rear disc brakes. This might have signaled that Porsche had something better in the pipeline. It did: a thoroughly overhauled version called *944*. With that, both 924s were withdrawn from the United States for six years but continued in production for Europe, the United Kingdom, and other markets.

Despite the 944, the 924 was far from finished. Indeed, an even more special Turbo appeared in 1981 to carry Porsche's flag among production sports cars in that year's running of the famed 24 Hours of LeMans. Called *Carrera GT,* but also known as the *924 Turbo Carrera,* it sported an intercooler and other engine modifications that lifted horsepower to 210, 33 above that in the roadgoing European model. A more prominent hood scoop was provided to feed air, and larger spoilers appeared at each end for better "airflow management." A lower and stiffened suspension with 911 Turbo wheels and tires nestled within bulging add-on fender flares. Performance was formidable: *Motor* in England got 6.5 seconds 0-60 and 150 mph tops. To many, the 924 now had the performance it should have had all along. Not surprisingly, perhaps, price was equally formidable at about $30,000, some $7000 above the standard issue. Today, though, it's a prized collectible, as only 400 production cars were built to complement a handful of racing versions.

Meantime, rumors were spreading of yet another "budget" Porsche, the so-called *918.* A decade of inflation and falling dollar/DMark

Previous page: The 944 (top) bowed for 1982 as a logical 924 evolution with styling obviously inspired by that of the 924 Carrera GT. Its new 2.5-liter engine was essentially half of the posh 928's 4.5 V-8, but very few parts were interchangeable. Still, the new four had the virtue of being Porsche designed and built, unlike the 924's Audi-sourced powerplant. It was also more potent and refined. Opposite page: A factory "phantom" drawing (middle) shows the basic front-engine/rear-transaxle layout shared by all versions of the EA425 project that produced the original 924. Porsche later built a literally cut-away 944 (bottom right) to highlight the many changes made to that model. Though exports were halted after '81, the standard 924 continued on sale in selected markets, as witness this 1983 German model (bottom left). So, too, the 924 Turbo (top), but only until introduction of the 944 Turbo late in 1985.

exchange rates had pushed the 924 far upmarket by 1980, and the betting was that Porsche would counter with a new lower-priced 914/924-style "cocktail" model. Most reports mentioned a Targa-roof two-seater bearing 924 styling hallmarks but based on the VW Scirocco chassis. Power would allegedly be supplied by the 1.8-liter VW four from the European Golf GTI (and the new-for-'83 U.S. Rabbit GTI), while the body would mix aluminum and steel panels with polyurethane bumpers.

In the end, Porsche resisted the "918." True, the mass exodus of British sports cars had left a tempting market gap at the $12,000-$15,000 level, but Zuffenhausen concluded that there was no point in competing there again. Undoubtedly influenced by American-born Peter Schutz, who succeeded Ernst Fuhrmann as company chairman in late 1981, the decision to avoid this particular niche was a logical one given the market of the day. Porsche was selling every car it could build, even at inflated prices growing more so every year. It had no need for anything new, let alone a cheaper car on which it would be tougher to turn a profit. As ever, future success seemed to depend on the time-tested Porsche formula of steady improvements to cars that were already superb.

But superb was not perfection, which helps explain Porsche's motivation for the 944. The 924 may have been a commercial success, but its credentials as a "real" Porsche were still widely doubted. Even the Turbo couldn't shake the VW/Audi heritage of its basic design—especially the engine, which still left something to be desired. And somehow, the fact that the Turbo was built by Porsche, not Audi, never got through to enthusiasts and critics.

Pride is a strong motivator, and Porsche has always been very motivated. Since the image problem seemed to rest with the engine, the obvious answer was to give the 924 a new one—a genuine *Porsche* engine. Then there'd be no question that it was Zuffenhausen's car, even if most everyone had forgotten that it had been designed there in the first place.

Almost as obvious was the new engine's source. The 924 had a slant four. The big 928 had an all-aluminum Porsche-designed 4.5-liter V-8. A V-8 is basically two slant fours put together, so why not slice the 928 engine in half for an all-Porsche four? Which, of course, is just what they did.

The result was an altogether superior car that lived up to its badge in a way the 924 couldn't. More important, the 944 reassured Porsche partisans that Zuffenhausen was still on course. Don

Vorderman, a critic not known for ready praise, called it "the best small sports car ever made."

It was certainly a much-improved four-cylinder Porsche—starting with muscled-up styling in the image of the short-lived Carrera GT. Fenders were aggressively flared to enclose broader 15 X 7 alloy wheels and 215/60VR15 tires, a deep airdam was integrated with the lower front sheetmetal, and there was a smooth new polyurethane nose. The 924's under-bumper air intake was retained, and a pair of standard foglamps was flush-mounted in the airdam. A 924 Turbo-style rear spoiler continued. Unlike the Carrera GT, whose fender flares and other panels were plastic, the 944 body was made entirely of steel. Despite Porsche's claim of extensive wind-tunnel work, the 944's "aero" touches lowered Cd to only 0.35, barely better than the 924's.

The engine was far more effective. Derived from the 928's V-8, it was a single-overhead-cam design with silicon-aluminum alloy block and crossflow aluminum head. Stroke was the same, too—78.9mm—but a 5-mm bore increase, to 100mm, took displacement to a little more than half the V-8's: 2479cc (151 cid). And for all the similarities, there were no interchangeable parts, though Porsche saved quite a bit of development and tooling money compared to a clean-sheet design.

The 944 engine was distinct in two more important respects. First, the 928's relatively simple Bosch L-Jetronic fuel injection gave way to the same firm's new state-of-the-art Digital Motor Electronics (DME) system with integrated computer management of injection and electronic ignition. Second, the 944 block employed twin counter-weighted balance shafts. These spun at twice crankshaft speed and in the opposite direction to dampen the vibrations (technically termed "coupling forces") inherent in inline fours of more than 2.0-liter displacement. (A Gilmer-type cogged belt drove the camshaft; a second belt, with teeth on each side, drove the balance shafts.)

The balancer idea was novel but hardly new, dating from 1911 and Frederick W. Lanchester in England. Moreover, Mitsubishi of Japan had recently resurrected it—with a patent. Porsche tried to avoid infringement by running its balancers in three bearings each instead of Mitsubishi's two but ultimately decided to pay a royalty estimated at $8 per car. As one Porsche executive said at the time, "There's no need to reinvent the motorcar."

On 9.5:1 compression, the U.S. 944 bowed with 143 bhp (SAE net) at 5500 rpm and 137 pounds/feet peak torque at 3000 rpm. The Euro version had

A more aggressive "face" and "telephone dial" wheels a la the 928 helped set the 944 Turbo apart from the standard offering. The tilt-up power sunroof (top) was an option. A rear spoiler (bottom right) was standard and was complemented by an underbody pan for smoother airflow to reduce drag. The hyperaspirated 2.5-liter engine (bottom left) was Porsche's most sophisticated and potent blown-four to date, with 217 SAE net horsepower in U.S. tune, courtesy of digital electronic ignition/fuel injection. The European version was scarcely different, reflecting Porsche's prevailing "one spec, one performance level" policy.

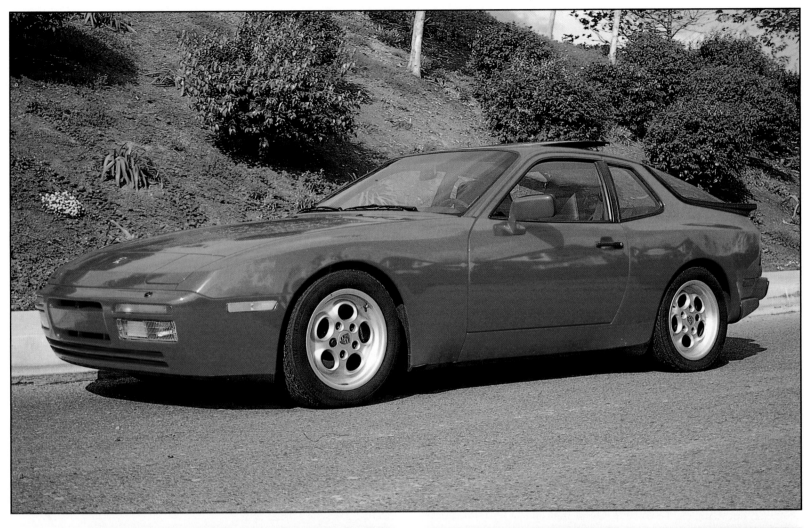

153 (160 DIN) on a tighter 10.6:1 squeeze. The factory claimed the American model would do 0-60 in 8.3 seconds, slightly slower than its transatlantic cousin. However, both would outsprint a 924 Turbo and were nearly as fast all-out (130 versus 134 mph)—yet without the blower's complexity. Strict weight control helped. The 944 engine weighed just 340 pounds dry, while the initial curb weight of 2778 pounds was just slightly higher than the Turbo's.

Porsche claimed no sweeping chassis alterations in turning 924 into 944—just the usual honing of spring/shock rates and anti-roll-bar sizes, plus attention to steering and transaxle mounts. The aforementioned beefier wheels and tires were standard equipment, as were the 924 Turbo's all-disc brakes. An optional sport package offered even stiffer shocks, limited-slip diff, and 7 X 16 alloy rims with 205/55VR16 Pirelli P7s.

The cockpit was much the same, too, though instrument markings went from white to yellow for easier reading, and a nice new tweed-cloth upholstery option made for a less sterile ambience. No-cost amenities were abundant, running to A/C, removeable sunroof, tinted glass, three-spoke leather-rim steering wheel, electric door windows, and heated power-remote side door mirrors.

A discouraging word was seldom seen in early road tests. The late Dean Batchelor remarked that a number of publications wrote about the 944 "as if employed by Porsche's advertising agency," and *Road & Track* was typical in judging the new "budget" model "worthy of the marque."

Predictably, perhaps, the engine earned the highest and most frequent praise. *R&T* found that "it fires up immediately and runs smoothly, even when cold. And Lordy, does it rev—right up to redline in every gear except 5th. There are no stumbles, flat spots, or resonance points. Furthermore, there's low- and mid-range flexibility that allows you to drop the revs as low as 1000 rpm in top gear and the engine pulls without protest."

The 944's handling was simply "terrific," according to *Car and Driver*: "You can drive like a hero without sweat popping out on your brow. The 944 is great because it responds crisply and decisively to every command, and it builds up to its limit in perfectly linear fashion. You won't find killer understeer here. And you won't find any nervousness at the limit." With standard tires, the 944 rounded *C/D*'s skidpad at an excellent 0.81g. *R&T*'s like-shod car did 0.818g.

Interestingly, *R&T* said the junior Porsche was now *more* than a match for the rival Datsun and Alfa. In fact, in a 1983 comparison test, the magazine picked it over that year's all-new Corvette, the Ferrari 308GTBi Quattrovalvole, and even the 928S. "...The 944 won simply by having so few weak points [and] the fewest complaints while being fun to drive and proving itself a useful, fine-handling, well built all-around car." In "sibling competition," the 944 "more than holds it own with the 924 and even the 911SC."

At just under $20,000 in the United States, the 944 looked like another bargain in Porsche performance, was praised because of it, and proved well-nigh irresistible. Sales were strong from the start, and the good folk in Zuffenhausen began breathing easier.

But they didn't rest, for the usual yearly refinements—and some significant evolutions—were on the way. The first appeared for 1984, when the original welded A-arms gave way to stronger alloy castings. Mid-1985 brought a handsome new 928-style instrument panel with more readable instruments, plus a smaller, round steering wheel to replace the never-liked oval helm. Also that year, the fuel tank grew to 21.1 gallons.

As if to answer speculation about the return of a blown junior model, Porsche released the 944 Turbo for 1986. Aside from the blower and correspondingly lower compression (8.0:1), its engine was basically stock, but it packed a healthy new wallop: in U.S. trim at the maximum 10.9-psi, 217 bhp (SAE net) at 5800 rpm and 243 pounds/feet of torque at 3500 rpm. It's worth mentioning that American-market engines were now nearly identical with Europe's, reflecting Porsche's "one spec, one performance level" policy.

Per longer-standing policy, the 944 Turbo was no halfway job. For example, new ceramic inserts in the exhaust ports kept gases hotter to provide more energy for the turbo and faster catalytic converter warmup for minimal emissions. The turbo itself (again from KKK) was not only water-cooled for efficiency but gained a small electric pump that circulated coolant through it after engine shutoff, thus avoiding oil coking of the turbo center bearing and possible damage. A boost-limiting bypass valve still supplemented the wastegate, but the DME electronics could now vary boost with rpm, providing more at low crank speeds where it's safe, less at higher speeds. DME also now controlled ignition timing in response to signals from engine sensors of incipient knock (detonation), a traditional problem in turbomotors.

Like newer 911s, the 944 Turbo had wider rear

Though the 944 accounted for most of Porsche's mid-Eighties four-cylinder sales, the 924 remained an important showroom attraction for Europe because of its lower price—the very thing that prompted U.S. introduction of the 944-powered 924S in 1987. Here, the standard German-market model of 1985, looking very much like the original 924 of a decade earlier.

wheels and tires: 16 X 8 and 225/50VR16, versus 16 X 7 and 205/55VR16s in front. Brakes were fortified with light-alloy four-piston calipers, and spring/shock rates were adjusted to suit the higher engine performance. Outside were distinctive five-hole "telephone dial" type wheels similar to the 928's, a revised nose with wide cooling slots and reprofiled bumper/spoiler, rear underbody pan (to smooth air exiting from beneath, again for better high-speed stability), and a more prominent rear spoiler. Cd was now 0.33, a useful if not startling reduction.

With all this, the Turbo had to cost more than the normal 944, and it did: initially $29,500 minimum. That was quite a "sticker shock," but Porsche eased the pain somewhat by throwing in 928-style seats with electric front and rear height adjusters, plus headlight washers and more uptown cabin trim. Options now included a power sunroof ($695).

The Turbo didn't overwhelm magazine types as much as the original 944, perhaps because it cost so much more and wasn't as easy to drive. *Car and Driver*, for instance, lauded acceleration and top speed but noted that "the Turbo feels more muscle-bound than powerful" at lower velocities. "Unless you punish either the tires or the clutch by starting hard enough to keep the turbo on the boil, the [car] feels sluggish off the line; flooring the throttle after normal clutch engagement produces little response for at least a second. And in top [fifth] gear, the Turbo requires 14.7 seconds to accelerate from 30 to 50 mph, versus 12.0 for the standard car."

Nevertheless, *C/D* judged the 944 Turbo as "not only fast but well rounded...very competitive with the 911 Carrera and 928S. [While it] makes its driver work harder to generate the straight-line performance that the others produce effortlessly...the Turbo delivers much of the 928S's comfort and refinement for about $20,000 less. And it demands less skill to drive quickly than the slightly more expensive Carrera."

A rather obvious price-and-performance gap between the two 944s suggested the need for something in between, and Porsche obliged in late 1986 with the 944S. The attraction here wasn't a turbocharger but a new twincam head with four valves per cylinder. Though similar to that of the recently introduced 928S4, no parts were shared.

Valvegear was unusual. A single-toothed belt drove the exhaust cam, which in turn drove the intake shaft via a chain between cylinders two and three. Other features included larger-than-944 ports and beautifully cast manifold runners for

both intake and exhaust. The result was not only more power and a fatter torque curve compared with the two-valve 944 but smoother power delivery than the Turbo and almost the same punch. The specific outputs: 188 bhp (SAE net) at 6000 rpm and 170 pounds/feet of torque peaking at 4300 rpm.

Model-year '87 also brought Bosch's four-channel anti-lock brake system as a 944S and Turbo option, surely one of the most worthwhile contributions to "active safety" ever devised. For passive safety, air bags for both driver and passenger became standard for the Turbo and optional for other 944s in the U.S., making these the first cars available with a passenger air bag at any price. The innovation may seem contrary to high performance, but it only reflected Porsche's longstanding concern for safety.

More pleasant '87 developments included higher-tech sound systems and a standard split-fold rear seat to enhance cargo-carrying versatility. A notable suspension change was switching from slightly positive to slightly negative steering "scrub" radius for improved steering control in a front-tire blowout or with one side of the car running on a lower-friction surface.

Conceptually, the 944S was a mix: Turbo-type wheels, normal 944 bodywork and features, in-between price. But while twin cams and 16 valves are always neat, the S generated more mixed reactions than even the Turbo. In a September 1987 report, *Automobile* magazine founder David E. Davis groused that "in the mountains, the 944S wants to be driven between 4000 and 6000 rpm in order to strut its stuff. The 944 Turbo is lazier...In traffic, however, the Turbo becomes finicky—it won't be lugged—and requires just as much shifting as the S."

But the S avenged itself on the track. "It is forgiving, neutral, pitchable," said Davis, "maybe the easiest car in the world to drive fast. It scrubs off speed obligingly, using both ends...Any tendency for the tail to come around is mild and controllable...The Turbo, on the other hand...requires both experience and finesse to be driven well at the limit." Davis put this down to tire differences: 215/60VR15s on the S versus the Turbo's unequal-size rubber (but an S option). "The two cars, so much alike to the casual onlooker, really define their quite different personas the moment a serious driver sits down behind their respective steering wheels."

Summing things up, Davis thought the S was the "true next step in the [944's] evolution...It's

Bowing Stateside for 1987, the 924S (bottom and top left) answered the pleas of American enthusiasts for a more affordable entry-level Porsche than the standard 944, which had been creeping up in price—like most everything else. At $19,900 to start, the S was more than fair value. The rear lip spoiler and 928-style "telephone dial" wheels (bottom and middle right) helped dress up the old styling, and included anti-theft locks. But the big attraction was the 147-horsepower 944 engine (top right), which combined with the lighter 924 platform to make the S even quicker than the base 944—to Porsche's embarassment.

The third variation on the 944 theme was the S model that appeared in Europe during 1986 (shown) and in U.S. trim for '87. Turbo styling combined with a new 16-valve 2.5 engine to make it a faster car than the base 944 but far less costly than the Turbo.

The 924S arrived in the U.S. for 1987 with a healthier helping of extras than earlier 924s. Among them were air conditioning, tinted glass, heated power door mirrors, "five-hole" alloy wheels; and power steering, windows, and antenna. Options included AM/FM/cassette stereo, electric sunroof, three-speed automatic transmission, and limited-slip differential.

lively, quick [the factory said 7.7 seconds 0-60 mph] and responsive. It has no vices. At $30,850, it is expensive, but we reckon it's money well spent. The 944 Turbo is lower and meaner-looking...and it transmits an entirely different set of signals to its driver. It feels heavy, but it is also very fast in everyday driving [6.1 seconds 0-60, 10 mph up on top speed at 152 mph]. The combination is an exciting one, but it really isn't a 944 anymore. It ought to have its own type number."

Meantime, Zuffenhausen had been wrestling with the perennial problem of how to keep at least one four-cylinder model reasonably affordable in the face of a declining dollar/DMark ratio it could do nothing about. There was also a need to perk up 924 sales in Europe, which had lately fallen off. Again, the answer was about as obvious as the 944 solution.

It materialized for 1987 in all markets, United States included, as an upgraded 924, also bearing an S suffix. Though it looked much like the original 924, right down to the old dash, it benefited from 944 chassis hardware and running gear, plus a good many standard extras (air, tinted glass, heated power-remote door mirrors, and power steering, windows, and antenna). With its lighter-than-944 shell and the smoother, more potent eight-valve 944 engine, the 924S had a higher top end than the old 924 Turbo and nearly the same acceleration. It also proved quicker than the base 944—to Porsche's embarassment. But the 924S was the answer to a prayer for many Porsche fans of lesser means. And by late-Eighties standards it was fair value at $19,900 to start.

For 1988, the U.S. 924S and 944 shifted to a catalyst version of the eight-valve 2.5-liter four, previously restricted to Europe, to gain 11 horses (for 158 total) and 15 pounds/feet of torque (to 155). Tighter compression (10.2 versus 9.7:1) and recalibrated DME did the trick. The factory said the manual-shift 924S was now 0.3-second quicker to 60 (at 8.0 seconds) and 3 mph faster all out (137 mph). Comparable 944 figures were 8.2 seconds and 136 mph (up from 131).

With one exception, the four-cylinder series was otherwise little changed for '88, though options proliferated: CD player, more elaborate 10-speaker audio, "soft look" leather upholstery. Another kind of option appeared in a Special Edition 924S and 944. Only 500 of each were built to assure exclusivity, but they were little more than the regular models with specific paint and interior and certain optional features included.

The aforesaid exception was the new 1988 Turbo

S, which swelled Porsche's four-cylinder U.S. line to no fewer than five models. Inspired by the racing 944 Turbos running in the European pro-am Porsche Turbo Cup series, it was another low-volume special, only this time the run was 1000, of which 700 came to America and 270 stayed in Germany. (We leave it to you to figure how many that left the rest of the world.)

It was worth latching on to, despite a stiff U.S. base price of $48,350. The reason was 247 bhp, up 30 from the normal Turbo, achieved via a bigger blower giving more boost (up to 11.7 psi). Suspension was upgraded to match in the usual Porsche way. So were wheels: new-design 16-inchers, with the rears growing to 9 inches in width. Wrapped around them were meaty V-rated Goodyear Eagle VR performance tires sized at 225/50 fore, 245/45 aft. Also included were the massive ABS brakes from the 928S4, with 12-inch front rotors and 11.8-inch units in back. Rounding out "standard extras" were limited-slip diff, "full-power" front sports seats, special cloth cockpit trim, fold-down back seat, headlight washers, and rear wiper. You also got premium audio, cruise control, and sunroof, but in a cagey move recalling Sixties Detroit, Porsche made those items "mandatory options," which inflated the true bottom line by $2157.

Still, Car and Driver's Tony Assenza termed the Turbo S "a bargain"—and not with tongue in cheek. After all, this was the most exciting 944 yet, with 0-60 coming in 5.5 seconds by C/D's watch, the standing quarter-mile in 13.9 at a racy 101 mph. "You'll have a hard time finding a GT machine that's as easy to drive fast and as easy to live with as the 944 Turbo S," said Assenza. "It's by far the stongest performing four-cylinder car in the world, and only a few cars of any stripe can match or beat its numbers. The same holds for its combination of mechanical smoothness, creature comforts and handling precision. Add all its virtues together and its least expensive competitor is the Porsche 928S4, which, comparably equipped, costs another twenty grand. See? We told you the 944 Turbo S is a bargain."

Motor Trend also branded the Turbo S a bargain. Though that magazine managed only 6.57 seconds to 60 and 15.1 seconds at 97.4 mph in the quarter-mile, dynamic behavior earned the usual five stars. Nevertheless, editor Jeff Karr couldn't resist chiding some nuisances Porsche hadn't addressed, "like having the single sideview mirror control joystick on the driver's door but positioning the left/right selector switch on the console. Or how about the tripmeter reset button disguised as a

Although the 924S changed little in 1988 European form (top, middle left, and bottom), that year's U.S. version adopted its catalyst-equipped engine to gain 11 horsepower and slightly quicker acceleration. The same change also benefited the standard 1988 U.S. 944. A redesigned spoiler and wheels marked the European '88 944 Turbo (middle right), but the model was overshadowed on both sides of the Atlantic by that year's new limited-edition Turbo S with no less than 247 horsepower (SAE).

vent control knob? They're probably still coughing beer out their noses in Weissach over that one."

If they *were* coughing in Weissach, it was likely over something far more serious: the sharp drop in U.S. sales that began in late 1987, aggravated by the biggest "crash" in Wall Street history. With its heavy reliance on the U.S. market, Porsche's fortunes depended more than those of most automakers on the health of the dollar. When the stock market plunged, the DMark soared, which only worsened the price pressure on all Porsche products. That and more aggressive sports-car competition explains why the firm's total U.S. sales plunged about 50 percent in just two years, dropping from an all-time high of 30,000-plus in calendar 1986 to under 16,000 by the end of '88.

There were problems in the executive ranks, too, and they're worth mentioning here. First, in late 1988, the Porsche board summarily dismissed *wunderkind* chairman Peter Schutz, some say because he clashed once too often with the Porsche and Piech families. But in his stead came Heinz Branitzki, a finance man who angered many old hands in Zuffenhausen by forcing longtime chief engineer Helmut Bott to take early retirement. Worse, Bott's hand-picked successor, Ulrich Bez, stirred up more ill feeling with a heavy-handed reorganization of the Weissach Development Center.

Bez also decreed several costly new programs that threatened to trigger a cash crisis. Among these were another low-priced VW-based sportster, Project 995; a 959 successor, called *965,* which was far more involved than the 911 Carrera 4 ultimately offered; and—talk about heresy—a V-8 four-door "sedan," Project 989, which would have to sell for no less than $93,000 to turn a profit. Meantime, sales kept falling, thanks partly to a stubborn U.S. recession. Porsche soon became the subject of takeover rumors, with Daimler-Benz most often mentioned as savior.

Fortunately for Porsche and its partisans, saner heads ultimately prevailed. Branitzki retired after only about a year, and Bez was soon fired. New chairman Arno Bohn was no more a "car guy" than Branitzki, but he could read a ledger, and he soon ended the spendthrift programs championed by Bez while seeking ways to "right size" the company for the vastly changed sales situation. Though more disagreements with the two "ruling families" forced Bohn to resign in mid-1992, his replacement was a good one: engineer and former production boss Wendelin Wiedeking. By that time, Horst Marchart, a 20-year Porsche veteran also well liked in Zuffenhausen, was in charge of

product development. Within two years, this new regime had trimmed the corporate payroll by about a third (from some 9000 workers to around 6600) and had started charting a new model course to take Porsche profitably into the 21st century while allowing it to remain proudly independent.

Even before these dark days—arguably the most difficult since Ferry set up shop in Gmund— Porsche had decided to reduce production of its four-cylinder models to match the decreasing demand. An immediate casualty was the 924S, dropped in late 1988 as too old and too costly to sell well against newer Japanese sporty cars and especially, Porsche thought, Volkswagen's forthcoming Corrado. As for the 944s, the plan was simple: Do everything possible to make them better while doing everything possible to keep prices down—which seemed virtually impossible.

Even so, the '89 models evidenced a return to Porsche's original "giant killer" role as a producer of premium sports cars that delivered far more performance than their looks implied. First up was a base 944 improved with a new 2.7-liter engine. This was basically the eight-valve 2.5 with a bigger bore (up from 100mm to 104), larger intake valves, higher compression (10.9:1), and, at last, Bosch DME ignition/injection. With all this, horsepower jumped by 15 to 162, and torque swelled to 166 pounds/feet, though the peak was now 1200 rpm higher at 4200.

Road & Track opined that these changes transformed "the [basic] 944's character to that of a more muscular and extroverted car." Indeed, the magazine's quarter-mile time was down to 15.7 seconds at 87.5 mph, and the 0-60 sprint was 1.2 seconds faster at 7.5. "Now [the 944] hustles with greater alacrity, in any gear, at any time, while requiring a lot less advance notice with the gearshift and accelerator. It simply has more flexibility and is more fun to drive."

The latest 944 was also more civilized, thanks to added standards like central locking, power heated door mirrors, power windows, an anti-theft alarm, and an electric tilt/take-out sunroof. Of course, the additions lifted sticker price—to $36,360 in the United States—but Porsche Cars North America (PCNA) took pains to point out that that was only 1.1 percent higher than an '88 model with comparable options.

Even so, *R&T*'s staff remained split on the value question, especially as interior appointments were still "not outstanding" for the class. "But both camps agree that the 944 is still a sensational machine and a worthy target for any manufacturer

A 944 Cabriolet was long rumored by late '87 when Porsche premiered it (middle left), but it wasn't widely available in America until model-year '89, when it was offered in new S2 guise along with a revised coupe. Both used a new 3.0-liter version of the eight-valve 944 slant-four with 208 SAE net horsepower (top right). The Cabrio came with a power top in all markets (middle right) and looked terrific with it down (European version shown top left). Assembly was done partly in a German outpost plant of American Sunroof. Regrettably, 1988 was the last year for a U.S. 944 Turbo (European model shown bottom left). The 924S (bottom right) departed late that year, a victim of Porsche's growing overall sales crisis.

The 944's conversion from coupe to Cabriolet dictated a specific rear end (top) that made for the first front-engine Porsche with a trunk. All S2s carried a rear underbody pan a la previous 944 Turbos. Less immediately obvious in the new Cabriolet was a slightly shorter windshield that gave a snug top-up appearance not unlike that of the 911 Speedster (above, left and right). Meantime, rising price, declining demand, and the advent of the replacement 968 conspired to kill the 944 Turbo (right) in all markets after 1989.

An all-around look at the open 944S2 in little-changed 1990 U.S. form. Its "top stack" was lower than the German Cabriolet norm but bulkier than those of most other modern convertibles, some of which hid their roofs entirely. This Porsche's $45,000-plus base price partly stemmed from a more involved assembly process than used for the 944 coupe. Seven-spoke wheels were featured on both S2 models.

who aspires to build a real driver's car."

Porsche moved the target higher in early 1989 with release of the 944S2 and a more potent 944 Turbo. The latter was essentially the previous S-model with a nicer price: $47,600—a *decrease,* crowed PCNA, of 4.7 percent on an "equipment adjusted" basis. Rear rolling stock was back to eight inches, but all tires were now Z-rated.

The S2 was something else. It, too, had the new standard goodies of the base and Turbo models, but it looked like a Turbo and was almost as strong, thanks to a 16-valve engine stroked to 88mm (on the 2.7's 104-mm bore) for no less than 3.0 liters, making it the world's largest four-cylinder in regular production.

Despite mounting corporate troubles, the S2 showed no less engineering care than any other Porsche. For example, the new 3.0-liter actually weighed 15 percent less than the old 2.5, thanks to joined cylinder sleeves without water jacketing, shallower jackets elsewhere, and thinner block walls. Switching from cast to forged aluminum pistons didn't save weight but did wonders for high-speed durability. A revised intake system gave a "pulse charge" effect for more high-end power (it was noticed above 4000 rpm) and a catalytic converter moved closer to the engine to shorten warm-up time for reduced emissions. An adaptive knock sensor and the addition of an on-board diagnostic system to allow tracing any intermittent faults in the Bosch Motronic engine computer rounded out the improvements. With all this, the big four now delivered 208 bhp at 5800 rpm in U.S. tune and 207 pounds/feet of torque peaking at a usefully low 4100. And that was on regular gas, despite tight 10.9:1 compression.

Motor Trend judged the S2 a fine piece of work. After testing a coupe in little-changed 1990 form, editor Jeff Karr enthused that the 3.0-liter "acts like a strong-running six instead of a hard-working four." And it did. At 6.62 seconds to 60 mph by *MT*'s clock, the S2 was a mere 0.05-second slower than the previous Turbo S and right up there with such vaunted performers as the latest Corvette and Mazda's turbo-rotary RX-7. What's more, said Karr, the S2 beat those rivals in the standing quarter-mile, logging 14.85 seconds at 95.2 mph. "Even though the [944] Turbo makes 247 hp at its peak, the S2 is quicker in the real world in all but the most demanding circumstances."

Price was definitely demanding at an '89 U.S. base list of $45,285, way above most every other car with similar performance. But Karr had an answer to that, too: "Porsche-ness." The S2's price

premium, he said, "buys something that can't be found for less money . . . an intangible too tough to label and impossible to measure with a stopwatch. Call it quality, call it elegance, but something there that makes the driving experience somehow more satisfying in the Porsche." High praise for a car whose basic design was over 10 years old.

But Porsche had prepared another dose of youthfulness in the form of its first front-engine convertible. Admittedly, the new S2 Cabriolet was a long time coming, announced in late 1987 but not genuinely available until early '89. Nevertheless, it charmed the most jaded critics despite an initial U.S. sticker of $52,650.

That price partly reflected a convoluted conversion process again involving Audi in Neckarsulm but also a new factory that had been set up by American Sunroof Corporation (ASC) in nearby Heilbronn. As *Car and Driver*'s John Phillips III described the process, unfinished coupe bodies "are shipped from Audi to ASC, where the tops are torched off. . . . The rocker sills and doorjambs are buttressed, and a pair of crossmembers are sandwiched by a *second* floorpan. In this half-finished condition, the S2 Cabrio goes back to Audi for its Porsche-built engine and drivetrain. And then it is shipped *again* to ASC, where it is fitted with a unique windscreen—2.4 inches shorter than the coupe's, which accounts in large part for the Cabrio's charming [911] 'Speedster-esque' appearance. At the same time, ASC installs plastic caps atop the rear fenders (for aesthetic reasons only) and fashions an entirely new rear deck, making this the first 944 with a trunk."

Unfortunately, there was scarcely room in that trunk for a deep-dish pizza. The coupe's token rear seats were omitted to make stowage space for the top, though that did leave a useful package shelf with a couple of lidded "gloveboxes" below. The top itself was rather vexing. As on 911 Cabrios, it was a multi-layered canvas affair, fully insulated and powered, but it folded into a bulky lump and only after being released from the windshield header with a rather clumsy little Allen-type wrench.

On the other hand, the droptop S2 was surprisingly draft-free at speed, even with the side windows down (also recalling 911 Cabrios). Porsche managed to hold the expected weight increase to just 123 pounds while preserving about 98 percent of the coupe's rock-solid structural feel. As a result, the new open S2 felt and acted much like its closed companion on straight and curved roads alike.

Neither the new S2s nor the "value-priced" stan-

Seeking higher four-cylinder sales in the wake of a drastic late-Eighties drop, Porsche restyled the 944S2 to become the 968. It arrived in late '91 for Europe as a Cabriolet (top left) and in still-familiar coupe form (middle and bottom right), both with definite 928 overtones. Dr. Ferry Porsche was pleased to pose with an early Cabrio (top right) around the time of his 82nd birthday. Besides newly altered appearance, the 968's big attraction was a 16-valve 3.0-liter four (bottom left) muscled-up to 236 horsepower (SAE net), thanks to Porsche's new "VarioCam" variable-valve-timing system.

dard 944 were enough to spark four-cylinder sales, and world production for the '89 series was a disappointing 8036. With Porsche's cash starting to run low, product efforts were increasingly focused on the more profitable 911 family, so it was no real surprise that the S2 coupe and Cabrio were the only 944s to return to U.S. showrooms for 1990. Both were virtually unchanged except for still lower prices. In reductions that came midway through the 1989 sales season, the coupe fell to $41,900, the convertible to $48,600.

It was a timely thing to do. *Road & Track*'s Peter Egan still thought the 944 "a true driver's car, with excellent (50/50) balance, superb brakes and responsive, linear steering with good feedback.... More than most of its competition, the 944 manages to feel both sophisticated and tough at the same time. And the current S2 is the best 944 yet.... Whether [the cabrio] is a good value . . . depends, I suppose, upon the ease or difficulty with which the buyer acquires this amount of money." *Car and Driver*'s John Phillips was less equivocal, calling the 1990 Cabrio "a real deutsch treat. But who will reach for his checkbook first?"

The answer wasn't long in coming, and it wasn't the one Porsche wanted, as four-cylinder production hit a new low of just 4104 units for calendar-year 1990. But there was nothing to do except carry on, so the S2 coupe continued into '91 with only a wing-type spoiler and a window sticker reading $1450 higher; the Cabrio was untouched, but its price rose by $1750.

Sales turned up a little in 1992, and the reason was called *968*. On the surface it looked like little more than a 944S2 restyled with 928 cues. (The restyle is credited to Harm Lagaay, by now in charge of Porsche's design studios.) There were even the same sort of exposed, laid-back headlamps that flipped up to vertical when switched on and 928-type tail styling. But although Porsche was running low on money, it didn't show, for the 968 was no less thorough a makeover than the 944 had been a decade earlier.

Improvements began under the hood, where the big twincam four was treated to a revised cylinder head with higher 11.0:1 compression, smoother intake passages, freer-flow exhaust, and a new wrinkle called VarioCam—Porsche's answer to the power-boosting variable-valve-timing systems on newer models from BMW and several Japanese makes. *Car and Driver*'s Pat Bedard thought VarioCam "at best inelegant—it amounts to a plastic rubbing block, controlled by the engine computer, that adjusts the length of the drive chain

between the intake and exhaust cams." Maybe so, but the idea behind it was sound. Below 1500 rpm, VarioCam allowed only a small amount of valve overlap for a smooth idle and low emissions. Between 1500 and 5500 rpm it retarded timing to promote better cylinder filling for more torque. Above 5500, timing was advanced for maximum power. With all this, the 3.0 muscled up to 236 bhp at 6200 rpm in U.S. trim and 225 pounds/feet of torque peaking at 4100—the highest torque output in the world for a non-turbo engine of this size.

Like the 944, the 968 transmission still sat near the rear axle, but the manual gearbox now had six forward ratios instead of five. And for the first time since 1989 buyers could have a four-cylinder Porsche with an automatic transmission. It was a good one, too, an adaptation of the 911's sophisticated four-speed Tiptronic, priced here at $3150. (See Chapter 3 for operating details.) Chassis-wise, the 968 was a tweaked carryover of the 944, but 17-inch wheels and tires were newly optional (at $1352). Rim widths were unchanged from the last S2s (7.5 inches fore, 8 inches aft), but the wheels looked like they'd come from the all-conquering 959, and the tires were run-flat Bridgestone Expedias, similar to those on the latest 911 Carrera 2. Continued for the coupe only was an optional sport suspension package with larger front brakes and firmer shocks with adjustable rebound damping.

There was little new inside, so the 968 inherited all the old 944 ergonomic quirks—but then, Porsche had only so much money to spend. Speaking of which, the four-cylinder line had been adding "boutique" options over the years, just like 911s. The 968 continued the practice, listing items like "partial leather" front seats (hide on wearing surfaces only, a stiff $668), heated seats, a CD player or changer ($1347 for the latter), headlight washers, and the beloved "paint and upholstery to sample" (price variable with outrageousness). More mainstream extras included a limited-slip differential ($895) and metallic paint ($803).

Happily, buyers didn't pay more up front, at least for the coupe. Because economizing measures in Zuffenhausen were starting to bear fruit, Porsche could price the closed 968 a whopping $4000 below the previous S2 model: $39,350 in the United States. That was a bit deceptive, however, because luxury tax and a few options would lift take-home prices to the mid-forties. And the 968 Cabrio was $3300 *more* than its S2 predecessor, a hefty $51,900. With that, *Car and Driver* predicted "price [is] the trip line where the 968 may fall on its face."

The 968 coupe and Cabriolet reached U.S. dealers in time for the '92 model year (top right and bottom). The coupe cost less than its 944S2 predecessor despite new standard features such as five-spoke wheels shod with run-flat tires, but the Cabrio was up $3300 to a hefty $51,900. Though the 968's "face" was clearly influenced by the 928's, some views showed a slight family resemblance with the 911 (middle left). On the other hand, the 968 instrument panel (top left) was a direct lift from the S2, so several ergonomic gaffes remained.

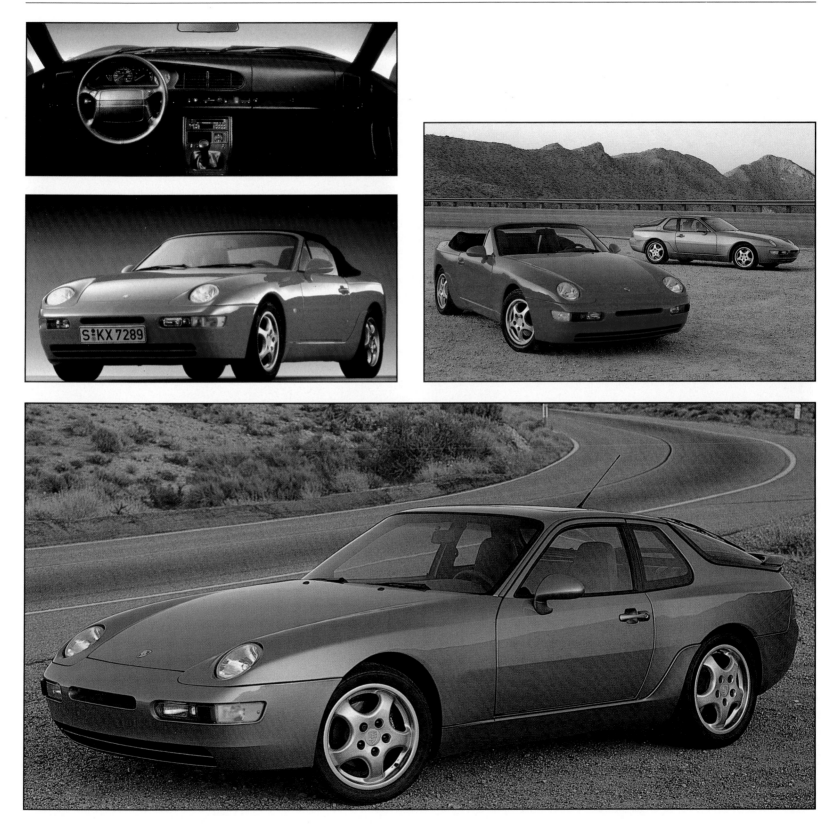

Like its 944S2 predecessor, the 968 Cabriolet (top and right) can be driven top-down with surprisingly little wind buffeting, especially with the side windows raised. Rocker-panel "cladding" harks back to the 944S and Turbo. The 968 has seen few changes since introduction, as seen in a '93-model coupe (above right). As noted, the cockpit (above left) also harks to the 944 but is nonetheless a reminder that Porsche was the first manufacturer to make dual airbags available on its American-market cars, starting with the 1987-model 944S.

The Club Sport coupe (top and lower left) debuted in 1993 as a special 968 confection for Europe and the UK. Suspension was lowered nearly an inch for handling, which earned raves from both road-testers and entrants in the European Porsche Cup series. Non-airbag steering wheel (above) was standard "over there."

Surprisingly, the fall never came. After selling just 862 four-cylinder cars in all of 1991, PCNA was relieved to deliver 1242 of the 968s—still small potatoes by even BMW standards, but a satisfying 44 percent increase. Total series production rose, too. Again, the number wasn't large, just 5238 worldwide, but it represented a 28-percent gain.

There were plenty of reasons to like the 968, though styling may have been the least of them. To most eyes it was clearly a 944 in a 928 suit, and not everyone approved. But road manners were still eminently rewarding, and cornering power was better than ever; *Car and Driver* reported a body-tugging 0.93g for its coupe with the optional suspension and wheel/tire packages.

There was more straightline go, too. Some observers questioned the need for six speeds in a car with such ample low-end torque, but as sixth was geared about as tall as the 944's fifth, the extra cog allowed closer spacing of the lower ratios for improved low-end snap. *C/D* clocked 0-60 at 5.6 seconds, *Road & Track* at 5.9. "Ten years ago," *C/D* recalled, "the 944 ate up 7.5 seconds getting . . . to 60 mph. . . . The [968's] penalty is a drop in our observed fuel economy from 26 mpg to 20." Well, Porsches *do* invite hard charging. As for the Tiptronic, it worked just as well here as it did in the 911, robbing a little low-end grunt in exchange for self-shift convenience.

The 968 would see virtually no change for the next three model years—including price. Was Porsche quietly taking a loss on its four-cylinder line? Probably not, though 968 sales have tailed off since introduction, and the premium sports-car market is still very much in flux as we write this in 1995, so a more likely explanation is that Porsche is simply biding its time pending another update—or an all-new replacement.

Which brings up the question of whether Porsche will persist with a "front-four" car into the next century. Informed opinion is divided so your guess is certainly as good as anybody's, but we hope Porsche won't give up. Despite being rooted in the humble 924, the 944s, and certainly the 968, prove that even a "basic" Porsche is something to treasure.

As for the old debate over whether any members of this clan merit the term "true Porsche," consider these words from *Car and Driver*'s Larry Griffin, written in March 1992: "In its basics, every Porsche provides the rewarding give-and-take that marks great machines. In a world sometimes aswirl with cars that sacrifice passion for 'perfection,' we see the 968 as another of Porsche's innumerable half-steps of progress on an emotional road. Just as after-images linger in the eye past the fading of the light, years from now some of us will still be able to call up accurate memories of how this car *went*. In that, if not in numerical test results or on the bottom line of price versus performance, the 968 is a winner out of the box."

Added power brought the 968 more punch in 1992 (top), *as well as an alarming 25-percent drop in mpg figures. Although no turbocharged 968 was available in the United States for 1993, examples did exist—and race—in Europe* (bottom). *This '93 968 Turbo RS wears racing slicks, suggesting that the car seldom, if ever, saw street duty.*

Flogging the 944

Given the unenthusiastic public reception accorded the Volkswagen-based Porsche 914, and the skeptical reaction to the front-engined, liquid-cooled 924 that followed, Porsche was unusually anxious for its 1981 offering, the 924-based 944, to get off on the right foot.

Late in 1980, British-based pr flack Michael Cotton whipped up an excited press release that began, "944: A NEW PORSCHE!" The copy continued, "The Porsche range will be extended next year when the new 944 goes into production. The 944, which has an entirely new Porsche 2.5 litre engine bristling with advanced features, will make its debut at the Frankfurt [Auto] Show in September and will go into production at the end of the year."

Porsche took particular care to educate the press and public about the 944's unique body; first, that it was constructed of galvanized steel and thus would not rust, and second, that it was a marvel of aerodynamics. Brochures highlighted the 944's slippery aspect, noting that considerable effort had been put into minimizing unwanted lift generated beneath the body.

Lessons learned from competition 924s, the press releases said, allowed Porsche engineers to cut down on the 944's wind noise, ensure a more efficient flow of rainwater off the body, and improve engine ventilation. A remarkable cutaway 944, split longitudinally, was created to display the car's myriad technical innovations.

Official Porsche photos were cleverly divided between low-angle racetrack shots emphasizing the 944's aggressive sheetmetal; and sedate, eye-level views snapped in formal gardens and similarly refined venues, suggesting that the 944 wasn't just a beast, but a proper pussycat, too.

Porsche's campaign eventually paid off, for the 944, and subsequent 944S, accounted for a considerable portion of an upsurge of U.S. Porsche sales in 1986.

The 928 Chronicle: Porsche Faces Luxury

In the early Seventies, Porsche chairman Dr. Ernst Fuhrmann, no small inventor himself, sweated along with his Zuffenhausen colleagues—not about what was going wrong (nothing much was in those days) but what *could* go wrong. Mainly they worried that the 911 just might stop selling (perhaps suddenly) before they could ready a replacement. Their concern was not unjustified. The 911 was then nearing its tenth birthday, no successor was in sight, and Porsche knew better than anyone that no car lasts forever. Even the evergreen 356 had run "only" 15 years.

As we now know, time was not running out on the 911 at all. The car is still with us, better than ever, and showing every sign of continuing into the next century. But Fuhrmann and company couldn't know that back then, and we can be glad. Perspiration and no little inspiration spurred their genius to produce a fabulous new Porsche unlike any that had gone before.

Other concerns prompted thoughts of a 911 successor. Most immediate was the trend to increasingly stringent emission, safety, and noise standards not only in the United States—then Porsche's most important export market—but in Europe, as well. This led to the idea that the air-cooled/rear-engine concept might not be able to keep pace—that it could, in effect, be legislated out of existence.

All this came together in project goals for a new model that, in the beginning at least, was seen as a 911 replacement. As Dean Batchelor recorded, it first had to have "all the quality and performance of previous Porsches" and "be capable of meeting any and all government regulations that might be conceived in the foreseeable future." The latter seemed to imply a water-cooled engine in front, which by then was seen as a given for all future production Porsches.

The new car would also have to be more refined, comfortable, and luxurious than any prior Porsche so as to compete with Mercedes and BMW. And it would have to play well in America, where more than half of all Porsches were sold. Of course, a long production run was assumed—at least 10 years—which called for styling that wouldn't quickly become dated.

Adding significance to these requirements, this would be Porsche's first "clean-sheet" road car. (The 356 was VW-based, the 911 had evolved from it, and the 924 was taken over from VW after this new project was started.) Considering that, it's amazing that the 928's basic concept was "worked out, deliberated and decided within a few days," as Fuhrmann later told author Karl Ludvigsen.

By late 1973, Porsche had decided on a relatively large-displacement, water-cooled V-8 up front, plus a rear transaxle, all-independent suspension, and all-disc brakes, the last two long-standing Porsche traditions by this time. Mounting the transmission aft would confer more even front/rear weight balance with the forward engine, plus a high polar moment of inertia to aid handling and high-speed stability. A 90-degree V-8 might seem rather "American," but Mercedes offered one nonetheless. And it had certain advantages over the 60-degree V-6 that was briefly considered (and may have given rise to rumors of a "new 911" with a front six): superior power potential and running smoothness, greater scope for future displacement increases, and compactness—important, because Fuhrmann wanted the characteristically low Porsche hoodline. Design chief Tony Lapine deliberately planned the styling to be futuristic and a little shocking, in line with his notion that if a car looks good right away, it soon starts looking old hat.

Though Porsche usually premiered new models at the Frankfurt *Automobil Ausstellung*, its traditional "home" show, it chose the Geneva Salon in March 1977 to introduce the 928. The choice was fitting, as the original 356 had been introduced there back in 1950. U.S. deliveries began late in 1977, in time for model-year '78.

What people saw was a sleek if rather heavy-looking 2+2 hatchback coupe unlike anything else on the road—a sort of German Corvette. That may seem an invidious comparison to Porschephiles, but it's logical, and not just because both cars have V-8s. For example, the 928's 98.4-inch wheelbase was just 0.4-inch longer than the contemporary Chevy's. Overall size was broadly similar, too, though the Porsche measured 10 inches shorter (175.7 inches) and offered "+2" seating where the 'Vette did not. Both were obviously high-style, high-performance sports cars, but the 928 was

Faced with the not unreasonable possibility that the 911 might one day lose its popularity, Porsche introduced the luxurious 928 as a potential replacement. The car made its debut at the Geneva Salon in March 1977, where it immediately caused a stir. The fresh styling, by American Tony Lapine, was one reason; the other was the car's V-8 (Porsche departure #1), which was water-cooled (departure #2) and located at the front (departure #3). Porsche purists howled but only the unreasonable refused to agree that the 928 was a luxurious beauty that went as good as it looked. The model seen here is a 928S, which was introduced in Europe for model-year 1979.

more weight-efficient, tipping the scales at just under 3200 pounds (versus 3500-plus). Undoubtedly, the 928's fixed-roof unit structure was lighter than the 'Vette's steel frame and separate fiberglass T-top body.

There was no doubting the efficiency of the 928 engine. It was not, as some thought, an adaptation of the contemporary 4.5-liter Daimler-Benz V-8. Displacement was close enough—4474 cubic centimeters versus 4520 (273 cubic inches versus 276)—but the Porsche unit was more oversquare with a bore and stroke of 95 X 78.9mm.

Pistons were iron-coated aluminum-alloy units running in linerless bores, made possible by casting the block in Reynolds 390 silicon-and-aluminum alloy, like the 911 engine. Again, the bores were electrochemically etched to leave silicon crystals as the wearing surface. The traditional forged-steel crankshaft ran in five main bearings, with forged connecting rods paired on common journals.

Naturally, there were no Detroit-style pushrods and rocker arms but a single overhead camshaft per cylinder bank, driven by a Gilmer-type belt. Though the banks sat at right angles, their cam covers were situated to make the installed V-8 look much like the 911 flat-six, which was possibly deliberate. The cylinder heads were made of alloy, for additional lightness. Compression was initially 8.5:1, and Bosch's reliable K-Jetronic injection fed fuel from a 22.7-gallon plastic tank at the extreme rear.

With all this, rated output was 240 DIN horsepower at 5500 rpm and 257 pounds/feet of torque peaking at 3600 rpm. U.S. models arrived with 219 bhp (SAE net) at 5250 rpm and 245 pounds/feet of torque (also at 3600) due to a more restricted exhaust system with catalytic converter for emission control (making this a 50-state car from the first) and minor retuning for operation on lead-free fuel.

A front-engine/rear-transaxle layout made as much sense for the posh and potent 928 as it did for the lighter, less powerful 924. And it worked just as well: Front/rear weight distribution ended up a near-perfect 51/49 percent.

The standard gearbox was a new Porsche-designed five-speed manual mounted ahead of the differential (not behind, as in the 924), and departing from past practice with a direct top-gear ratio (1:1). Alas, it also had a racing-style shift gate like early 911s, with first to the left and down, out of the normal H. Porsche engineers explained that the V-8's ample torque permitted routine starts in second gear, so first wouldn't be needed that much and should thus be "out of the way." Most owners

felt differently.

Daimler-Benz did provide one major component: the no-extra-cost three-speed automatic, wearing a housing designed by Porsche. Both transmissions pulled a long-striding 2.75:1 final drive.

Power went through a special Fitchel & Sachs twin-disc clutch of fairly small diameter (200mm/7 inches). This was chosen to match the rotary inertia of a thin, rigid driveshaft carried in a torque tube. A helper-spring release kept clutch effort at a manageable 33 pounds.

Nowhere was that thoroughness more evident than in the suspension. Geometry looked ordinary but wasn't. Up front were unequal-length lateral A-arms, with the lower one mounting a concentric shock absorber and coil spring that passed through the upper arm to an attachment point above. An anti-roll bar was standard.

Rear suspension was more novel. *Road & Track* described it as "upper transverse links, lower trailing arms, coil springs, tube shocks, anti-roll bar." Porsche proudly called it the "Weissach (VEE-sock) Axle," after the site of the company's new Development Center not far from Stuttgart.

Britain's *Autocar* noted that each lower arm "takes braking and acceleration torque loads as well as helping the ball-jointed single top link locate the wheel laterally. The bottom [arm] has its inboard pivot axis inclined outwards at the front, like a semi-trailing arm, to provide a measure of anti-squat. And at the front body pivot, it has a sort of double joint [actually an articulated mount]. The give of this in a corner under braking and decelerating forces [that ordinarily result in] an oversteer-inducing toe-out [instead] makes the outside rear wheel toe-in slightly [and] thus counters the usual accidental oversteering self-steer in the case where the driver who has entered a corner too fast lifts off, or, worse, brakes."

Like so many Porsche innovations, the Weissach Axle was an elegant solution to a thorny problem, and it marked a first for toe-compensating rear suspension in a production car. Other manufacturers would devise their own solutions, including full rear-wheel steering, but it would take them at least a decade to follow Porsche's lead.

ZF supplied the 928's rack-and-pinion steering, which, unusually for a Porsche, came standard with power-assist. The assist was also predictive in that it varied with vehicle velocity: minimal at highway speeds for proper effort and optimum control, maximum at low speeds for easy parking. Gearing was reasonably quick at 3.1 turns lock-to-

Above: *The 928's lie-flat headlights were undoubtedly inspired by a similar design seen on the 1966-73 Lamborghini Miura. The Porsche lamps rotated up and forward when in use, creating a "froggy" look reminiscent of another great car, the 1958-61 Austin-Healey Sprite.* **Opposite:** *American auto writers quickly embraced the 928, some naming it "the best car ever" by 1979 (top). Porsche was anxious to show off the 928's technical innovations and created cutaway versions to give up-close views of the engine, suspension, brakes, and door panels.*

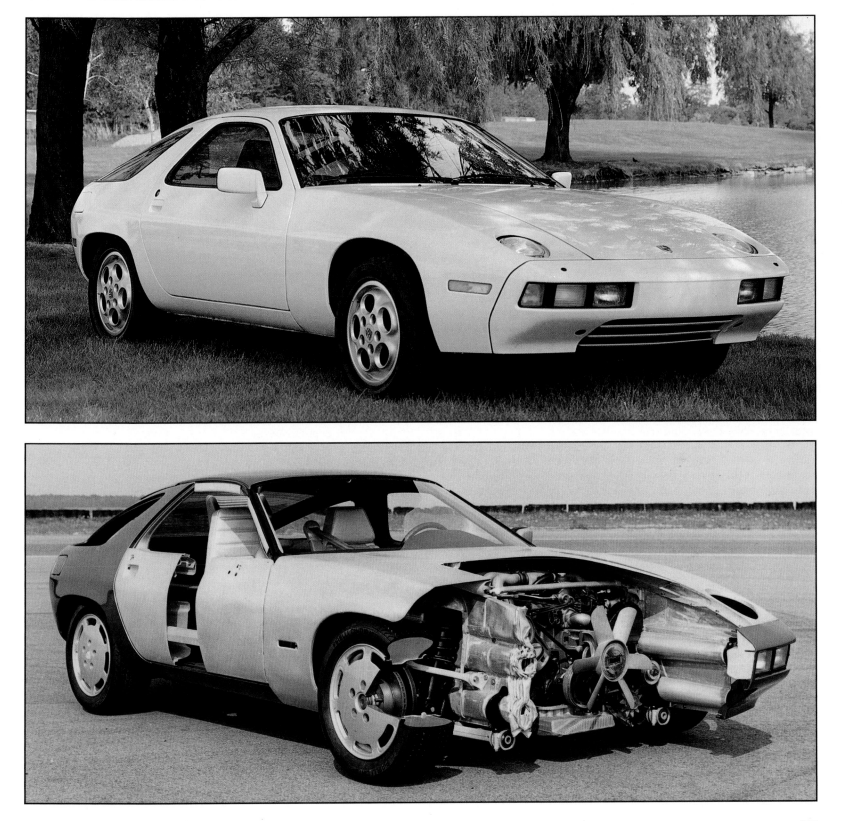

lock. Again for better control (and foreshadowing the later 944), negative steering roll (or "scrub") radius was designed in to counter sudden changes in steering torque in situations like a front-tire blowout.

The 928 rolled in on low-profile, high-performance 225/50VR16 Pirelli P7s mounted on special "telephone dial" cast-alloy wheels. These state-of-the-art tires worked with the high-tech suspension to give the 928 uncanny cornering stick. "They hang on to absurd limits," exclaimed Autocar, "and combined with the drama-free way the car simply understeers ultimately, it is easy to dismiss the 928 as almost dull in a corner. And then you think about how fast you are going through the corner."

In fact, the 928 suspension was so remarkably compliant, absorbing most every kind of irregularity, that critics could hardly believe the race-car-like cling in hard driving. "True, those tires are harsh over sharp inputs," observed Road & Track, "and they're also noisy on all but the smoothest asphalt surfaces, but otherwise the ride is wonderfully supple and well controlled. The softness of the suspension on our California freeways had some drivers expecting a floaty, wallowy ride on fast, twisty undulating roads. Nothing could be further from the truth."

The big vacuum-assisted all-disc brakes proved equally capable. They could rein in a 928 at up to 1g deceleration and, in R&T's tests, a mere 139 feet from 60 mph. "One wonders how much the very handsome, wide-eyed wheels help in keeping the fade performance good," added Autocar. "Few cars have such nakedly obvious discs . . . a piece of functional design that makes the car look all the more what it is—ideally functional."

Acceleration was nothing less than Porsche-brilliant. Despite its heft, a five-speed 928 would reach 60 mph from rest in 7-8 seconds; the automatic version took perhaps a tick more. The standing quarter-mile flew by in 15-16 seconds with manual, the speedo reading about 90 mph. Top speed was 135-145 mph, more than most owners would typically use.

Not that they didn't have a right to expect super performance, because the 928 was super expensive, arriving in the United States at a heart-stopping $26,000. "Hardly a bargain," sniffed R&T in 1978, by which time the price had ballooned to $28,500. "But clever engineering doesn't come cheaply, and few automotive design teams are more clever than the one residing in Zuffenhausen, West Germany."

Porsche was a bit sensitive about the controversy generated by the 928's styling, taking great pains to explain its benefits to customers and dealers alike: "The 928 was designed to have as many Porsche styling points as possible and to be clearly different from other sports cars," said a 1978 dealer training booklet. "Then there was the safety legislation [to consider]. . . . And, of course, acceptable aerodynamic values had to be reached. . . .

"The 928 styling with a fastback is an intentional continuation of Porsche tradition in that it is aerodynamically superior, because of the comparative short front end and a gently tapered and rounded tail, guaranteeing low air turbulence. As well as improving directional stability, the large-surface tail end also means a large passenger compartment and an outstanding amount of headroom for rear seat passengers in a sports car. We also believe that rounded forms are more interesting than clean-cut lines, which can be absorbed immediately and do not have anything new to offer the observer. The 928 looks different from each angle and remains interesting."

Porsche suggested that its sales people offer this retort to prospects dubious about the looks: "Naturally, every observer will need a certain amount of time to get accustomed to the unusual styling of the 928; but a car which is technically different from other cars has the right to look different, don't you agree?" Styling director Lapine later allowed that even Dr. Fuhrmann didn't like the 928 when he first saw it, though he did later.

As time passed, the 928 no longer seemed so strange. As Lapine intended, time and tastes caught up with it, "worn-bar-of-soap" shape, curvy flanks, body-color bumpers, flared wheel-arches, and all. Even the side-window shapes would be rendered commonplace by imitators like the mid-Eighties Chrysler Laser/Dodge Daytona.

One element was borrowed: exposed headlamps that "stood up" when switched on and "lay down" (in recesses) when switched off, resting just below hood/fender level. At least Porsche borrowed from one of the best, the magnificent mid-engine Lamborghini Miura of the late Sixties. As Porsche explained, the design had advantages, enhancing aerodynamics while ensuring that the headlights were cleaned each time the car was washed. Also, the design was cheaper to build than the hidden lamps of the 924 and later 944. But most of all, it made for an unforgettable face, which may explain why layback lights appeared on the 944's restyled 1992 successor, the 968. Something else not found on most other cars were separate driving and fog lamps, catering to most every nighttime condition.

As with other Porsche models, the 928 lent itself to aftermarket conversions. This 1983 model by California-based D.E.C.I. was turned into a convertible that looked nearly as much like a 944 as a 928.

The 928 cockpit was the most sumptuous yet seen from Porsche, with all the usual luxury-car features and a few that weren't. Among the latter were a tilt-adjustable steering wheel that moved the entire instrument cluster with it, thus ensuring good gauge visibility at all times, and air-conditioning that cooled not only the interior but the glove compartment. And as for the back-seat sun visors, well, just put them down to Teutonic thoroughness. At the very least, they were perfect blinders for occupants who got nervous at 125 mph.

Those rear seats were individual buckets and definitely of the "occasional" sort for adults; small children fit much better. As on previous Porsches, the backrests could be flopped down for extra cargo space. Between the rear seats was another glove locker, and each door had map pockets concealed beneath armrests that could be pulled in four inches for closer support in spirited driving (an idea from R&D director Professor Helmuth Bott). Nobody liked the "op-art" checkerboard cloth on seats and door panels, but it wouldn't last, and hide upholstery was available from the start.

Instrumentation was Porsche-complete, with a large, central speedometer and tachometer flanked by oil pressure/voltmeter and fuel/coolant temperature gauges. A vertical extension of the tunnel console swept up gracefully into the main panel, with a small clock at its base, surmounted by radio, climate controls, and, topmost, a large air vent. Additional vents were located in the upper front portions of the armrests, which also flowed into the dash. *R&T* complained about the air vents' meager output but said "the heater, like the 911's, will practically fry eggs and burn toast."

Left of the center vent was a bevy of warning lights for a central monitoring system. This kept track of all the usual items plus fluid levels, exterior bulb failures, and brake-pad wear. A malfunction illuminated the appropriate lamp, which spelled it out in words (like "wash fluid"), plus a large red master light simply labeled "!". One pressed a button to turn off the master, which was reactivated when the driver next switched on the ignition. If a fault was serious, the master light wouldn't extinguish at all until the problem was fixed.

Also on the 928's lavish list of standards were a vacuum-operated central locking system, power windows, headlamp washers (activated with the windshield washer when the lights were up and lit), cruise control, a rear-window wiper and wire-element electric defroster, electric remote-adjustable and heated door mirrors, and a four-speaker stereo radio/cassette. Besides the aforesaid leather trim

(which would be progressively expanded over time to include door panels and headliner), buyers could add an extra-cost electric sliding sunroof, limited-slip differential, and factory-fitted burglar alarm.

Porsche initially promoted the 928's structural safety, even claiming that the stout B-pillars functioned in the same manner as the 911 Targa's rollbar. The 928 was indeed robust but, as noted, a little portly despite the use of aluminum for doors, hood, and detachable front fenders. The large, weighty hatch window did nothing to keep weight down.

No matter, for the 928 was built to go the distance. Reflecting Porsche's early-Seventies research into "long life" technology, the steel body/chassis was protected on both sides with the new hot-dip galvanizing process then being applied to 911s (see Chapter 3). Moreover, brake lines were sheathed in copper-nickel iron alloy, and fuel lines were treated with chrome and then plastic-coated. By 1980, Porsche would offer a six-year warranty against lower-body rust in addition to its normal new-car warranty for all U.S. models, following a program inaugurated in Europe a few years earlier. The only requirement was that the car be inspected once a year at a participating Porsche dealer. Coverage remained in effect even if the car changed hands during the six years—yet another expression of Zuffenhausen's commitment to top-quality craftsmanship.

For 1979, the 928 began the inevitable Porsche process of logical, progressive evolution to higher levels of comfort, performance, and refinement. The monitor warning lights moved to the instrument cluster on all models, but the big news was a more potent new 928S for Europe. A 2-mm bore stretch (to 97mm) brought the V-8 to 4664cc (284.6 cid); with dual exhausts and an interim compression boost to 10:1. Horsepower swelled to 300 (DIN) at 5900 rpm and torque to 283 pounds/feet at 4500 rpm. Also new were flat-face wheels with circumferential slots for better brake cooling, a front "chin" spoiler beneath the large under-bumper air intake, a small black-rubber spoiler at the base of the rear window, and bodyside rubbing strips.

Autocar had found the original 928 slightly lacking in the "*real* raw performance which the 911 Series had taught us to expect" but had "no doubts now." The S's 0-60 mph time was just 6.2 seconds, top speed 152 mph, and the standing quarter-mile a 14.3-second 97-mph trip. Noting that Britons had a choice of 300-bhp Porsches that year, the magazine advised: "If you want raw excitement . . . there is still nothing to touch the [911] Turbo—a truly fantastic car. . . . If it's refinement that matters, then there is no

Besides chopping the top, D.E.C.I. modified the '83's front end for improved aerodynamics.

alternative to the Jaguar XJ-S. If refinement doesn't matter too much, and you can bear the road noise, then the 928S offers a tremendous amount of marvelous motor car which has restored our faith in Porsche's abilities to adapt their formidable skills to the ways of the front-engined Grand Tourer, for that is what the 928S most certainly is."

The action shifted to America for 1980. A half-point compression increase, improved emissions control (via an oxygen sensor and a three-way catalyst), revised valve timing, repositioned spark-plugs (moved 4mm closer to the combustion chamber centers), and adoption of more sophisticated L-Jetronic injection yielded only one extra horsepower but 20 more pounds/feet of torque: 265 at 4000 rpm. Top speed was harder to measure on the feds' new 85-mph speedometer, but *Road & Track* estimated 140 mph for its automatic-equipped test car. It also reported small gains in economy and off-the-line performance (0.3-second faster to 60, for instance)—nothing to write home about, but at least they weren't losses. Some 220 pounds *were* lost via a lighter alumimum torque tube and a hollow (instead of solid) transmission mainshaft and front anti-roll bar.

Several items became optional in the United States for 1980: radio/cassette, rear wiper, headlight washers, and the big wheels and tires (replaced by five-inch-wide rims with 215/60VR15 rubber). New extras included six-way power driver's seat (with a pair of rather hard-to-reach rocker switches on the cushion's outboard side) and automatic temperature control for the climate system. Base price was close to $38,000 now, though that included leather seating and a pliable cargo-area cover that rose with the hatch. Late that season, Porsche offered an extra-cost Competition Group that brought over all the goodies from the European S except its engine.

There was also a second U.S. offering for 1980: the Weissach Edition. Sales were deliberately limited to 205 copies, all with Champagne Gold metallic paint, matching alloy wheels, electric sunroof, fore/aft spoilers, and two-tone leather interior, plus a matched three-piece luggage set valued at over $1000. An electronic-tune radio/cassette and the auto climate control were also included, as was a small commemorative plaque ahead of the shift lever. The Weissach would continue through mid-model-year 1982.

The 928 took a breather for '81, though further emissions fiddling brought another incremental mileage gain on U.S. models. Not that fuel efficiency was a 928 strength—Porsche never intended

that. Still, the addition of an economy gauge for 1982, the year's only significant change, was a telling admission in the wake of "Energy Crisis II" (1979-80). It registered instantaneous mpg in normal driving or fuel use in gallons per hour at idle or very low speeds.

Car and Driver's Pat Bedard termed the magazine's all-black 1981 test 928 "the triple distillation of evil, the baddest machine on any block. . . . But contrary to appearances, the 928, even with the so-called Competition Group, is a mannerly device lacking all the frenzy that characterizes rear-engined Porsches. . . . It's also a graceful performer on the track, something I wouldn't say about the 911 or any other road car in its class. In fact, I can't think of another car that offers as happy a combination of road comfort and ultimate handling." In short, the 928 was still everything Dr. Fuhrmann intended—and more.

During 1982, Porsche discontinued the original 4.5-liter 928 in Europe. This left only the 4.7-liter S, which finally arrived in America for 1983. On higher 9.3:1 compression, horsepower rose to 234 (SAE net) at 5500 rpm and torque to 263 pounds/feet at 4000 rpm. However, price rose, too—to 43 big ones to start—but at least that heady sum included the Competition Group.

To maintain a semblance of fuel economy, Porsche lowered final drive to 2.27:1 with both transmissions. The optional automatic was now a four-speed, again from Daimler-Benz, with a better spread of ratios for overall performance; the five-speed's four lowest cogs were more closely spaced for the same reason. A happy sign of an improving U.S. economy was the return of 160-mph speedometer scales.

In 1983 U.S. S trim, the manual 928 dropped to a claimed 7.0 seconds in the 0-60 dash, but it climbed to 146 mph all out; the automatic's numbers were 8.5 and 143 mph. As usual, magazine test results tended to bracket these official figures. Here's what *Car and Driver* and *Road & Track* got with their five-speed models:

	C/D	R&T
0-60 mph (sec.)	6.2	7.0
0-100 mph (sec.)	17.8	19.3
0-¼ mi. (sec.)	14.7	15.4
Mph at ¼ mi.	94	92
Top speed (mph)	144	136
Lateral accel. (g)	0.80	0.818

Discrepancies nothwithstanding, this was real Corvette and Ferrari stuff. But C/D's Rich Ceppos rightly observed that mere numbers couldn't cap-

The 1985 928S (above) ran with a 288-horsepower 4.7-liter V-8 that had been introduced for '83, but now with the bore stretched an additional three millimeters. Peak torque came in at 302 pounds/feet, at a usefully low 2700 rpm. Sixty mph came up from rest in less than six seconds. Anti-lock brakes became standard for 1986 (opposite page) and helped bring the 928 to a stop from 70 mph in just 175 feet. Luxury continued to be emphasized nearly as much as performance, and the "+2" rear seat, although cramped, did give the 928 more utility than most other comparable performers.

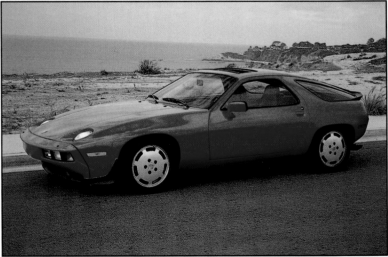

ture the Porsche's "double-agent personality: a killer instinct coupled with luxocar civility and the kind of bulletproof solidity you'd normally associate with a Mercedes. . . . The feeling around these parts is that the 928S actually gives you your money's worth in today's inflated market."

R&T mostly agreed: "The 928S is simply a marvelously competent car . . . as close as anything to being the complete automobile as understood in the year 1983. . . . It's a judgment call to say a car this expensive is worth it, but at least the 928S gives you a good deal of substance to go with its costly image."

And Porsche was about to add new substance. While the U.S. 928 was all but unchanged for 1984, Europe was treated to a Series 2 version fortified in more ways than one. Bosch's advanced new LH-Jetronic injection teamed with electronic ignition and sky-high 10.4:1 compression to lift the 4.7-liter V-8 to 310 bhp (DIN) and 295 pounds/feet of torque, gains of 10 and 12, respectively. Porsche claimed 10-12 percent better fuel economy, though you couldn't prove it by *Autocar,* whose test S2 proved "patently" thirstier than previous 928s. But who cared? Top speed was now a thrilling 158 mph. "Even with all that luxury, you think the car is still too expensive?" the magazine asked. "Get behind the wheel of the 928S Series 2, drop the clutch, floor the accelerator . . . and think again."

Even better was the arrival of an anti-lock braking system (ABS) as standard equipment. Subsequently adopted by a number of other manufacturers, ABS does what any good driver would at the first sign of a skid: "pump" the brakes to get a locked wheel rolling again. The difference is that ABS does this more rapidly than any human can—up to 15 times a second in this case—and only at the affected wheel (via electromechanical means in response to signals from wheel-mounted sensors). That sort of braking is beyond human capability; the result is a virtual absence of skidding (except on hard-packed snow or gravel) no matter how hard the driver might push the brake pedal. Steering control is thus maintained. As past 928 brakes had been occasionally criticized for front- and/or rear-lock sensitivity, ABS was a worthwhile addition, mating beautifully with the Weissach Axle to set a new standard of active safety.

The 928S continued its upward bound for 1985. Porsche stretched bore another 3mm and—the big attraction—doubled the V-8's valves and camshafts. The result was superb: 4957cc (303 cid), plus 10.0:1 compression made possible by the four-valve head with spark plugs centrally located

above new pentroof combustion chambers. SAE net horsepower came in at 288. Torque swelled to 302 pounds/feet and peaked at the lowest crank speed yet, 2700 rpm.

Wonder of wonders, America got the revised 32-valve 928S *before* Europe—and a lot of new thrills. *Car and Driver* clocked just 5.7 seconds to 60, a mere 13.5 seconds to 100 mph, 14 seconds at 102 mph in the standing-quarter, and 154 mph flat-out. "These are amazing figures for a car with extremely tall economy-oriented gearing," *C/D* observed dryly. ". . . [A] substantial improvement over its predecessor."

Braking was somehow better, too, even though ABS had been left in Germany (it became standard Stateside for '86). *Car and Driver* termed the system "reassuring, thanks to linear performance, well-proportioned front-to-rear balance, and excellent modulation. These characteristics contribute to the 928S's ability to stop from 70 mph in just 175 feet. Perhaps even more impressive is [its] ability to absorb triple-digit speeds without fading or emitting any disconcerting squeals, groans or odors."

There were few other changes for 1985, though Porsche now extended its rust warranty to an impressive 10 years. Inevitably, price was more impressive, too: a cool $50,000. Still, only a few, much costlier Italian exotics were in the same performance league, and the 928S was far more reliable, comfortable, and practical.

Amazingly, an even better 928 was on the way. It arrived for 1987 in all markets except Australia as the S4 (denoting a "fourth series"). "Porsche raises the price and rewards of automotive hedonism one more time," said *Car and Driver.*

And how. Emissions-legal horsepower was now 316 at 6000 rpm, torque 317 pounds/feet at 3000 rpm. This was accomplished with revised cylinder heads with larger valves, combustion chambers that were shallower by 3mm, a narrower valve angle (27.4 degrees versus 28), altered valve timing, and a new, more compact two-stage intake manifold. The last comprised twin resonance chambers or tracts—one long, one short—feeding air to the intake pipes via a Y-shaped passage from the throttle body. Below 3500 rpm the engine breathed only through the long tract; above that, depending on throttle position, a butterfly valve in the second tract opened to increase airflow. Porsche claimed this setup ensured at least 300 pounds/feet of torque from 2700 to 4750 rpm, a "fat" torque curve, indeed.

Putting the power to the ground was a larger-diameter single-disc clutch instead of the previous

Another aftermarket house, Germany's DP Motorsport, gave an '86 928 (above) an aggressive makeover that included a vented hood, fender flares, and hard-to-miss DP graphics. Inside was a hands-free telephone.

For 1987 Porsche introduced the 928S4 (above); the "4" denoted "fourth series." By this time, the 928 was challenging the 911 for the title of "fastest Porsche." With 316 horsepower and a new, two-stage manifold, the 928 was indeed a screamer—and it stopped with ferocious competence: In one test an S4 was brought to a halt from 60 mph in just 137 feet.

dual-disc unit. The ABS brakes also got attention, with a shorter-travel booster and larger pistons for the front calipers.

Further bolstering S4 performance was the 928's first facelift, a minor one that reduced aerodynamic drag. Fog and driving lamps were newly flush-mounted in a smoother nose cap that added 2.3 inches to overall length, and the chin spoiler was now fully integrated with it. A revised cooling system featured thermostatically operated radiator shutters that opened only when needed to minimize drag in high-speed driving. Twin variable-speed electric fans replaced a single engine-driven fan that consumed more power. A "detached" wing-type spoiler flew above a smoother tail (again with flush-mount lamps). Also easing airflow were deeper rocker panels, a new belly pan beneath the engine, a bonded-in windshield, and wipers that parked 20mm lower than before.

All this added "down" to a drag coefficient of 0.34, versus 0.41 for the original 928 and 0.38 for the previous S. That was commendable considering that, in Porsche tradition, the rear tires had grown wider than the fronts: 245/45VR16s versus 225/50VR16s (on respective rim widths of eight and seven inches).

The S4 cockpit remained familiar 928-style. Body-hugging sports seats were still available, but there were two new options for the standard power seats. One was electric lumbar support adjustable for height as well as firmness. The other was "Positrol," a memory system that stored the positions of seat, lumbar support, and even the door mirrors for recall at the touch of a button. Both were available for either the left or right seat which, as in '86, could be fitted with heating elements as a separate option.

As before, and as with recent 911s, Porsche would decorate a 928 interior to special order in any materials and/or colors a customer wanted. One example was done completely in ostrich leather for Jordan's King Hussein.

In all, the S4 was the kind of thorough, timely update expected of Porsche. With it, the 928 was even more of what it always had been: a luxurious, supremely comfortable high-speed tourer capable of astounding performance on straights and curves alike. Porsche said the manual S4 would reach 60 mph in 5.7 seconds, but *Road & Track* got 5.5. And though claimed top speed was now no less than 165 mph, Al Holbert, longtime Porsche racer and chief of Porsche Motorsport in the United States, took a virtual stock S4 to 170 mph his first time out in a series of USAC-certified speed runs at Bonneville in

August 1986. He eventually coaxed the car to 171.110 mph in the flying mile and 171.296 mph in the flying kilometer, both new world records for normally aspirated production cars.

With that, the 928 vied with the vaunted 911 Turbo as the fastest production Porsche—and not just in acceleration. The S4 achieved truly incredible stopping distances in *R&T*'s March 1987 road test: 137 feet from 60 mph, 234 feet from 80. "That's shorter than any production car we've ever tested save the Ferrari 412, which does [80-0 mph] in 230."

The 928 celebrated its tenth birthday with the 1988 model year, yet changes were restricted to standard three-point rear seatbelts and driver's-seat Positrol, plus a newly optional factory cellular-telephone hookup and warmer-looking "Supple Leather" upholstery. Price, however, was drastically changed, especially in America. After several years of relative stability, the dollar began another retreat against the German Deutschmark, which forced Porsche to raise sticker prices twice on all its U.S. models during the 1988 season. The increases added up to about 6 percent across the line, which didn't sound too bad except that it meant paying up to $3800 more for a 928, which ended the year just $620 shy of $70,000 before options. On top of that were the new U.S. gas-guzzler and luxury taxes.

That more than anything explains why Porsche sales began a full-fledged slide in 1988, with the biggest losses coming in the ever-important U.S. market. The 928 was the biggest loser among Porsches, with total production plummeting from just over 8000 for '89 to barely 4100 for 1990.

The '89 base price was higher still at $74,545, but the car itself was a virtual rerun. The only differences involved a new, standard 10-speaker sound system and an automatic transmission with a shorter final drive, revised intermediate gear ratios, and higher full-throttle shift points, all for improved standing-starts.

As explained in earlier chapters, a management crisis compounded Porsche's dwindling sales and cash reserves as the Nineties approached. Yet even as the firm struggled to get back on track, the 928 continued to evolve, even if reduced development funds meant that progress was somewhat slower than before.

Still, there was no shortage of worthwhile improvements. For example, the 1990 models (no longer called *S4*) sported standard dual air bags as well as two features pioneered by Porsche's recently deceased 959 supercar. One was a variable-ratio limited-slip differential, comprised of a multi-

disc hydraulic clutch with electronic controls linked to the ABS wheel-speed sensors. Based on sensor input, the diff could vary its lock-up from 0 to 100 percent to compensate for traction loss as well as variations in cornering and braking loads.

The other improvement was a tire-pressure monitoring system. This used a separate set of sensors, housed within the wheels, to warn when pressure in any tire fell below a set level, as signaled by a light in the central array.

Yet even with these pluses, the 928 cost not one extra penny in the United States, Porsche holding the price line on all its 1990 models in hopes that the dollar would soon firm up. Unfortunately, the greenback wouldn't strengthen for awhile because America was entering a sharp new recession, making Porsche's decision to forgo another price hike all the more laudable.

Extra power packed into manual-shift 928s was achieved in the time-tested Porsche way of revised cam profiles and altered intake system. The result was a boost in horsepower—to 326 at 6200 rpm—and some 200 extra revs to work with. Torque, however, was unchanged and still the same as the automatic version's 317 pounds/feet. With that, Porsche's official performance claims proved optimistic for once. Where the factory said 5.6 seconds 0-60, *Road & Track* replied 6.1—a 0.6-second deficit from the magazine's previous S4 result. The self-shift version was claimed to need 6.0 seconds flat, but *R&T* clocked a comparatively disappointing 6.3.

Despite the 928's undeniable abilities, Porsche was worried by a growing perception of the V-8 Porsche as a dinosaur in the automotive world of 1990—a too-heavy, too-thirsty, and never-too-practical tourer that had been allowed to live too long with too few meaningful changes. Perhaps that's why Garrat Lai felt compelled to defend it in *Road & Track*'s *1990 Sports & GT Cars* issue. "The 928 set the standard for its class," he argued, "embodying the very definition of the luxurious sports car. Moreover, it heralded a number of changes in automobiles. Rounded, aerodynamic shapes are now the norm, and the entire genre of luxury-sport automobiles came into being shortly after the 928. Many cars . . . now incorporate rear suspension geometry designed to emulate Porsche's Weissach axle. Furthermore, the large engine is making a comeback, borne witness by BMW's V-12 [and] a crop of V-8s from Japan. It's true [the 928] has undergone little more than cosmetic changes over its lifetime. But it may hardly be called a dinosaur. Just think of it as a little ahead of its time."

Car and Driver found the 1991 edition needed no defense, even though nomenclature was about the only thing that had changed. "GT" now denoted the manual model, and a revived "S4" tag identified the automatic version. Granted, editor Art St. Antoine took note of the 928's "reputation as something of a poseur's Porsche—a car seen less often carving up mountain roads than being proudly handed over to the country-club valet." But he then promptly declared the GT "a deadly serious *driver's* car. In its quest for pure performance, Porsche has chiseled off most of the 928's remaining soft edges." He almost sounded surprised, but then with the 928's slower development pace, *C/D* (and some other "buff books") hadn't visited the car in a while.

No matter. As usual with Porsches, the numbers spoke volumes. Despite absolutely carryover specifications—and *R&T*'s 1990 numbers—*C/D*'s GT rocketed "from 0 to 60 mph in just 5.2 seconds and through the quarter-mile in 13.7 seconds at 104 mph—improvements of 0.1 and 0.2 second, respectively, over . . . the five-speed 928S4 we tested in May 1987. (Not a bad showing for a 3603-pound 'luxury' GT, eh?) Top speed is up a full 10 mph to 169 mph at the engine's 6600-rpm redline."

And road manners were better than ever. The GT "shines when you give it the spurs," St. Antoine reported. "The control efforts are finely honed for speeds above 80 mph; the steering arcs with reassuring heft, the shifter chunks solidly through its racing-pattern H, and the clutch takeup is smooth and positive. Spin the speedo to autobahn speeds and the GT really comes into its own. Suddenly, the beefy body feels not chubby but secure [and the car] is far more agile in curvy-road dicing and slicing than you'd expect. . . . Porsche has tamed the old 928's tail-happiness; the GT understeers resolutely through hard bends, tucking in neatly even if you suddenly snap off the throttle."

Yet for all that, St. Antoine judged the 928GT too potent and pricey for all but "the serious" and "the solvent." Then again, "Porsche plans to sell only about 100 . . . in the U.S. this year. That should tell you plenty about this car's mass-market appeal."

And however limited, the 928's appeal *was* still on the wane. Porsche Cars North America (PCNA) moved just 620 of the 1990 models and a mere 262 of the '91s (including, one presumes, those 100 GTs). Though total production took an uptick to 5238 for calendar-year 1991, it dropped back to 3389 in '92, when U.S. sales were a minuscule 181.

Part of that decline was due to an abbreviated

The "S4" designation was dropped for 1990 (above and opposite, top right and bottom). Dual air bags were now standard, and manual-shift models were now rated at 326 bhp. A skilled driver could take a manual-shift 928 from 0-60 mph in less than six seconds; the same sprint could be managed by the automatic transmission in six seconds flat. Luxury was still a dominant feature although, as before, the rear seat was best reserved for the very young or very limber. Ferry Porsche celebrated his 75th birthday in 1984, and the company celebrated the event by surprising him with a one-of-a-kind stretched 928 (opposite, top left) designed with full four-passenger capacity; note the custom headlamps. Ferry Porsche, who still owns the car, stands at the base of the windshield.

model year in which both the GT and S4 were virtual reruns. But Porsche jumped the '93 season in the spring of '92 by releasing a pair of more potent replacements called *928GTS*.

The letter *S* implied a more-powerful Porsche, and the GTS was. Stretching stroke from 79.9 to 85.9mm (3.11 to 3.43 inches) upped total capacity to an even 5400cc (329 cid). Bolstered by even tighter 10.4:1 compression, horsepower swelled to 345 bhp achieved at a usefully lower 5700 rpm. Torque rose, too, to 369 pounds/feet, but the peak was now 4250 rpm for both models—a lofty 1250 rpm above the previous year's automatic S4. Less noticed but still appreciated were a stronger clutch, a crankshaft with eight main bearings instead of six, lighter con rods and pistons newly forged instead of cast, and slightly softer shock absorbers for reduced ride harshness.

Appearance was modestly updated for the GTS. The rear wing was reshaped and newly available in either black or body color, smoother 959-type door mirrors appeared, and the tri-color taillights were linked by a half-height red reflector. More subtle changes included a 2.7-inch wider rear track and a two-inch broadening of the rear flanks to accommodate wider 255/40ZR tires on new five-spoke 17-inch wheels like those of the latest 911 Turbo; front rubber also widened, to 225/45ZR17. (Respective rim widths were 7.5 and 9 inches.) The bigger wheels allowed larger front brakes designed to cope with the extra power; Porsche specified the beefy 12.7-inch rotors of the 911 Turbo. Rear-disc diameter remained 11.77 inches, and hefty four-piston calipers continued at each wheel.

For all that, *Car and Driver*'s test of the manual GTS showed little change from previous GT results. The 0-60 dash actually took 0.1-second longer at 5.3 seconds, as did the standing quarter-mile (13.8)—but then, Porsche only claimed 5.5 for the manual model and 5.6 with automatic.

Zuffenhausen quoted a top speed of 171 mph, versus *C/D*'s reported 169 for the previous GT.

But none of this really mattered, for *C/D* seemed about the only U.S. magazine that cared to test a 928GTS on home soil. Perhaps that's because the V-8 Porsche was by now such a negligible part of the American scene. Indeed, calendar '93 sales were just 121 units. The '94 total was even lower: a paltry 84.

Still, Joe Rusz needed no persuading to try the GTS for a "First Drive" report in *Road & Track*'s July 1992 issue. Though a loyal 911 fan—and longtime 911 owner—he remained impressed with the 928 but bemoaned its evident fate. "This may be your last chance to own one of the world's finest *Gran Turismos*," he intoned. "Also, one of the most underrated. And unappreciated. . . . That the 928 hasn't caught the public's fancy may be due to the popularity of the 911 Carrera, which continues to be Zuffenhausen's best-selling road car. Also the oldest. The 928 . . . has been with us for a mere 15 years. Perhaps some designs take a bit longer to catch on."

Rusz was being kind. The fact was that by the early Nineties, and for all its splendid abilities, the 928 had lost much of its old sales magic—and, of course, it wasn't a "volume" car to begin with. Higher prices for the GTS iteration only made things worse: nearly $81,000 on its U.S. debut, rising to $82,260 by model-year '95.

So while the rear-engine Porsches, and maybe even the four-cylinder models, steam full speed toward a new millenium, the 928 may not make it, thanks to falling sales in recent years and Porsche's inability to fund a major redesign, let alone a replacement. Then again, it's been with us nearly 18 years at this writing, so it's had a good long life even for a Porsche.

Of course, we always knew it would have to disappear *one* day, whether by whim or necessity. As we said, Porsche knows better than anyone that no car lasts forever. But when that day dawns, the 928 will pass into the realm of truly collectible automobiles and will be recognized as a pathfinder not only for Porsche but for an entire breed of fast, roadable, luxurious touring machines—and one with an unsurpassed engineering pedigree.

Reliable figures reveal Porsche built 17,710 of the 4.5-liter 928s and 16,777 of the 4.7-liter models. Tallies aren't available for the 5.0- and 5.4-liter series, but they're surely much lower. With values on early models still falling toward easy affordability, and given the likely high survival rate for all 928s—Porsches *do*, after all, tend to end up in caring homes—the message for collectors is clear: Get yours now before these cars are "discovered," and then hold onto it. For all its many breaks with tradition, the 928 is and always has been a "true Porsche," and that makes it something to treasure.

Since its introduction in 1977, the 928 had proved itself a true Porsche—not merely beautiful but luxurious and impeccably engineered for flawless high performance. Examples from model-year 1990 continued the tradition, but 928 sales were hurting because of price—an unavoidable bogey that Porsche felt compelled to pass on to its customers. Although prices were held at 1989 levels for '90, the tab still started at more than $74,500—rarefied territory indeed. So rarefied, in fact, that the inevitable had happened by mid-decade: Production of the 928 was halted. Still, the ride was glorious while it lasted.

The Porsche Racing Chronicle: The Crucible of Competition

Part I: The Production Racers

"Racing improves the breed." It's an old saw but a valid one that Ferdinand Porsche passionately believed. So did his son, Ferry, and most of their associates. The marque they founded and built into an enthusiast's icon has always been planted foursquare on the world's raceways. Porsche has won more races—and more kinds of races—than any of its rivals.

Winning a single race, of course, merely proves that an existing car is sound and perhaps lucky. More impressive is a lengthy history of racing and winning. It proves a manufacturer has a commitment to improving its product. Porsche's dedication to motorsports has been day after day, year after year, decade upon decade. And nowhere is this dedication more evident than in the incredible stream of production-based competition cars that have been part of Porsche history from the start.

The very first one, in fact, appeared barely a month after completion of the prototype 356/2. It was a silver roadster driven by Herbert Kaes in an open road race at Innsbruck, Austria, on July 11, 1948. This "racer" wasn't in the least modified, retaining a normal windshield and road wheels. It could do only 84 mph flat out, but the little 356 won its class. With that modest success began the unprecedented story that has seen production-based Porsches win nearly every type of contest they have entered.

Porsche's earliest competition successes occurred mainly in rallying—the European kind where speed on "special stages" is crucial. In 1950-51, Porsches with 1.1- to 1.5-liter engines racked up class wins in the Swedish Rally (twice), the Alpine and Tavemunde rallies, and the demanding Tour de France. These winners were most often specially prepared Gmund coupes carrying a 356SL designation. A 1.1-liter carried the colors on the difficult Liege-Rome-Liege Rally in '51, Huschke von Hanstein and Petermax Muller finishing second in class after achieving close to 100 mph on only 46 horsepower. The following year, the 1.5-liter coupe of Helmut Polensky and Walter

Schluter won the event outright, and other Porsches finished third, fourth, ninth, and tenth overall. Porsche first contested the Rallye Monte Carlo that same year, and one coupe completed the trans-European road portion of this always-treacherous rally without a single penalty point.

The later Super 90s and Carreras went on to even greater things. Though too numerous to list here, their championship rally wins stand as exciting testimony to their stamina and performance under the most trying conditions.

As for track racing, Porsche first assaulted the prestigious 24 Hours of Le Mans in 1951. Though the plan was to run four 356SLs, two were damaged in practice, and a third, pieced together from those and another car, crashed during the race. But Auguste Veuillet, the French Porsche distributor, had better luck in the aluminum-bodied Gmund coupe he'd persuaded Ferry Porsche to let him run. With nothing more than careful tuning and aerodynamic fender skirts all-around, it won its class at an average 73.5 mph and finished 20th overall against much more potent machinery. Veuillet returned in 1952 with a 1.5-liter car, increased his average speed to 76.7 mph, and again finished first in class and 11th overall.

Porsche's emergence in U.S. competition was spurred by Max Hoffman, the energetic Austrian who almost singlehandedly introduced the country to import cars. In fact, Porsche's American racing debut came in October 1951 with Hoffman's own drive in a 356 Cabriolet to a class win at the Mount Equinox hillclimb in Vermont. He later brought over three Le Mans-prepped coupes, though they didn't do as well: Their best showing was in July 1952 at Torrey Pines, California, where John von Neumann (who would later set up Porsche's West Coast sales operations) won the 1500-cc modified class.

The 1.5-liter cars fared better in Europe. A highlight was the 1953 running of the Mille Miglia, the formidable 1000-mile dash up and down the "boot" of Italy. Driven by Count "Johnny" Lurani and rally ace Konstantin "Tin" Berckheim, a modified 1.5 beat every car in its class and finished 46th overall.

These early victories prompted development of

Ferdinand Porsche's first attempt at a racing machine was the Volkswagen-based Type 64 of 1939. Although the German government told Porsche that VW (i.e., state) components could not be put to private use, Ferdinand and son Ferry pressed on. Three 64s were built, each with a VW chassis, aluminum body, and tweaked engine. Top speed was estimated at 95 mph. The cars were readied for competition in the 1939 Berlin-to-Rome race, which was canceled because of the outbreak of war late that summer. Ironically, the Type 64s served "state" purposes after all, for they were eventually driven by Nazi VIPs. Opposite page: The true Porsche racing tradition began in 1951, with competition 356s. The car first raced at Le Mans in '51 and won the 1100-cc class.

the Type 528/1500 Super competition engine, initially with 70 DIN horsepower, though it soon had more. It would ultimately power the first Type 550s sports racers, thus beginning the legend of the competition Spyders.

As its cars improved, Porsche widened its horizons. A squadron of Type 550RS prototype coupes and 1.5-liter production cars went to Mexico in 1953 for the third *Carrera Panamericana* (Mexican Road Race). The 550s finished 1-2 in the "Light Sports" class of this ultra-long-distance open-road grind, while a 356 managed eighth overall and first in the production class at an average 83 mph. The latter was really more impressive than it sounds, for the class was then wide open and the cars that placed higher than the little 356 were all larger and considerably more potent: Mercedes 300SLs, Ferraris, Lancias. The 550s repeated their class-winning performance in 1954 at the final Carrera.

The 356A, Speedster, and 1500GS Carrera greatly swelled Porsche's numbers in U.S. production-class racing. Dr. Richard Thompson, the "flying dentist" later to gain fame piloting competition Corvettes, kicked things off in 1954, the year the Sports Car Club of America (SCCA) first ran national championships. Thompson wound up the season in a tie with Art Bunker for the F-Production (F/P) crown, both men driving 1500 Super Cabriolets. The light and competitive Speedster gave the same title to Bengt Sonderstrom the following year, after which F/P became a Carrera parade. Porsche's stranglehold on the class didn't end until 1960, when SCCA no longer classified cars strictly by engine displacement.

The Speedster proved an ideal race car almost from the first. In 1954 John von Neumann teamed with Erich Bucklers in a 1500 Super to take eighth in the Torrey Pines six-hours the Saturday after Thanksgiving, then won the 1500-cc production class on Sunday. Speedsters have been winning ever since, though they're too valuable these days for anything but carefully staged contests between vintage machines. Yet it's still not uncommon for a Speedster to rocket up Mt. Equinox (now a venue for the Vintage Sports Car Club of America) in fine time or for a well-driven example to run newer iron right out of a road race.

The SCCA's juggling of classifications directly affected the 356 Carrera. Though faster than most everything else in C-Production (C/P), the 356 wasn't normally a match for the small-block Corvettes in B-Production (B/P). This explains a dearth of championship crowns after 1960, when Bruce Jennings won C/P going away. After that,

the Carrera was bumped up to B/P. Even so, Jennings made many incredible assaults on the fiberglass Chevys and occasionally beat them, even in the rain. Road-race crowds, of course, were usually pro-import and cheered Jennings on, which didn't make Corvette fans very happy. SCCA returned the Carreras to C-Production in 1964, and they again dominated, Jennings winning the championship. Richard Smith was Pacific champ in 1965's divisionally divided standings, then national winner in '66. The torch then passed to the 911, but the Carreras, like the Speedsters, are still seen in competition occasionally—and they're as awesome as ever.

European Carreras were mostly in charge of the International Automobile Federation's (FIA) displacement-based 1600 GT class during 1959, but possible challenges from the Lotus Elite and Alfa Giulietta prompted Zuffenhausen to commission 20 special lightweight bodies from Scaglione in Italy. That *carrozzerie* was also supplying bodies to famed engine tuner and race-car designer Carlo Abarth, who became the ostensible builder. Thus was born the Abarth-Carrera GTL.

Though based on the 356B, the GTL looked more like an overgrown version of one of Carlo's Fiat-based coupes. Bodywork was executed in fragile aluminum and bereft of all but the essentials, including bumpers. The cockpit was Spartan, with plastic side windows raised and lowered by simple leather straps. When the first Italian-made GTL arrived in Zuffenhausen, the Germans found their Teutonic physiques didn't fit until some substantial alterations were made! But nobody really minded, because this was the fastest Porsche yet.

Bodywork aside, the Abarth-Carrera was all Porsche. Power was provided by the 1587-cc engine from the roadgoing 356B Carrera, with double coils and distributors to deliver the spark and a pair of twin-choke Weber downdraft carbs. This engine was a marvel of complexity, with four camshafts driven by nine intermediate shafts, 14 bevel gears, and two spur gears. Crankshaft and rod bearings were roller type, but the camshafts ran in plain bearings. Output depended on exhaust system. The tamest setup was good for 115 horsepower; a "racing exhaust" liberated 128 bhp and a "Sebring extractor" design released 135 bhp. To counteract the engine, the brakes were large-diameter aluminum drums with cast-iron liners.

The GTL's first outing came in 1960 at Sicily's mountainous Targa Florio, where Paul Strahle and Herbert Linge placed sixth overall and first in class. GTLs finished 1-2-3 in the 1600-cc Sports

Top: A 356 driven by Otto Mathé plows through a turn at the '53 Internationale Osterreichische Alpenfahrt. These 1.5-liter racers were remarkably durable, able to run trouble-free for thousands of kilometers in a single race. Above: A 356 Sauter-Roadster, photographed in 1951. Note the race-ready windscreen. Opposite page: The racing 356 was based on production cars; the 550, in contrast, was purpose-built for competition. Early versions ran with 1100-cc engines capable of 98 bhp; later ones, such as the 1954-57 models seen here, had more flexible 1500-cc engines. The 550s raced in closed and open body styles. The coupes were particularly aerodynamic and went fast in races where speed was vital; the open models were better suited to endurance contests where visibility was crucial. Top row: 1954 550 Spyder; 1955 550 Spyder, with driver Hans Herrmann. Middle: four-cam 1955 550 RS. Bottom row: 1957 550A-CS.

Class at that year's Nurburgring 1000 Kilometers; the top finisher, a prototype with Porsche's ring-disc brakes, was a creditable seventh overall. There were also class wins in the Sebring 12 Hours and at Le Mans, where a GTL came in 11th overall.

For 1961 the new Type 692/3A engine was installed, with plain bearings swelling the rpm band to 7800. In this form, the highest-tuned GTLs (for Sebring) delivered 140 bhp. Class wins and/or high overall finishes came that year at the Targa, Le Mans, Sebring, and the Paris 1000 Km.

Records are incomplete, but 15 of the 20 GTLs built were apparently sold to private parties. One of these "customer cars" became the first GT car to lap the 14-mile 'Ring in under 10 minutes. A later 1600 example was timed at 138 mph on the Mulsanne Straight at Le Mans, and factory driver Linge felt it might do five mph more.

Porsche engineers were preoccupied in this period with their ultimately unsuccessful assault on Formula 1, so the Abarth-Carrera became the workhorse racer. Porsche had homologated it in the production 1600- and 2000-cc GT classes, and a 2.0-liter version appeared at Daytona in 1963. On Saturday, Huschke von Hanstein, Zuffenhausen's well-known driver/engineer, ran to seventh overall and first in class in a 250-mile contest around the tri-oval. The next day, in a three-hour battle on the infield road course, Joakim Bonnier and Bob Holbert finished seventh and eighth overall and 1-2 in class, with a privately entered GTL right behind.

The Abarth-Carrera hadn't been planned for the 2.0-liter and none were originally built with it, the engine being retrofitted as the needs of competition dictated. All GTLs were built with drum brakes, the Porsche-made ring discs being installed later along with the bigger engine.

For a time, the Porsches most favored for GT racing were the 356B/C Carrera 2s and a lightweight evolution, the 2000GS GT. The latter was mainly for factory teams, which nicknamed it "the wedge" because of its special droop-snoot body with squared-up roof. Many privateers continued to run GTLs (one won the Twin 400 at Bridgehampton, Long Island, in 1962), though by 1964 the new 904 GTS was clearly the Porsche of choice for long-haul contests.

But the GTL had enjoyed an exceptional career. Karl Ludvigsen wrote: "Not until the Seventies did [the name Carrera] regain the original sense of a high-performance variant of the normal production Porsche."

Porsche's fresh 911 design took up arms as the company's production-class warrior for the decade beginning in 1964. SCCA initially put the new model in Class D, where it had little real competition. Jerry Titus won the 1966 D/P title going away in a mildly "prodified" 911 sponsored by Porsche dealer and racing enthusiast Vasek Polak. At Le Mans, meantime, a 911 that had been driven to the race over public roads finished 14th overall—after which it was driven home again, one of the more impressive performances for a race-and-ride sports car to that time.

From the first, special equipment was available for turning the 911 into a track star at relatively low cost. Early examples include suspension package W171, with anti-sway bars, special brake pads, and a driver's footrest. There were also two engine kits, one comprising special carb jets and venturis and rudimentary carb filters, the second with blue-printed heads and manifolds. Together they raised output to 175 bhp to make the 911 formidable in C-Production. Alan Johnson owned that class in 1967-68, as did Milt Minter in '69, after which Datsun took over with its 240Zs. Johnson also won the GT class at Sebring '67 and that year's SCCA national championships at Daytona.

Back in Europe, the 911S was earning fame in the GT Hillclimb Championship and numerous rallies. Vic Elford and David Stone, two expert Englishmen with a 911T, won Porsche its first Monte Carlo Rally in 1968, a triumph Zuffenhausen had long sought. The four-cylinder 912 was also on the scene. Polish driver Sobieslaz Zasada won the 1967 European rally championship and outlasted 375 rivals for an outright win in the Argentine Grand Prix, a 2000-mile open road race that broke more cars than not.

Just barely stock was the 911R, conceived by Ferdinand Piech in 1967 to stretch various rules in rallying and GT racing. The first three Rs had fiberglass bumpers, front fenders, doors, engine cover, and front "hood." Thin-gauge steel was used elsewhere. Hinges were aluminum, and the side and rear windows were Plexiglas. The cockpits were noticeably detrimmed. Fenders were flared to allow wider tires, and twin oil coolers were fitted. The engine (Type 901/22) was much like that of the Type 906/Carrera 6 endurance racer, with the same valve timing, oversize valves and ports, chrome-plated bores, dual ignition, and two triple-throat Type 46 Weber carbs. On 10.3:1 compression, output was 210 bhp at 8000 rpm and 152 pounds/feet of torque at 6000 rpm. One of the 911R's first triumphs was an enduro at Monza: 10,000 miles, 15,000 and 20,000 kilometers, 72 and 90 hours at an

Top and middle: *Porche's 356B 2000 GS/GT bowed for 1960 and was produced through 1963. The car seen here is a '63 model. Body design, by "Butzi" Porsche, earned the car a novel nickname, Dreikantschaber, which means "triangular scraper." The car's 1996-cc four produced 155 horsepower at 6600 rpm; power ran through a four-speed gearbox and limited-slip differential. In 1963 a 2000 GS/GT took third in the Targa Florio, and first in class. Later that year, one finished fourth overall and first in class in the Nurburgring 1000 kilometers.* **Above:** *The 356's production successor, the 911, quickly proved itself a terror in competition. Here, drivers Bjorn Waldegaard and Lars Helmer take on the snow at Monte Carlo 1970.*

Top: *A dirty and battered 911 Carrera negotiates a bit of non-road during the Paris-Dakar rally.* Middle: *Working with a 3.0-liter six, the 1973 Carrera RSR produced 330 horsepower at 8000 rpm, good enough to take seven national and three international championships in its debut season. The #8 car seen here won the 1973 24 Hours of Daytona and the 1973 Targa Florio.* Above: *As its name suggests, the 1974 911 Carrera RSR Turbo/2.1 had a 2.1-liter turbocharged six. What was not immediately apparent was the car's prodigious power output: 500 bhp at 7600 rpm. Fender extensions and an enormous rear wing helped keep the 911 RSR planted on the track. The car took second at Le Mans 1974, and the same at that year's Watkins Glen race.*

average 140+ mph, thus earning Porsche five world records in the 2.0-liter class.

In mid-1967, Porsche assigned the Stuttgart firm of Karl Baur to build 20 more 911Rs, using standard-gauge steel and adding quick-fill fuel tanks and deep bucket seats. The plan was, eventually, to build 500 for homologation in FIA's Grand Touring category. But the sales department didn't think it could move that many, so the project ended. A shame, as there's no telling what the car might have done in GT or SCCA B-Production. Running in the prototype class, one 911R managed an outright win in the 1969 Tour de France, thus demonstrating reliability equal to its performance.

A horde of 911s, factory and private, would continue to do well in major rallies and enduros. A team of 911Es finished 1-2 in the 85-hour Marathon de la Route, held on the taxing Nurburgring in August 1968. The 911S of Bjorn Waldegaard and Lars Helmer gave Porsche another outright Monte Carlo win in 1969, and the car repeated the feat in 1970, when 911s also took second and fourth.

Meanwhile, the intrepid Sobieslaz Zasada had followed his Argentine caper with private entries for the East African Safari rally in 1969 and again in 1970, so Porsche decided to field a three-car team for 1971. These had 180-bhp engines, extra fuel tanks, raised suspensions, beefy torsion bars, and full rally gear. The raised suspensions made shock-absorber rods vulnerable, and two cars had to retire, but Zasada drove the remaining S to fifth place despite an erratic ignition system. Zasada tried again in 1973, and Waldegaard gave it a shot in '74, but neither nailed a win, and Porsche wouldn't achieve outright success in a cross-country rally until the mid-Eighties.

The 911 went on winning major races and rallies through the early Seventies, thanks to a profusion of lightweight competition derivatives. Porsche produced four for the 1970 season alone: 2.2- and 2.3-liter 911STs for production classes; S 2.4, for the Tour de France; S 2.2 Safari, the East African rally version; and the S 2.5, which saw action in rallies *and* track events and was the most powerful, with up to 270 bhp. Though the deviations from stock specifications among these cars are too detailed to list here, suffice it to say that all were basically 911s carefully modified for specific purposes.

That the modifications were possible at all testifies eloquently to the amazing versatility and stamina of the showroom product, reason enough to highlight a few of the 911's more notable successes of these years. Besides the fabled triumph at Monte, 1970 brought outright victories in the Swed-

ish Rally (again campaigned by Waldegaard and Helmer, who managed their third straight victory in that event), the Austrian Alpine, and the Danube and Arctic rallies. In 1971, a 911 was first in GT and sixth overall at Le Mans. The following year, Porsche won the GT championship and FIA Cup for GT cars in Europe and, in America, took the GT Challenge in IMSA (International Motor Sports Association) and the Six Hours of Daytona. Zasada was runner-up in the '72 East African Safari; Gerard Larousse managed likewise at Monte Carlo. The following year brought victories in the Baltic Rally and the tough Circuit of Ireland. Privateers and weekend racers would add many more wins to the 911's scorecard—and continue to do so today.

By 1973, the factory's emphasis shifted to a new sort of 911 weapon based on the reborn Carrera. The first was the Carrera RSR, the all-out version of the roadgoing RS described in Chapter 3. Besides the usual modifications, its flat-six was enlarged to 2806 cubic centimeters (171.2 cubic inches) for an astounding 308 DIN horsepower at 6200 rpm on 10.5:1 compression. The RSR had a splendid career in Group 4, beginning in 1973:

Targa Florio, 1st (Muller/Van Lennep)
Daytona 24 Hours, 1st (Peter Gregg/Hurley Haywood)
Sebring 12 Hours (Gregg/Haywood)
European GT Champion (Claude Ballot-Lena/Clemens Schickentanz)
IMSA GT Champion (Gregg)
SCCA Trans-Am GT Champion (Gregg)

The RSR's beefed-up six was enlarged with some difficulty during the season for the Martini Racing Team, expanding to 2993cc by a further bore increase to 95mm. With 315 bhp, it beat everything in sight at a four-hour Le Mans contest, blasting down the Mulsanne Straight at up to 179 mph.

The beat went on in 1974:

European GT Champion (John Fitzpatrick)
IMSA GT champion (Peter Gregg)

There was also a wild new Group 5 RSR 3.0 with up to 330 bhp (DIN) and very purposeful body alterations: even wider rear fenders with fore and aft air ducts, wider front fenders with trailing-edge vents, and a large air dam with integrated oil cooler. This version was run mainly by the Cologne-based teams of Erwin Kremer and George Loos (Fitzpatrick alternated between them in Group 4) and would shortly lead to even greater things.

RSRs again won everywhere in 1975, including fifth overall at Le Mans and first at the Daytona 24 Hours (again Gregg and Haywood). Porsche claimed another GT championship in IMSA and Europe (the latter courtesy of Hartwig Bertrams), as well as that year's European hillclimb crown (Swiss driver Jean-Claude Berling) and the FIA GT World Cup. The IMSA title came despite determined efforts from BMW and even General Motors to end their yearly embarrassment at Porsche's hands. Gregg/Haywood won eight of the 14 events. Porsche drivers also took the second and third spots. Last but not least, Porsche was 1975's German rally champ. On these high notes ended the era of the normally aspirated 911 and its derivatives.

Meantime, the humble little 914 had been earning its share of glory, with most of the factory's efforts predictably centered on the Porsche-powered 914/6. Competition versions were often tested on rally routes, but the emphasis was on track racing, not rallies, which were 911 territory.

The American "Porsche + Audi" organization made a lukewarm 1970 effort in SCCA C-Production, the always hotly contested class then dominated by the Datsun 240Z and Triumph TR6, both amply supported by their makers. The 914/6 proved competitive, winning four of seven divisional championships, but was overpowered by the Z-cars at the national runoffs, where John Morton's Datsun prevailed. Porsche factory backing then melted, and though the mid-engine model later repeated as champ in several divisions, it never captured the national crown.

For a time, the special 914/6 GT carried Porsche's colors in European Group 4 events. Ultra-wide rolling stock and bulging fenders (actually welded-on extensions) identified it. The engine remained at 2.0 liters but was highly modified, with Weber carbs instead of fuel injection, special heads, dual ignition, high-dome pistons, and aluminum cylinders. Horsepower was between 210 and 220 (DIN), and suspension and brakes were appropriately upgraded.

Four 914/6 GTs performed well at the 1970 Nurburgring 1000 Kilometers, finishing 2-5 behind the class winner, a 911L. A single car contested that year's Le Mans enduro, where it surprised everyone by taking first in class and sixth overall in a gale-lashed ordeal of severe attrition. Driven by Guy Chasseuil and Claude Ballot-Lena of France, it averaged 99.27 mph and 13.56 miles per gallon, good for second in the Index of Efficiency. 914/6 GTs breezed home 1-2-3 at the Marathon de la Route (two run-

ning in Group 6 because of their extra-wide tires and fender bubbles). Another pair, driven by Prince von Hohenzollern and Gunther Steckkonig, finished 1-2 at the Osterreichring, earning enough points for Porsche to clinch the international GT trophy. But smiles turned to frowns when a GT assault on the 1971 Monte Carlo Rally was stopped cold by the Alpine-Renaults, which gave away 400cc yet were faster than the 914s.

Back in the States, the 914/6 fared better in IMSA's 1971 GT Challenge. Gregg and Haywood dominated in the Brumos Porsche car (sponsored by Gregg's Jacksonville, Florida, dealership), which won two of the six rounds outright, making Porsche the under-2.5-liter champ. The SCCA, however, stopped the 914's fun the following season by moving it to B-Production, the category dominated by Allan Barker's Corvettes between 1969 and '72.

Meanwhile, back at the Zuffenhausen ranch, racing had bred some exciting new animals. Porsche's success in taming turbochargers for its 1100-hp Can-Am and Interserie racers (detailed later) had its roadgoing result in a turbocharged 911, the Type 930, and competition versions started appearing almost immediately. Following the Martini & Rossi team's 1974 foray with a 2.1-liter development car, Porsche introduced a Group 4 Type 930 for the 1976 season. Logically tagged 934, it had a basically stock body with pop-riveted fiberglass fender flares and a huge front airdam, plus a whale tail rear spoiler. To meet the minimum weight standard (1120 kg/2740 lbs), the road car's power-window lifts and many other amenities were actually left *in*.

Suspension was suitably fortified with coil springs atop gas-filled Bilstein shock absorbers, and hard plastic replaced rubber in control-arm bushings. Both front and rear anti-roll bars were adjustable to suit various tracks. Tires were Goodyear racing specials, and brakes were borrowed from the fearsome 917 racer, with cross-drilled discs and finned wheel cylinders (for heat dissipation) and twin master cylinders.

Because Group 4 required a near-stock engine, the 934's main mechanical changes from 930 specs were higher turbo boost and different valve timing and overlap. In the interest of reliability and, again, to suit different track requirements, boost pressure could be varied (to a maximum 18.5 pounds/square inches) via a dashboard knob. An interesting fillip was water-cooling, not for the engine but to handle the hotter turbo-compressed air and improve volumetric efficiency. It took the form of what we now

Top: *Driver Sobieslaz Zasada piloted a 911S to the 1967 rally championship on a route that stretched from Lyon to Charbonnieres.* Middle: *Decades later, 911s dominated Carrera Cup events.* Above: *The frequently maligned Porsche 914 made its mark in competition, in 914/6 racing guise. With a six-cylinder engine pumping out 210 bhp, good for a top speed of 149 mph, a 914/6 finished sixth overall at Le Mans 1970.* Opposite page, top and second from top, right: *The 1977 935/2.0 "Baby" was based on the 935 Group 5 racer. Running with a 1.4-liter six-cylinder turbo rated at 370 horses, the Baby won the 1977 German championship race at Hockenheim.* Other photos: *The 935 proved itself the preeminent endurance racer between 1976 and 1981. This 1978 variant, the 935/78 "Moby Dick," cranked out 750 horsepower and won that year's 1000 kilometers at Silverstone.*

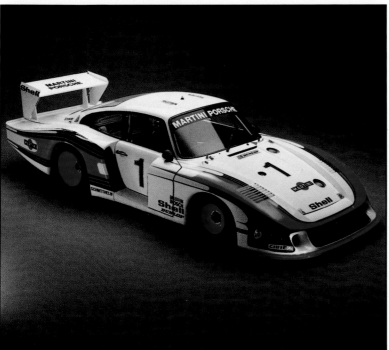

call an air-to-water intercooler, with a water/alcohol cocktail as the cooling medium. The cooler itself was located in the front airdam, much like the oil coolers on earlier Carrera RSRs. Another departure was retention of the road car's Bosch K-Jetronic fuel injection, again modified for racing.

All this (literally) boosted horsepower to a rated 485 (DIN) at 7000 rpm; by 1977 it was up to 540. Torque was a prodigious 420 pounds/feet at 5400 rpm. Porsche built 31 of these 3.0-liter "customer" cars (officially Type 934 Turbo RSR) and sold every one for about $40,000 apiece.

For Group 5 there was an even wilder evolution dictated by class requirements. Called *935*, it was based on and resembled the 930 because FIA rules precluded purpose-designed cars. This resulted in so-called "silhouette" racers that looked like street models—but only somewhat. For performance, the 935 towered over the 930 the way a 911 did over a VW Beetle.

The first two 935s built were factory prototypes with hardly a trace of 930. Doors, fenders, deck, hood, and spoilers were fiberglass; windows were Plexiglas. Porsche shaved so much weight, in fact, that it had to add 154 pounds to meet the required minimum (970 kg/2138 lbs sans fuel). Naturally, all the ballast went up front, resulting in a fine 47/53-percent front/rear weight distribution.

Things were surprisingly stock inside except for a single racing bucket seat and the mandatory roll cage. A big 8000-rpm tach dominated the dash, surrounded by turbo-boost and other gauges. A central lever allowed the driver to adjust rear anti-roll bar stiffness to suit weight-distribution changes as fuel was used. The front bar was adjustable, too. Suspension comprised adjustable front coil springs made of titanium (replacing the normal torsion bars) and rear trailing arms. Brakes were basically 934 with extra cooling ducts. Rear tires were an eye-popping 19 inches wide, the fronts 16 inches, all mounting on racing rims 14½ inches in diameter.

Group 5 imposed a sort of "handicap" on turbo-engine displacement, which was multiplied by 1.4 for comparison with normally aspirated engines. As the latter were limited to a maximum 4.0 liters, Porsche debored the 930's flat six to 92mm and 2857cc, equivalent to exactly 3999.8cc to meet the rules. More engine tweaks were allowed than in Group 4, so Bosch mechanical injection replaced K-Jetronic, dual ignition and many lightweight internal components (such as titanium con rods) were fitted, and boost pressure was set at 19-22 psi. Result: 590 DIN horsepower at 7900 rpm and 434

pounds/feet of torque at 5400.

In their 1975 debut season, the 935s had front bodywork much like that of the 930 and 934. But the following year brought the first of the now-famous hidden-headlamp "droop snoot" cars, with a lower and smoother *Flachbau* (flat profile) front developed in Porsche's Weissach wind tunnel. Rear bodywork became unbelievably wide and wild for both European and American events. Besides an assortment of radical scoops and ducts, the later 935/77 and 935/78 versions had huge spoilers, sometimes bridging tall shark-like fins molded into the rear quarters. Other cars wore finny "strakes" fared into the upper rear roof and extending aft to form short struts on which the wing mounted. Configurations varied among the different teams, but all were sure to attract attention at any race.

Their performance certainly did. With the long-tailed "Moby Dick" of 1978, the 935 was producing an incredible 845 bhp at 8200 rpm, thanks to developments like four valves per cylinder and water-cooled cylinder heads.

Needless to say, the 934 and 935 had incredible performance. *Road & Track* tested both in 1977 with these results:

	934	935
0-30 mph (sec)	3.9	1.6
0-60 mph (sec)	5.8	3.3
0-80 mph (sec)	7.7	4.4
0-100 mph (sec)	10.1	6.1
0-¼ mi (sec)	14.2	8.9
Speed at ¼ mi (mph)	121.5	133.5

Porsche's hopes of a GT championship were temporarily dashed in 1976, when IMSA initially banned turbocars (the ban was lifted at mid-season). There was no such problem in the Trans-Am class, however, where Porsche won the championship, with George Follmer first in points (with a 934), followed by Hurley Haywood, both of Holbert Racing.

The 935 had similar troubles with the FIA when, after taking the first two events in the European GT series, the cars were forced to run with the 930's rear spoiler, which required adapting the 934's "waterworks" for proper cooling. Despite some mid-season stumbles after these and other modifications, Porsche managed to take the Makes Championship late in the tour by outlasting BMW's winged CSL coupes at Watkins Glen. As this was the first time a hyperaspirated car had won the title, the 935 started a revolution. From

Top and middle: *Fitted with a 2.5-liter turbo good for 410 bhp at 6500 rpm, Porsche's 944 GTP Le Mans took seventh place in the 1981 event—a quite credible showing for a new engine. In addition, the GTP spent just 56 minutes of the race in the pits, the least time of any entrant. Above: The 944 evolved from the 924 and picked up turbo power late in 1985. Seen here is a racing version in 1988 Turbo Cup competition.*

The Type 718 RS 60 Spyder of 1960 was an improved version of the 718 RSK that made its debut in 1958. By 1960, the 718's 1.6-liter four had been upgraded from 148 bhp to 160. The car performed well at a variety of long-distance venues, including the 1960 Targa Florio (first place) and Sebring (first and second); it won the European Hillclimb championships in 1960 and '61. In the top photo, Umberto Maglioli puts a 718 RSK through its paces at the 1000-kilometer race at Nurburgring, 1957.

here on it took a turbo to win in Group 5—a Porsche Turbo.

And 935s continued to win and dominate every series. Again, the record is too long to detail, but highlights include three consecutive Makes titles 1977-79 and an outright victory at Le Mans 1979—the first by a production-based car since the 1953 Jaguar C-Type's. In North America the 935 was IMSA GT champion in 1978-80 and took the 1979 SCCA Trans-Am title. Its last victory occurred in March 1984 (first overall in the Sebring 12 Hours). By then the baton had passed to the even more specialized 936, 956, and 962, though they, too, relied on engines firmly rooted in that of the original 911.

Remarkably, the basic 911 itself continued making motorsports history. One hero was the 961, competition cousin to the miraculous, high-tech 959 (see Chapter 3). Its first outing was the car-killing Paris-Dakar Rally of 1986, which it won going away. The 961 also did well in its first track appearance, the 1986 Daytona 24 Hours. Had not a series of tragic accidents ended the Group B rallies for which it was originally designed, production might have gone higher than the 25 units Porsche planned to build. But as we've seen, its technological precepts would live on in the later 911 Carrera 4.

As for the stalwart standard models, their tally of victories never seems to end. Highlights of recent seasons include 15 race wins in IMSA's Supercar category for the 911 Turbo, leading to three straight Manufacturers Championships: 1991 (driver Hurley Haywood), '92 ("Doc" Bundy), and '93 (Hans Stuck).

We cannot leave the faithful old 911 without celebrating the special accomplishment of one particular four-wheel-drive model driven in SCCA's high-speed PRO Rally events by California cinematographer Jeff Zwart. Though the venerable rear-engine Porsche has generally been outshone here in recent years by front-engine cars, which are more forgiving of the sudden surprises on gravel roads that make this branch of the sport so exciting, Zwart relished the challenge. After a couple of learning seasons, he scored his first overall victory in 1994, followed with two more, and wound up second in points to Audi's perennial champion Paul Choiniere. Not bad for a working stiff who couldn't make every round of the series.

Midway through the season, Zwart took his faithful (if increasingly battered) 300-horsepower Carrera 4 on a little side jaunt to Colorado, where he temporarily treated it to a turbocharged 450-bhp engine, lowered its ride-height, and won his

class in the Pikes Peak Hill Climb. Porsche is the car of the enthusiast, and there can't be many enthusiasts who get more enjoyment from their Porsches than Zwart.

As for Porsche's own front-engine cars, they've certainly been successful in their way. The 924 participated in many major rallies, and though it never managed a win, it did post a creditable 20th overall in the 1979 Monte Carlo against a horde of more powerful rivals. Racing was a more successful venue, the 924 earning national SCCA D-Production championships for "Doc" Bundy in 1980 and Tom Brennan in '81. The latter repeated in 1985, when the category was known as GT-3.

But the model's big triumph was the first-in-class and remarkable sixth overall scored by a 924 "prototype" at Le Mans 1981. Manfred Schurti and Jurgen Barth drove the car, which was actually a sneak preview of the new 944 announced two weeks later. Based on the European 924 Carrera GT, the prototype was powered by a 16-valve version of the new Porsche-designed four, thus providing a very early look at the new-for-'87 944S engine (though no one outside Porsche then knew that, of course).

When the 924 Turbo appeared, Group 4 versions were developed for Europe, with a basically stock body mounting fiberglass doors and hatch as well as Carrera-style flared fenders to accommodate racing footwear. DIN horsepower was 310-320 with Kugelfischer injection. One of these cars proved faster than even the quickest RSR Carrera in 1980 tests at Le Mans. Two years later, Doc Bundy and Jim Busby rode to GT-class glory in the legendary French event with a 924 Carrera Turbo running on street tires.

Speaking of the street, the four-cylinder Porsches have earned many honors in what quickly became known as "showroom stock" racing. Interest in SS racing rose dramatically in the early Seventies, when IMSA president John Bishop began reviving the kind of "run what ya brung" competition so popular in the early postwar years. By mid-decade, the SCCA had established a professional SS class of its own, and Ken Williams captured the 1980 national crown with his 924. In 1985, a separate Escort Endurance Series (named for a brand of radar detector) was formed for SS cars in SCCA. IMSA's counterpart was the Firestone Firehawk Challenge.

Because SCCA allowed Corvettes in SS, the 944s initially fared none too well overall. But they dominated the Firehawk Challenge, winning the championship in inaugural '84. The 944 repeated in 1985, with Walt Maas and John Milledge taking five of the eight events. That same year, the 944 Turbo was SCCA showroom-stock champion, and non-turbo models grabbed the Escort series. Firehawk success rolled on, with 944S2s winning championships in 1991, 1992, and 1994 for a total of 37 race victories through the end of that season.

The "Longest Day" 24-hour enduro at the Nelson Ledges course in Ohio doesn't count toward the SS championship but has provided several interesting Porsche anecdotes. The first running, in June 1981, saw a well-prepped 924 outlast a variety of rivals, including a squad of Ford EXP/Mercury LN7s piloted by *Car and Driver* and *Road & Track* staffers. In 1982, a then-new 944 blithely repeated the victory (this time, beating the *C/D* and *R&T* crews, who were running prototype Mustangs). The following year, a new 944 Turbo was entered but didn't win—sending the Weissach gnomes racing to devise improvements that were eventually incorporated on production models. Then, in 1984, the SS class was won by a stock 944 with 23,000 miles on the odometer.

Further improving its four-cylinder breed, Porsche conjured up a special 300-bhp 944S, then an even wilder 944 Turbo GTR; both were intended for the SCCA's more liberal Street Stock series. The former was a lightweight flyer with fiberglass bodywork and an aluminum-tube frame with stock 944 suspension and the big cross-drilled brakes from the 962. Top speed exceeded 160 mph. The Turbo GTR, the first Porsche designed and built for American road racing, was the same formula bolstered by full competition suspension and an engine coaxed to 575 bhp by Andial of California. That was good for around 175 mph.

Even the luxurious, V-8-powered 928 has a track credit or two. In December 1982, a European model covered over 3700 miles at an average of 155 mph on the Nardo track outside Brindisi in southern Italy. Establishing themselves as "the world's fastest Sunday drivers," the international team of Gerhard Plattner (Austria), Peter Lovett (Great Britain), and Peter Abinden (Switzerland) experienced no real problems, requiring only replacement tires. With less than half the horsepower of the Porsche 956 that won the 1982 LeMans, the 928 actually went faster on the circular track. And mention should be made of Al Holbert's speed records at Bonneville in 1986 (see Chapter 6).

Recently, of course, the eyes of Porsche fans have smiled on the race debut of the new 993-Series 911. What is certain to be a continuation of the "old" car's near-infinite record of victories has already begun, with six race wins and the championship in

the SCCA's World Challenge for 1994.

There are many more examples we could cite, but the point is clear: Porsche learns from competition and, perhaps more intensively than any other make, applies that experience to the cars it sells.

Part II: The Sports Racers

As a company founded by a man who had chosen to demonstrate his Lohner electric by setting a record time on the Semmerling hillclimb course in September 1900, Porsche was a group of people with racing fever in their blood. Modified production sports cars were never going to cool their brows. As early as they could manage, they began creating special sports cars specifically for racing—and for high-intensity research and development of production components.

Type 550 Spyder

Porsche's first purpose-built racing model was powered by Ernst Fuhrmann's four-cam version of the air-cooled opposed four that would motivate the exciting 356 Carrera sports coupe. The first move toward this model actually was made not in Zuffenhausen but some 100 miles to the north, in Frankfurt. Walter Glockler had been a successful racer of motorcycles and 1.5-liter cars in the prewar years. He was also a capable engineer and after the war decided to build and race a car of his own design. Constructed at his large VW distributorship in Frankfurt and completed in 1950, it looked so much like the eventual 550 Spyder that Glockler has always been credited as its "father."

Measuring just 78 inches long, Glockler's *Eigenbau* ("own construction") was a smooth, lozenge-shaped roadster with a tubular frame. An 1100-cc Porsche engine, modified to develop 53 DIN horsepower on alcohol, was mounted amidships, ahead of the rear-wheel axis. This layout, chosen for optimum weight distribution, naturally followed that specified by Dr. Porsche himself for the much bigger, vastly more powerful Auto Union Grand Prix racers of the 1930s.

Glockler's special immediately proved itself, winning the German 1100-cc championship in 1950-52—same car, different drivers. Glocker then went on to an improved body and a 1500 Porsche engine with 90 bhp. The result, called *Glocker-Porsche*, captured for Germany the Bugatti-class records on France's Monthlery track in 1952. With all this and more, Porsche's reputation as a builder of durable, race-winning components was firmly established.

In contrast to its RSK predecessor, the 718 RS 60 Spyder had a larger windshield, larger-diameter drum brakes, and a real trunk in the tail. The chassis was a steel-tube space frame, with independent suspension; torsion bars were used in front, coil springs at the rear. A five-speed gearbox helped put the power to the track. When Joakim Bonnier and Hans Herrmann drove an RS 60 to victory in the 1960 Targo Florio, they finished more than six minutes ahead of the 3.0-liter Ferrari that finished second.

Though a 356 won its class at the 1951 Le Mans 24 Hours, Ferry Porsche and Karl Rabe concluded that their production pushrod engine would no longer be enough for endurance events. Accordingly, Rabe and Fuhrmann explored the potential of a competition 1500 with four camshafts placed atop the cylinder barrels to serve the four widely spaced sets of valves. A prototype designated Type 547 was on the Zuffenhausen dynamometer by spring 1952, but minor development problems delayed mating it with its intended body/chassis, a new design created expressly for racing and coded project 550.

To fill the gap, the Type 550 platform, a coupe style from Weidenhausen in Frankfurt, was fitted with a souped-up Type 528 pushrod engine for the 1953 season. It promptly won the *Eifelrennen* at the Nurburgring and distinguished itself on other European circuits.

The four-cam was ready by August 1953, and it propelled former Auto Union pilot Hans Stuck to a class win in the Freiburg hillclimb. But its first real test was the gruelling Mille Miglia the following spring, when Hans Hermann and Herbert Linge drove to victory in the 1500-cc sports class. By this time the car was known as a Spyder, meaning a light, high-performance sports car. Porsche referred to it as 1500RS (RS for *rennsport*, racing sport).

Like Glockler's special, the 550 Spyder had a tubular frame (with slight kickups front and rear) and a smooth, low-slung open body. Wheelbase was a compact 82.7 inches, weight a shade over 1200 pounds. A front-mounted oil radiator, four-speed Porsche gearbox, Ross-type steering, and Porsche's usual all-independent torsion-bar suspension were on hand, along with three mechanical features unique even to Porsche: a double-admission cooling blower, large separate oil tank, and dry-sump lubrication.

Spyder body production shifted several times after *Karosseriebau* Weinsberg built the first few hulls. It was late 1954 by the time all the engine problems were sorted out, and privateers had been waiting months for the Spyder. What they ultimately got was the Type 550S (Sport), the "customer" model with bodywork supplied by Wendler of Reutlingen and priced at DM25,000 or about $5500. A factory car driven by Huschke von Hanstein finished eighth overall in the Sports Car Grand Prix at Caracas, Venezuela, battling a field of Maseratis and Ferraris.

Several options were offered for customer Spyders: center-lock wire wheels (modified and laced by Glocker), the necessary axle and hub adapters,

and chrome center-lock disc wheels to match post-1954 brake drums. A later catalog listed lightweight rims for the factory RS, saving about 4.5 pounds per wheel. Swiss engineer and Spyder owner Michael May offered Porsche a specially designed airfoil to improve rear-end adhesion, but management rejected this forecast of the later Chaparral wing on the grounds that it obstructed driver vision.

By the mid-Fifties, factory-sponsored Spyders were exceeding 120 mph with a degree of reliability unknown to most competitors. Ken Purdy wrote: "So fantastically durable were these cars that it was only in the most trying races, say the 24-hour Le Mans or Sebring, that they demonstrated their uncanny ability to run flat-out hour after hour while ordinary attrition strewed the dead-car park with blown-up examples of lesser makes. As the hours passed, spectators at long-distance events came to realize that there were two dominant sounds in the cacophony of passing exhaust howls: the high scream of the Ferraris and the lower-pitched booming of the Porsches."

But competition was rife in those days, and by mid-1956 it had prodded Porsche to produce an improved Spyder, the 550A. Retaining much of the original's appearance, it packed 135 DIN horsepower on 9.8:1 compression (previously 9.5:1), a new five-speed gearbox, and double-jointed swing axles with lower fulcrums. Fuel capacity for long-distance events, always a Porsche specialty, was 28.6 gallons from a main tank and auxiliaries. Plug reach was increased to ¾-inch and a Hirth roller-bearing crank was installed along with lightweight cylinder barrels. It all made for a very free and fast-revving engine that was seemingly unbreakable.

Yet the Spyder was also surprisingly tractable off the track (if less than practical as a road car). In fact, many of the 100-odd built for FIA homologation are around today, having seen little or no race action but admired as much for their functional beauty as their performance.

Predictably for a Porsche, the Spyder evolved progressively through higher power and more sophisticated design. The 550A, for example, not only had more horses but a lighter, chest-high steel-tube space frame. A works training car now known as the RSK Spyder was tested the following year, when the 550 gave way to the new type.

Type RSK 718/1500 and RS60

This highly evolved model became available in early 1958. The K referred to a new front suspen-

Porsche did not experiment with fiberglass bodies until 1964, when the technology was put to use on the Type 904 Carrera GTS. One hundred 904s had to be built to satisfy homologation requirements; in all, 116 were assembled, with an additional four kept on hand for spare parts. The sleek design by Butzi Porsche was distinguished by an elongated nose, "flying buttress" roofline, and kammback tail.

sion that deviated from Porsche practice in having angled upper members that suggested that letter. Variable-rate coil springs concentric with the shock absorbers replaced the Spyder's rear torsion bars, resulting in more neutral handling. Driven by the famous Jean Behra, a 1500RSK with 142 bhp (DIN) and single-seat bodywork won the 1958 Formula 2 contest at Rheims, France, besting 14 Coopers, three Lotuses, three OSCAs, and a six-cylinder Ferrari. It could reach 155 mph at 8000 rpm. Porsche also won that year's European Mountain Championship with the 718 *Bergspyder,* a special hillclimb version.

For 1959, the RSK was upgraded to a 1.6-liter four-cam with 148 bhp (DIN) at 5800 rpm. It debuted at that year's F2 race in Monte Carlo, where Wolfgang von Trips crashed it on the first lap. Rear suspension underwent a major change at season's end, with a new coil-spring/wishbone layout very much like that of the 718 F2 car, in keeping with Porsche's policy of applying competition experience to "production" vehicles.

By that point, the Spyder had apparently reached its full potential. Porsche placed third in the world sports-car championship in 1958 and '59—amazing for 1500- and 1600-cc challengers to machines with up to 3.0 liters. And Porsche again showed its hillclimb prowess in '59, finishing 1-5 in that year's international championship.

The "K" designation vanished for 1960 in favor of *RS60.* Expected FIA rules changes for 1962 prompted a wait-and-see attitude in Zuffenhausen, so the Spyders were little changed in the meantime. Wheelbase was stretched by 100mm (3.94 inches) for '61, wider 16-inch-diameter wheels replaced the previous 15s, and the cars were fitted with both 1.5- and 1.6-liter engines. Twelve cars went to private racers; four stayed with the factory. With the trend toward more cylinders now underway and Porsche increasingly busy with its eight-cylinder Formula 1 car, the Spyder program was halted in early 1962.

Inevitably, Spyders weren't built like production Porsches. Bodies were hammered out of aluminum over wooden forms, and during the entire nine years of production, assembly work was carried out by perhaps only a dozen selected artisans. With care and many years of experience, they put each car together piece by piece.

The Spyders were surely the ultimate expression of the three characteristics that most clearly defined early Porsches: air cooling, rear engine mounting, and giant-killing power derived from midget-size displacement. They also proved the

Most 904s ran with 180-bhp four-cylinder engines, but some went into action with six- and even eight-cylinder powerplants. A four-cylinder 904 captured the 1964 Targa Florio; other 1964 victories included the 1000-kilometer race at Nurburgring and the Tour de France.

worth of simple, lightweight construction, being both fast and ironclad reliable in the most gruelling of races. They testify to the formidable engineering skill Porsche could muster even in its earliest days.

Type 904 Carrera GTS

The Spyder's day was over by 1963. With competition in the "big leagues" heating up, Porsche saw that it was time for more specialized racing machines that owed less to road-car technology. The car that marked this historic turn was the 904 Carrera GTS. It was the last competition Porsche with anything like a "stock" engine, and thus the last that might be used on the street—if you insisted—yet it set the pattern for every "deluxe" competition Porsche to follow.

Which is a bit surprising because, except for a fiberglass body, the 904 broke no new technical ground. David Owen wrote that it "was beautiful, but it wasn't as aerodynamically efficient as it could have been. It was tough . . . but it wasn't as light as it should have been. And it used the old four-cam four-cylinder engine, stretched in this case to 1966cc [120 cubic inches] and producing (ultimately) 195 bhp [some sources list 185 DIN] ahead of the rear wheels." The 904's boxed-rail chassis, said *Car and Driver,* "might be straight out of Frank Kurtis' design book."

All true enough. Yet the 904 was one of the prettiest Porsches of all time: low, sleek, exquisitely shaped. And it went like almighty clappers. "Time and again," Owen continued, "in races like the 1964 Rheims 12 Hours, the Porsches would come roaring home just behind the big Ferraris." With it, Porsche returned to prominence in international sports-car competition.

Work on the 904 had begun in 1962, when a wood body buck was built to a design by Ferdinand "Butzi" Porsche, grandson of the company founder and creator of the 901/911. This was sent in February 1963 to Heinkel, the aircraft firm, which returned the first finished body the following November.

Certain 904 elements were influenced by Porsche's abortive 804 Formula 1 car, notably the all-around double-wishbone suspension. The rear employed four-link geometry, with upper and lower pairs of parallel trailing arms and reversed wishbones. Telescopic shocks and coil springs appeared at both ends in lieu of lateral torsion bars. Steering was the new ZF rack-and-pinion mechanism from the recently announced 901/911, which also supplied the 904's five-speed transaxle.

Brakes were outboard Dunlop/Ate four-wheel discs; tiny drums were provided inside the rear rotors for the handbrake *a la* the 356C.

To speed pit stops, bodywork behind the doors was a one-piece assembly that lifted up on rear hinges, and the engine could be easily removed for more serious servicing. Such convenience didn't extend to body repairs, however, as Porsche found it extremely difficult to fix broken panels quickly.

FIA rules at the time required 100 units to qualify a car for GT-class racing, and Porsche completed that number of 904s by April 1964. The first six were retained as factory team cars and were eventually seen with four-, six-, and eight-cylinder engines. The first dozen or so customer cars went to the United States, where the racing season started earlier than in Europe. Unfortunately, only these 100 would be built. All were quickly snapped up, leaving many would-be buyers disappointed.

Fitted for road work, the 904 greeted its driver with a full set of gauges dominated by a 9000-rpm tachometer. Deep bucket seats didn't adjust, but pedals did. Different size seats were available to further accommodate various physiques. A huge single wiper swept laterally on a pantograph arm for maximum coverage.

It all sounds quite civilized, but the Carrera four didn't like stop-and-go traffic, and the car as a whole wasn't as successful for touring as it was in racing. Most 904s now used on the road have been retrofitted with 911 engines, which does nothing for a cockpit that was never designed for relaxed highway cruising and totally lacks sound insulation. But then, this was a racing car—a real one.

"Ze machine," cracked *C/D*'s Brock Yates, "ist chust an oldt Carrera mohtorr vis only 130 horses. Ist much better vis too-litah 180-horrsepowerr rracing enchine. . . . Oh sure, only 130 hp. It didn't seem hardly enough to do any more than pool all our blood along our jellied spine, break our glasses across the bridge of our nose and leave the impression of our belt buckle on our stomach." Huschke von Hanstein, giving Yates his first 904 ride, was doing 100 mph three blocks from the factory. "You're sure President Johnson does this?" Yates asked. "Ja shoor—look!" Huschke removed both hands from the small wood-rimmed wheel. "The 904 tracked along as steadily at 120 mph as a Yankee Clipper."

Test results showed 0-60 mph times of 5.5-6.1 seconds and a 160-mph observed top speed. And no surprise when you realize that, pudgy though it was, the 904 was the first Carrera with a sub-10 pounds/bhp weight-to-power ratio: about 8 lbs/

bhp—smack dab in muscle-car territory. And it could run at 160 all day long if necessary, as reliable as Big Ben.

The quadcam Carrera engine may have been 10 years old by then but was at its developmental peak, while the mid-engine layout made for superb handling. Though the highish weight reduced the 904's effectiveness in short-distance "sprint" contests, it proved no great handicap in longer races on less-than-perfect surfaces. A 904 might not outrun competitors, but it could almost certainly outlast them.

Successes both factory and private came quickly for the 904, with longer events the predictable forte of this almost too-sturdy machine. Clutch problems prevented a finish at Sebring 1964, the car's debut outing, but things went better a month later when 904s ran first and third in the Targa Florio, leading a fleet of Ferraris and Shelby Cobras. Next came a third overall in the Nurburgring 1000 Kilometers. Five Porsches contested Le Mans that year and all finished in the top 12, the highest placing seventh overall. In the Tour de France, 904s ran third through sixth (behind a brace of Ferrari GTOs) and were first and second on handicap.

For 1965, Porsche fitted a revalved Carrera engine with a reprofiled camshaft. Horsepower went up again in 1966 via higher compression. As mentioned, a few 904s were seen with more than four cylinders: the 2.0-liter flat six from the 911, tuned for up to 210 DIN horsepower, and the potent 2.2-liter Type 771/1 eight, derived from the 804 F1 engine of 1962, with up to 270 bhp—more than double the initial 130.

The 904 was nothing if not versatile, and it did well in major rallies. For example, Porsche acquired the services of ace Mercedes driver Eugen Bohringer for the 1965 Monte Carlo. One of only 22 of 237 starters to finish, he placed second overall in one of the snowiest Montes ever.

Though costly by 1964 standards at $7425, the 904 was a remarkable bargain, all things considered. A pity that more weren't made.

Type 906 Carrera 6

Another production-based powerplant appeared in Porsche's next "deluxe" racer, only now it was the 911 flat-six. It, too, was mounted amidships in an all-out competition machine, the first Porsche designed by Dr. Ferry Porsche's young nephew, Ferdinand Piech, who'd helped develop the engine.

The 906 was built around an ultra-light tubular space-frame topped by a very streamlined body

Porsche's competition use of fiberglass bodies continued with the 1966 Type 906, a lightweight racer that made excellent use of the 210-220 bhp generated by its air-cooled six; top speed was 165 mph. The car was designed by Ferry Porsche's nephew, Ferdinand Piech, who broke with Porsche tradition by utilizing wing-style doors. The 906 debuted at Daytona 1966, where it finished sixth overall—a splendid showing for a new vehicle.

with an overall height of only 38.6 inches. The engine, turned 180 degrees from its 911 position, was quite similar to the production unit in basic design but significantly lighter, making extensive use of magnesium and aluminum alloys. With dual ignition, 10.3:1 compression, two triple-throat Weber 46IDA carburetors, and special manifolds and exhaust system, this Type 901/20 put out 210-220 bhp (DIN) at 8000 rpm and 145 pounds/feet peak torque at 6000 rpm. Clutch and transaxle were 911-based, and specific gearsets were devised for various tracks and race distances.

The first outing for the 906 was the 1966 Daytona 24 Hours, where a dark-blue car finished sixth, beaten only by a factory team of fleet Ford GTs and a single Ferrari. The lead car at Sebring spun out, but 906s nailed fourth, sixth, and eighth. At the Targa Florio that year they ended up 1-3-4-8. Ford's huge 7.0-liter GTs dominated Le Mans, but the 2.0 Carrera 6s were right behind, 4-5-6-7.

The Carrera 6's lineal successor was the 1967 Type 910/6, which used the same engine in an even lighter space-frame topped by more handsome and slippery fiberglass bodywork. There was also a 270-bhp flat-eight variation, the 910/8, powered by the 2.2-liter Type 771/1 engine. One of these appeared at the 1967 Targa Florio, where 910/6s placed second and third. Six-cylinder cars also finished high at Daytona, Sebring, Monza, and Spa, while a trio cleaned up at the Nurburgring 1000 Kilometers. A 910/8 might have led them home but suffered an electrical failure on the last lap. Porsche outscored Ferrari in 1967 Manufacturers Championship points, helped by a class win at Le Mans by one of the new 907s, but Ferrari prevailed because only the best five races counted.

Racing developments came thick and fast in the late Sixties; those from Porsche were mostly logical evolutions. Thus, the 904's suspension and brakes went into the 906, whose frame was lightened and modified for the 910. Next came the 907, which started out as a more aerodynamic 910, with the same six- and eight-cylinder engines and somewhat smoother bodywork, again in K (*Kurzheck*, short-tail) and L (*Langheck*, long-tail) guises. The next step was the 908, basically a 907 with a new and simpler 3.0-liter flat eight.

Type 908

This is the car that put Porsche in the big time, turning the make into a contender for overall wins instead of just class honors. 908 development was prompted by the FIA's 3.0-liter displacement ceiling on prototype-class racing for 1968, which followed an earlier move by the Le Mans organizers after Ford's giant GTs swept the 24 Hours for the second time in 1967. Porsche probably didn't influence these decisions, but racing manager Huschke von Hanstein was certainly close enough to keep track of them.

Work on the new engine got underway in July 1967. With 2977cc (181.6 cid) and a formidable 350 DIN horsepower, it was exactly right for the new formula. Though less powerful than leftover Ford GT40s, which could still use 5.0 pushrod engines, the four-cam Porsche was sufficiently lighter and was faster overall on most tracks.

Piech and his engineers faced but one obstacle in developing the Type 908 engine: money. But an expensive ground-up design wasn't necessary. Instead, the team simply added two cylinders to the 911 engine, changed to magnesium-alloy construction, bolted on twincam cylinder heads, and stretched bore by 5mm (to 85mm). Completing the transformation were a titanium-alloy flywheel and titanium con rods. Putting power to the ground was a hefty transaxle with six forward speeds for coupes, five on the later (1969) 908 Spyders. Porsche insiders jokingly termed this the "injection gearbox" because lubrication was via an oil jet directed at each pair of gears.

Outside, the first 908s were difficult to distinguish from 907s—mainly because they *were* 907s with aerodynamic refinements; only minimal chassis modifications were needed to accommodate the new engine. But after a "907/8" won the Daytona 24 Hours, Porsche shifted from 13- to 15-inch wheels and tires, which made for higher front fenders and reduced aerodynamic efficiency.

High-speed stability was one of several problems that plagued the 908s in '68. By mid-season, the K-body had acquired a strut-mounted rear wing with suspension-controlled flaps, Porsche's first use of such a device. An earlier K won the Nurburgring 1000 Kilometers, which would be the 908's only victory that year. Continued teething troubles, particularly with the new transaxle, prevented further wins. Meanwhile, the 5.0 Fords took Le Mans a third time.

This underwhelming performance led to some personnel changes at Weissach. The charming Huschke von Hanstein stepped down as racing manager but continued as a consultant. His successor, Rico Steinemann, picked up new drivers: Britain's Richard Attwood and Brian Redman, Formula 2 maestro Kurt Ahrens, and rally aces Pauli Toivonen, Bjorn Waldegaard, and Gerard

Porsche fielded a variety of sports racers in the late Sixties. From the top: Type 906; 1969 Type 908/02 Spyder, at Hockenheim; 1967 Type 907, an aerodynamic variant of the 910; 1968 Type 907 LH Longtail. 907s ran with both six- and eight-cylinder engines.

More Porsche racers from the late Sixties; top and bottom: 1968 908 Shorttail, a 3.0-liter, 350-horse terror that finished first overall at Nurburgring, 1968; middle two photos: a pair of 1969 908/02 Spyders, of the sort that finished 1-2-3-4 at the '69 Targa Florio at Sicily. New regulations for prototypes with engines of up to three liters decreed that windscreens no longer had to reach a certain height, a rule of which the Spyder took full advantage.

Larousse. The result was one of the most daunting factory teams in the business.

Steinemann decided to use the open Spyders for shorter courses, long-tail coupes for fast tracks like Monza, and 908Ks for in-between venues. He also decided to ignore events that did not count toward the championship. As far as Steinemann was concerned, it was win or nothing and let the privateers worry about non-point matches.

Not everything went Porsche's way in '69. The initial contests at Daytona and Sebring were plagued by breakdowns, and Ford won again at Le Mans—albeit narrowly, Hans Hermann dicing back and forth with Ford's Jacky Ickx during the race's last hour and just missing the win by about 100 yards. In other races, though, the plan worked: 908s finished 1-2 at Monza, 1-2-3-4 in the Targa, and 1-2-3-4-5 at the 'Ring. In short, Porsche won the Makes Championship handily, trouncing Ford 76 points to 26. And 908s would continue doing well. In 1981—12 years after the first examples appeared—a 908/80 won the Nurburgring 1000. Few machines can claim as long a competitive lifespan.

Type 909 Bergspyder

A sister to the 908, the 909 Bergspyder was designed specifically for the hill climbing, or "mountain racing," popular in Alpine Europe (*berg* meaning mountain in German). It lasted only a year, after which Porsche withdrew from hillclimbs to concentrate on Makes Championship road racing in 1970, but for as long as it campaigned, it was unbeatable.

Not that Porsche had anything more to prove. Edgar Barth had won the European Hillclimb Championship in 1959, 1963, and '64 in stubby, purpose-built versions of the Type 718 and RS 60/61. Gerhard Mitter followed by winning it in 1966-67 using similar open derivatives of the 906 and 910.

The 909 evolved from the 910 Bergspyder of 1967, with the same aging but still capable 2.0-liter flat-eight (Type 770/0) coaxed up to 275 bhp (DIN), as high as it would go. Weighing a hair under 950 pounds (feathery for a race car), the 909 could see 155 mph on the straight. With extra-wide tracks (57.9/57.6 inches front/rear) and a compact 89.1-inch wheelbase (versus the 908s' 90.6 inches) it was simply amazing on the curves.

As on the 910 Berg, bodywork was low and squat but even more streamlined, with a pair of small downward-pointing "spoilerettes" on the nose and two up-tilting flaps on the tail. Beneath was a tubular space-frame that placed engine and

driver relatively far forward. In fact, the driver's legs actually extended over the centerline of the front anti-sway bar. Titanium was used extensively in the all-coil suspension and for the fuel tank.

Mitter made it three in a row by winning the '68 Hillclimb Championship. But the triumph was overshadowed because teammate Ludovico "Lulu" Scarfiotti, the greatest of the contemporary Italians, was killed at Rossfeld when his 909 leaped off the road and plastered itself against a tree. It was the first death at a Porsche racing wheel. In the wake of Lulu's loss, Mitter decided he'd had enough of the hills.

Type 917

Though just recently elevated to top-rank contender, Porsche so enjoyed life at the summit that it soon turned to its biggest, fastest, and most successful sports-racer yet—a car that would recall as no other the screaming silver streamliners of pre-war Grand Prix fame. The mighty 12-cylinder battlewagon launched in 1969 would so completely dominate the sport that nothing else could be properly compared to it. Today it's been enshrined with the Grand Prix Mercedes and Indianapolis Offenhausers as one of racing's giants. We can only be speaking of the 917.

The FIA's 3.0-liter limit for prototypes in '68 had been intended to curb Ford, but a loophole was allowed to remain in order to appease owners of leftover GT40s homologated with 5.0 engines. These were given their own class, called Group 4, for which a key requirement was minimum production of 25 within one year.

The minimum-production requirement turned out to be a key point, because Porsche decided to call the FIA's bluff. The politicos thought nobody would go to the expense of building 25 special 5.0 cars. Porsche, though, realized it was already building more than that number of 3.0 prototypes just to maintain its fleet. So mere numbers would be no problem. Beyond that, the technical challenges—and perhaps the political dare—were irresistible.

The 917 chassis was basically that of the 908, enlarged and strengthened for the new engine. It wasn't feasible to make the eight into a 12 simply by adding cylinders; that would have meant a long crankshaft subject to excess torsional vibration. Porsche sidestepped the dilemma by splitting the new crank into two six-cylinder lengths with gear clusters at the middle to take power to the camshafts, the air-cooling blower, and to the clutch (via a jackshaft in the sump).

Other than that and some new castings, the 917 twelve retained the 908's reciprocating parts and its 85-mm bore and 66-mm stroke. The result was 4494cc (274.2 cubic inches)—an increase in capacity of exactly 50 percent. (During research, Porsche also built a flat-16 engine of similar size, but never raced it.)

Thanks to their experience with lightweight engines and chassis, Porsche designers kept curb weight very close to the 800-kg (1764-pound) Group 4 minimum. In fact, the 917 ended up so light—and its engine so powerful—that the design team found it unnecessary at first to use the full 5.0 liters allowed. With 10.5:1 compression, the 917 as raced at Le Mans and Spa in 1969 packed 580 bhp at 8400 rpm and 375 pounds/feet of torque at 6600 rpm. This plus extreme lightness promised to make this the fastest car in the class, and the FIA knew it.

Porsche duly presented the 917's homologation papers. What followed is one of those stories race fans love to tell about bureaucratic regulators. Porsche had more than the minimum 25 cars under construction when the FIA's International Sporting Commission (*Commission Sportive Internationale; * CSI) first visited, but the inspection team demanded that the cars be ready to roll before the 917 would be certified. After a marathon effort by all hands, 25 fully finished cars were lined up in a Le Mans-start sort of formation for CSI's second look on April 21, 1969. The Porsche folk offered a box of keys and invited their guests to drive any one at random. The inspectors meekly declined.

Porsche again raced *kurz* and *lang* versions of its latest fiberglass-bodied streamliner. As before, aft sections could be exchanged to suit distance and track conditions. The long-tail, designed for high-speed circuits, had a drag coefficient of 0.33, good for 236 mph at Le Mans. Both *Hecks* incorporated suspension-controlled aero flaps, though they caused intense debate and were banned at some '69 events. Without them, the 917 was a real handful at racing speeds.

Like the 908, the 917 needed a full season to be completely sorted out. One car led at Le Mans for 20 hours before retiring with a cracked bell housing, leaving Jacky Ickx in a Gulf-sponsored, John Wyer-managed GT40 to make it a narrow four straight for Ford over Herman's 908, as described earlier.

Suitably impressed, Porsche invited Gulf-Wyer to campaign a team of 917s for 1970. A second team, Porsche-Salsburg, was operated by Ferry

Porsche's sister, Louise Piech. The Martini Racing Team would also field its first 917 in 1970, at Le Mans, a purple-and-green monster for Larrouse/Kauhsen.

Inevitably, these teams simply dominated Le Mans with their 917s, sweeping home 1-2-3. Confounding the wind-tunnel crew, which had labored long and hard on a special 917 LH (*Langheck*) just for this race, the winner was a short-tail Porsche-Salzburg entry piloted by Dickie Attwood and veteran Hans Hermann. Though marred by crashes and the death of a corner marshal, it was the crowning moment of Hermann's career. He retired from racing soon afterward, depressed by the tragic events, but his work was complete, his greatest ambition realized. The victory was just as sweet for the Austrian team. The land that 22 years before had given birth to the strange teardrop-shape 356 had produced a winner in the world's most prestigious road race.

Having won every 1970 contest except Sebring, the Targa, and the Nurburgring 1000, the 917s were now "the cars to beat," as Don Vorderman put it. But in 1971, nobody tried. The one apparent challenger was Ferrari's 512M, faster and lighter than its 512S of 1970—but not as fast or as light as the 917 of any year.

To thwart any potential threat from the Italian quarter, Porsche engineers decided to take advantage of their remaining half-liter, bringing the twelve first to 4907cc (299.4 cid), then to 4998cc (305 cid) for 600 and 630 bhp, respectively. The 5.0, found to be the more reliable, was selected for Le Mans '71. But Ferrari elected not to contest the Manufacturers Championship that year, so Porsche again won all the big races—Daytona, Sebring, Monza, Spa, the Osterreichring, and Le Mans—on the efforts of Gulf-Wyer and Martini Racing. The latter took over from Porsche-Salzburg and repeated its triumph at the Sarthe circuit, with drivers Helmut Marko and Gijs van Lennep.

A memorable factory entrant at Le Mans '71 was the 917/20, a low-drag special built to see whether the L-body's superior aerodynamics could be achieved without a long tail. This rather bloated-looking coupe with vast lateral overhang was developed by the SERA design office in France and chosen over a rival proposal by Porsche's own stylists. Porsche consoled the stylists by letting them paint and decorate the thing, which they referred to as "Big Bertha" and "The Pig." The latter nickname was particularly appropriate, as the car was finished in a bright piggy-pink with dot-

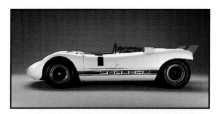

The 1968 Type 909 Bergspyder (top two photos) *was more of a rolling test bed than a full-on racer. It competed only in a pair of hillclimbs, winning neither. But the car's unusually low center of gravity and center-mounted engine were innovations that were successfully exploited by competition Porsches throughout the Seventies. The 910/8 Bergspyder of 1967* (third from top) *was purpose-built for hillclimb competition. To save weight, it was fitted with fiberglass body panels over an aluminum space frame Other weight-saving innovations included a small, 15-liter fuel tank and a battery made of silver instead of lead. 910 Spyders scored eight wins and six second-place finishes during the 1967 hillclimb season.*

No other competition Porsches shine as brightly as those comprising the 917 series, inaugurated when the company decided to contest Group 4, where engine displacement was restricted to five liters. The 917s had no real competitors; only Ferraris had a ghost of a chance against them. From the top: 1969 917/10K, a superb handler; 1970 917 Shorttail, a big-bore 12-cylinder developing 580 horsepower; 1971 917 Shorttail, magnesium-framed, with a 600-horsepower 12; 1972-74 917/30 Experimental, developed for the Can Am race series and running with a 5.4-liter 12 good for 850 horses at 8000 rpm.

ted lines to mark off various sections, as on a butcher's diagram. When "Bertha/Pig" crashed, few tears were shed by the disdainful Porsche styling group.

The end of the 1971 season ended the 917's Group 4 career. As Porsche knew from the outset, 5.0-liter sports cars wouldn't be eligible for the Makes Championship beginning in 1972. All due credit, then, to Weissach's determination to build a winner—and the speed with which they did it.

Porsche built 37 Group 4 917s, and many survive today. Count Gregorio Rossi of Martini & Rossi had Porsche put one in concours condition (painted silver, like its German forebears of decades past) for display at his Paris offices. Porsche itself salvaged the "Pig" and treated it to a complete restoration in 1985. Today it rests in the Porsche Museum alongside long- and short-tail 917s and 908s, assorted Bergspyders, the 908, 910, Carrera 6, 904, and all the rest.

But the 917 was far from finished after '71. It was ready, in fact, to write more history in the Canadian-American Challenge Cup.

Types 917/10K and 917/30

Established by the Sports Car Club of America (SCCA) and Canadian Auto Sport Clubs (CASC) in 1966 as North America's premiere road-racing series, the Can-Am was initially run under what amounted to Formula Libre ("free formula") rules that permitted almost anything at all. This noble principle was compromised over the years, but at the time Porsche came in the rules were still surprisingly liberal. Competitors had to qualify as FIA Group 7, which basically required little more than fenders and some semblance of a cockpit. There were certain restrictions on aerodynamic aids, weight, and engines (nothing below 2.5 liters, no gas turbines), but the series was otherwise wide open.

On paper, the 917 was not good Can-Am material. Up to that time, the dominant cars had been powered by relatively cheap, uncomplicated American V-8s, mainly from Chevy. Practicality dictated an off-the-shelf engine for Porsche and the biggest one available was the 917's. (Weissach again contemplated its flat-16, which stood to deliver about 2000 horsepower with turbocharger, but progress with the 12 rendered it superfluous.)

Porsche had tested the Can-Am waters as early as 1969, building two open Spyders designated 917PA (for Volkswagen of America's Porsche + Audi division). One was sent to North America

late in the season. As expected, it was no match for the Detroit V-8s, its best finish being a third at Bridgehampton. The chief obstacle was the competition's tremendous low-end torque.

Once ousted from the Makes Championship, Porsche turned in earnest to development of a Can-Am 917, approaching the project from two directions. One was an enlarged 5.4-liter 12-cylinder that showed a useful gain in torque but only 30 more horsepower than the 5.0-liter version. The second approach was turbocharging via an Eberspacher system boosting at 18-20 pounds per square inch. Though considerable work was required to ensure reliability, the turbo released astonishing power: 850 bhp (DIN) from the original 4.5-liter, 950-1000 on the 5.0. Having helped with development, Penske Racing agreed to campaign the 5.0-liter version of what Porsche called the Type 917/10K (K for *Kompressor*), with Mark Donohue driving.

Donohue went to Germany to work with chief program engineer Helmut Flegl. "I've got a unique relationship in this project," Donohue said, "a kind . . . I've never had before. Helmut Flegl . . . is capable in every respect. I can talk to him. I can say things to him and he to me and we understand each other perfectly. . . . I've never really had a relationship like that before." Donohue added, "When Porsche ships you a car, it's not like with McLaren or Lola. With a Porsche, you unload it off the airplane, put the key in the ignition, turn it on and you race it. . . . We've never seen a car so complete."

The affable Donohue thus summarized a close, friendly partnership with Porsche over months of trial and error in bringing the 917/10K to a race-ready state. For example, the extra power required a completely new gearbox, strengthened chassis, improved cooling system, and deeply finned, vented aluminum disc brakes. The team was also mindful of weight. A secret here was a tubular space-frame of magnesium alloy instead of aluminum. (Questioned hard by *Road & Track*'s Pete Lyons, Donohue quipped that the material was "Unobtainium.")

Lyons pointed out that the 917/10's great strength wasn't engine power (McLaren M20-Chevys had almost as much) but cornering power. As developed by Donohue and Porsche engineers, the body created tremendous downforce to glue the tires to the road. This naturally created a lot of drag too, but the engine had enough pull to overcome it. Stopwatches proved that Donohue "was a lot faster than anybody else in the corners," Lyons

wrote. "By a factor of 5 percent—which is a bunch."

With such a well-prepared car, the Penske team proved virtually unbeatable by McLaren or anyone else. One of the turbo relief valves denied Donohue the opening race at Mosport and during testing for the next, Road Atlanta, inadequately fastened rear bodywork caused a crash that injured one of Donohue's knees. It also destroyed the only magnesium chassis frame, and no more were built. Penske called in George Follmer, who duly went on to win in Georgia, then at Mid-Ohio, Road America, Laguna Seca, and Riverside. Donohue came back later in the season and ran a second, new car to win at Edmonton. But Follmer had scored too often to avoid taking the Can-Am Championship. In Europe, Leo Kinnunen matched this performance in similar Interserie competition to give Porsche its third championship in a row (after non-turbo 917s won in 1970-71).

Over the winter of 1972-73, Donohue and Flegl lengthened the chassis, improved the body, and switched to the turbo 5.4-liter, which by spring was pumping out 1100 bhp at 7800 rpm and 810 pounds/feet of torque at 6500 rpm. (These were merely the nominal outputs. At 32-psi boost, the dyno showed an amazing 1560 bhp!) With this new and better car, the 917/30 (the K was left off as redundant), the '73 Can-Am was a virtual Donohue cakewalk: six of eight rounds.

It began to seem that every time Porsche started dominating competition, authorities would rewrite the rules to even things up. That's just what they did for the 1974 Can-Am season, introducing fuel allowances and thus effectively barring the turbocars from yet another series. But Petermax Muller took the Interserie—and won it again for good measure in 1975 with a turbocharged 908/03. With that, Porsche had achieved supremacy in almost all forms of road racing.

One final triumph awaited. At NASCAR's high-banked Talladega speedway in August 1975, driving a specially prepared 917/30 fitted for the first time with intercoolers and rated at 1190 bhp, Donohue set a new closed-course speed record of 221.160 mph, breaking A.J. Foyt's 217.854 set with a Coyote-Ford Indycar. It would be Mark Donohue's last hurrah. Ten days later he died of injuries suffered when his Formula 1 Penske crashed at the Osterreichring. He had accomplished great things, for Porsche and motorsports in general, and was sorely missed.

Though the 917 had no place left to race, Porsche stood ready to tackle anything the fickle FIA could throw at it. When a sports-racer in the new Group 6 class was needed for 1976, its engineers promptly reeled off a fabulous contender.

Type 936

Here, Porsche returned to its mainstay powerplant, the 911 flat-six. Group 6 allowed two options: a normally aspirated 3.0-liter or a turbocharged engine with a handicap of 1-to-1.4. The latter calculation yields 2142cc (130.7 cid), and that's precisely what Porsche built. Designed mainly for short hauls, this engine could tolerate a 20-psi boost providing a maximum 520 bhp (DIN) at 8000 rpm—242 bhp per liter! The sizzling little six naturally rode ahead of the rear wheels, tied to a 917-type transaxle. Suspension and steering were also in the 917 mold, as was the aluminum spaceframe. Bodywork was a new Spyder style that looked very much like a cleaned-up, slicked-down Can-Am 917, dominated by a huge air intake above and behind the cockpit (Can-Am rules had banned this sort of tall scoops) and equally large tailfins cradling an adjustable airfoil.

The 936 had a splendid first season. The climax was Porsche's triumphant return to Le Mans, where Jacky Ickx and Jochen Mass drove the winning car. The 936 also collected the World Sports Car title that year. It then repeated as Le Mans winner in 1977, giving Porsche its fourth outright victory at the Sarthe, with Ickx, Hurley Haywood, and Jurgen Barth sharing the driving.

Types 956 and 962

For 1982, the FIA established a new Group C category. At the same time, America's International Motor Sports Association (IMSA) spawned a North American counterpart called Grand Touring Prototype (GTP). This joint move was in some ways a return to the kind of way-out factory sports racers that had so thrilled fans in the old days of big-engine Le Mans and unlimited-engine Can-Am cars, so perhaps it was no surprise that Porsche's entries—the 956 for Group C, the 962 for IMSA—evoked good memories.

Imposing and very smooth, they looked much alike. The difference was the 962 had an extra 100mm (3.94 inches) in wheelbase toward the front to satisfy IMSA's rule that a driver's feet remain behind the front-wheel centerline. For once, a rule brought about a real improvement, for the longer wheelbase added stability that 956 drivers felt right away on jumping into a 962.

Porsche began development of the 936 series in 1976, intending to contest the World Sports Car Championship. The 1977 936/77 Spyder (top) had an air-cooled turbocharged six; note the enormous air intake above the cockpit. Although Porsche concentrated on its Group 5 car, the 935, in 1977, it did enter a 936 Spyder in that year's 24 Hours of Le Mans, which it won for the second year in a row. The 1980 936/80 (middle) was essentially a carryover, but the 936 received a new engine for its next iteration, the 1981 936/81 Spyder (bottom). It ran with the same chassis and body as before, but now had a six-cylinder "boxer" engine that was air- and water-cooled. A 936/81 driven by Derek Bell and Jacky Ickx stormed to victory at Le Mans 1981, finishing 14 laps ahead of the second-place car, a Rondeau-Ford.

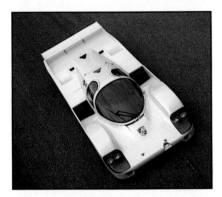

Thanks to new regulations, Porsche's 956C (for "Group C") series (top three photos) did not have to be declared a "prototype" for a future production car. The 2.6-liter turbocharged six made 620-630 bhp, and had enhanced stability thanks to a monocoque chassis and ground effects (both firsts for Porsche race machines). In 1982, its debut season, 956s dominated Le Mans, coming in 1-2-3. It continued to rack up wins through 1985. From that point, Porsche switched to the 962C (above), which first competed in 1986. The durable 962 regularly defeated quicker competitors.

Because Porsche already had the essentials, these new twins came together with astonishing speed, the 956 racing a little more than a year after budget approval that came on June 22, 1981. Peter Falk had replaced Manfred Jantke as racing manager, aided by development engineer Norbert Singer, engine designer Valentine Schafer, and body/chassis expert Horst Reitter.

Salvaging work from the aborted first six-cylinder Indy effort (described later in this chapter), Schafer endowed the 935/76 engine with a special racing version of the Bosch Motronic integrated electronic ignition/fuel injection system. Result: 620-630 bhp (DIN) at 8200 rpm. Reitter produced a riveted-and-bonded aluminum monocoque frame that was 50-percent stiffer than that of the Indy car, and that met Group C rules for driver-protecting "crushable" structures. This was overlaid as before with plastic panels, only now they were made of reinforced Kevlar carbon-fiber. Curb weight came in only 20-50 kg (44-110 pounds) over the 800-kg (1764-pound) minimum, though some suggested the frame could have been lighter still. The only other change from 936 chassis specs was double-stiff springs to avoid unwanted "porpoising" at racing speeds.

Like the 917s, the 956 was raced in long- and short-tail forms. The former, for Le Mans, had a 0.35 drag coefficient; the latter, measuring 0.42, was for other Makes races. Hidden beneath was a rules-restriction version of the "ground effects" underbody profile now used to create downforce in Formula 1 and Indy cars. Fuel economy in enduros was a concern, so compression ratios were varied between 7.1 and 7.5:1 during the season, as were boost pressures, which ultimately settled at 1.2 bar/17.6 psi.

Unlike the 917, the 956 was a winner from its very first race. Ickx and Derek Bell (who drove a 956 "test mule" faster than any previous Porsche in tests at France's Paul Ricard circuit) led a 1-2-3 Le Mans sweep in a season that brought Porsche another Makes championship and made Ickx the world's top endurance driver. Porsche added three more Le Mans victories and three consecutive championships in 1983-85, after which it switched to the 962C.

That development of the 962 stemmed from the North American GTP series. Al Holbert Racing had been Porsche's main standard-bearer in the IMSA wars (his Porsche-powered March won the '83 championship), and Holbert himself participated in much of the 962's development. Also on

board were Alwin Springer from Andial of California and Jurgen Barth and Valentine Schafer from Weissach.

Aside from bodywork—distinguished by a shorter nose, tail, and underbody configurations on the longer wheelbase—the 962's chief distinction was its powerplant. Initially this was the 2.8-liter all-air-cooled 934 unit, with single turbo and ignition. In this form the 962 scored its first win, at Mid-Ohio 1984, but the team was already working on a 3.2 extension for needed extra power.

Problems with the Motronic engine management precluded a winning season in '84, but the 962 came into its own the following year, walking away with the GT championship. It repeated in '86, giving Holbert (by now director of Porsche Motorsport, the firm's North American racing arm) his fifth IMSA driving title. That same year, Derek Bell captured his second endurance-driver's title with a 962C.

This basic design would enjoy a long and successful life. Victories were too many to list here, but they included IMSA championships through 1988. In fact, 962s continued to race through the GTP's swan-song season in 1993, and managed to pick up one final win that summer, albeit in the temporary absence of the all-conquering Dan Gurney Racing Toyota Eagles. Then, at the beginning of 1995, a 962 converted to Spyder bodywork and detuned to meet new IMSA regulations picked up a surprise victory against faster but less durable Ferraris in the Daytona 24-Hour enduro.

Indeed, this prince among Porsches remained so effective for so many seasons that an incredible number—at least 180—were made, and not only by the factory. Holbert Racing was just one of several operations that built their own variants of the 962 chassis. Between them, all these teams racing all these cars for all those years honed and polished the weapon into one of the finest, fastest, most reliable, most easy-to-work-on, most enjoyable-to-drive race cars in history.

For a very lucky few enthusiasts, the 962 was one of the most exciting road cars ever. Porsche itself and a number of private tuners have turned out a few 962s tamed—just a little—for the street.

They aren't very practical cars and they certainly can't be described as economical, nor will their sales figures ever excite bean-counters, but these incredible raced-then-ridden road rockets bring the Porsche sports racing story to a satisfying full circle. As always, Porsche means performance on road and raceway—often literally on both.

The Future Porsche Chronicle: New Beginnings

This chapter could have been titled "Back to Basics Part III," for there are two and only two cars in Porsche's immediate future. Although both are new, one takes the marque back to its roots, at least in spirit. We're talking about the much-discussed mid-engine *986* convertible, born of the boffo 1993 "Boxster" concept car. No less intriguing is the car known as *996* within the halls of Zuffenhausen but most everywhere else as "the next 911." Expect the former by 1996, the latter in 1997 or '98.

As for the 928 and 968, they're history. In fact, the V-8 Porsche will go out of production by the time you read this, and the 968 will bow out later in favor of the 986.

If this sounds like retrenchment, it's also just good business. After all, in the parlance of poker, it's the wise player who knows when to hold and when to fold.

Fate dealt Porsche a bad hand in 1988-94, arguably the most troubled period in the firm's history. That drama was just unfolding in 1988, when the Auto Editors of Consumer Guide® observed: "Now, suddenly, Porsche seems to be falling apart. With the dollar's precipitous drop against the Deutschmark in 1987 [stemming partly from the October Wall Street crash] came the first [U.S. sales decline] most anyone could remember, unmasking an overreliance on the American market and long-standing internal dissention among company managers. Things seemed so serious, in fact, that Porsche became rumored as a takeover target."

As we know, a takeover hasn't happened; to the joy of all who love its cars, Porsche remains proudly independent. But the events of 1988-94 have forced it to become a very different company: smaller, more efficient, and—though it may strain belief—even more focused. Which explains why the slow-selling 928 has been consigned to the ages (and to collectors), why a productionized Boxster is replacing the 968 as the "entry level" Porsche, and why the 911 is being reborn to carry a cherished concept into the new century.

But let's not pass over Porsche's difficulties without noting the two vital lessons they teach to businesses that would be successful in a world economy growing ever more interdependent.

Lesson one: It *is* possible to price yourself out of your market. Lesson two: Don't expect all your sales eggs to come from one basket.

Before looking at the cars of Porsche's tomorrow, we'll consider some facts about Porsche today. As ever, it's one of the world's smallest automakers with anything like volume production, only that volume is about two-thirds less than it used to be: down from a mid-Eighties peak of some 50,000 cars a year to just under 16,000 for the firm's fiscal 1993-94 (the last year for which figures are available at this writing). Revenues have also declined, if not as much, going from DM3.2 million to a modern low of just over DM1.9 million before making a modest but welcome recovery to DM2.34 million in 1993-94.

Income might have dropped even more were it not for Porsche's engineering consultancy business, which has remained vigorous despite the sudden drop in worldwide car sales and has thus come to play an increasingly large role in corporate earnings. Indeed, it was this as much as Porsche's car-making assets that prompted those late-Eighties rumors of a "benign takeover."

In character and financial importance, Porsche's engineering business mirrors that of Britain's Lotus. Both operations are world renowned and remain separate from each firm's production-car activities. The bulk of Porsche's contracts continue to involve major clients ranging from SEAT in Spain (now part of Volkswagen-Audi AG) to the People's Republic of China.

That's right, China, the last great commercial frontier. In 1994, the Beijing government invited several Western companies to submit proposals for a low-cost, easily mass-produced car as a prelude to expanding its native auto industry. Porsche Engineering put forth its best thinking, which culminated in a small notchback sedan with front-wheel drive—nothing at all like Porsche's pricey, high-powered sports cars, but a perfect *volkswagen* for a new time and place. We suspect the great *Herr Doktor* would understand it completely. Here was proof, if any be needed, that for all its recent troubles, Porsche remains unsurpassed for inventive flair and technical genius.

As before, Zuffenhausen earns *no* money from

Porsche's Boxster wowed auto-show crowds in 1993—and no wonder, for it's as daring a concept as any offered in recent years. And yet it's clearly a Porsche, and part of a tradition of engineering excellence that stretches back generations. Although the Boxster will never see production, many of its innovative ideas will come to fruition in the 986, Porsche's internal designation for its upcoming, entry-level mid-engine convertible.

Porsche Design, the industrial design and marketing concern famous for leather goods, Carrera sunglasses, watches, and other premium-price personal gear. That company has always been a separate entity, established by Butzi Porsche after papa Ferry removed the family from direct involvement with the car business in 1972, when Porsche KG (limited-partnership company) became today's Porsche AG (*Aktiengesellschaft,* public stock corporation).

Indications at this writing are that Porsche's sales and earnings should continue on a slow but steady upward track as the 21st century approaches. Credit for this turnaround is largely owed to Wendelin Wiedeking, the veteran Porsche engineer and onetime production boss who took over as company chairman in October 1992. As noted in Chapter 5, he swept into power intending to slash production costs and payroll by up to 30 percent to match the firm's reduced sales volume. He succeeded. Wiedeking also convinced the Porsche board to float a stock issue in early 1994 to help finance the 986 and 996.

Those two new models were the second part of Wiedeking's comeback plan. As the chairman told Georg Kacher for the August 1993 issue of Britain's *CAR* magazine: "We must cultivate the 911 because it is the backbone of our business. At the same time, we must develop an entry-level car priced below [$40,000]. This segment is six times bigger than the one the 911 competes in. As soon as we have the new baseline Porsche in the showroom, I guarantee you that our production will double to over 30,000 vehicles per year."

Perhaps, but never again will Porsche rely on just one market to supply so much of its income. Or so says Fred Schwab, who became chief executive officer of Porsche Cars North America (PCNA) at about the time Wiedeking moved in at Zuffenhausen.

Schwab replaced Brian Bowler, who was unable to stem the U.S. sales slide after succeeding PCNA's first chief, John Cook, in late 1988. Not that Bowler didn't try. Among his more salient efforts: cutting staff at PCNA's Reno headquarters by no less than 25 percent and overseeing formation of an in-house financing arm, Porsche Credit Corporation (PCC), in mid-1992.

PCC made great sense. After all, if Porsches had to cost a lot, why not make it easier for people to buy them? PCC has done just that by offering fixed-rate loans of up to seven years on new models (most lenders still don't go beyond five years), as well as leases of two to five years. And if the customer's budget won't stretch to a new Porsche, there's always the alternative of a used one. To make that idea attractive, PCNA began a one-year/unlimited-mileage warranty program for qualifying "pre-owned" Porsches built after 1985 that have traveled no more than 125,000 miles. Buyers pay a fee and must do business with an authorized dealer, but this supplemental plan covers over 500 parts and kicks in only after the original new-car warranty expires.

PCNA wasn't quite out of the woods when Schwab stepped in. Yet by early 1995 he was able to announce the first upturn in U.S. Porsche sales since 1986—and that PCNA was back in the black after several years of heavy losses. Of course, the 993-Series 911 did wonders to spark American sales, yet dealer profits and overall earnings also improved despite the price restraint Zuffenhausen had exercised since 1989. But then, as Schwab said, "Porsche AG is now building them for less," a nod to Wiedeking's belt-tightening measures as well as Schwab's own efforts to further trim overhead in Reno.

Still, Schwab told the press in early 1994 that PCNA "will never again achieve its sales levels of the 1980s." The reason, he explained, was Zuffenhausen's "right sizing" for annual production of no more than 30,000 cars, a level the new regime deemed realistic for a company of Porsche's size producing costly cars for the less predictable high-dollar market of the late Nineties. Of those 30,000, Schwab felt, the United States might take up to a third by the turn of the century—still a sizeable chunk of Porsche's total business but less vulnerable to Stateside economic woes, as when American buyers accounted for more than 50 percent of Porsche sales.

It was also in early '95 that Schwab promised a "new Porsche model every six months for the next several years." But he was probably counting body and engine variations. As noted at the beginning of this chapter, only two basic cars are in Porsche's near-term future. Happily, they should assure that future in no uncertain terms.

Of the two cars, by far the most significant is the 986. As the new "budget" model, it's the car Porsche is counting on to generate most of its sales and profits into the new millenium. Fortunately for all concerned, the 986 looks like a winner, even if it looks a bit different from its parent, the Boxster.

That concept car was greeted with huge enthusiasm on its January 1993 unveiling at Detroit's North American International Auto Show. That was a surprising change of venue given Porsche

From the start of the Boxster's development, Porsche viewed the car as vital not simply to the company's image, but to its future, as well. Price hikes of all Porsche models had led to falling U.S. sales that stood to be revitalized if the Boxster—and the production car to which it would lead—were well received. The well-appointed two-place cockpit had its share of fanciful ideas, such as gold-on-cream dials and petite cooling fans nestled on the console behind retro-look mesh screening.

tradition, but one that underlined the production car's mission of rebuilding the U.S. sales base. Porsche termed the Boxster "a futuristic sports car study," yet in its "rear mid-engine" layout and smooth, compact two-seat convertible package it recalled the pioneering 356/1 that Ferry Porsche and Erwin Komenda had built over 40 years before. And though the Boxster's lines were completely new, there was a clear stylistic link with the great competition 550 Spyder and RSK/RS60 of the mid-Fifties.

The similarity was precisely the intent of designer Grant Larson, Montana-born but raised in Mequon, Wisconsin, where he sometimes dusted cars in the museum of industrial designer Brooks Stevens. After studying at the famed Art Center College of Design in Pasadena, California, Larson launched his professional career with Audi. A few years later he moved to Porsche, working under chief designer Harm Lagaay. As Larson told *Road & Track*'s John Lamm, the Boxster was influenced by many things, but most of all by "Porsche history."

It was thus no surprise that for all its newness the Boxster—with its sloped nose, curving flanks, and neatly rounded tail—was unmistakably a Porsche. Press releases termed the proportions "concise" and called particular attention to the relatively long wheelbase and short overhangs dictated by the mid-engine configuration. Most everyone else just thought the Boxster looked terrific.

R&T's Lamm noted a close size similarity between the Boxster and its illustrious racing forebears. Compared to the 911, the Boxster was shorter overall by 6.9 inches (at 162), lower by 3.2 inches (48.8), and wider by 3.5 inches (68.5), but five inches longer in wheelbase (at 94.5). Front/rear track dimensions were 57.9/58.5 inches, up 3.6/4.4 inches from those of the evergreen rear-engine Porsche.

The Boxter hunkered achingly close to the ground on 17-inch wheels with chrome outer rims and copper-tone five-spoke centers. Wheel wells tightly embraced Z-rated tires (205/50s front, 225/45s rear) to enhance the ready-for-action air.

As the template for a new production Porsche, the Boxster was more functional than most concept cars. Its manual soft top, for example, was fully engineered to fold neatly out of sight beneath a hinged hard cover behind the cockpit. Yet this was no Spartan 356 Speedster, as Porsche fitted power windows, dual airbags, air-conditioning, even a cellular telephone, trip computer, and on-board navigation system.

Still, there was no shortage of fanciful ideas. The

instrument cluster, for instance, was a five-dial type *a la* 911, but the gauges were nearly impossible to read with their gold numerals and cream-colored backgrounds (at the least the pointers were legibly black). A center console held the shifter, as well as a pair of individually adjustable fans with protective mesh over exposed blades that looked incapable of generating anything more than a puff. A similarly tiny fan winked from the leading edge of each upper door panel. Interior door handles were leather-wrapped tubes—real "retro," though Porsche said they were part of a modern side-impact protection system.

More thoughtful were the twin bucket seats that looked alike but weren't. The driver's was more heavily bolstered for better lateral location and thigh support, while the passenger's chair was wider, flatter, and given a greater range of adjustments, plus a zippered storage pocket on the back. Luggage space was sparse in the tail, but a useful pair of fitted travel cases could be stowed behind the seats. A real high-tech touch was the LCD dashboard screen for displaying trip data, clock, and additional operating instruments, as well as controlling the cell phone, audio system (complete with CD player and graphic equalizer), and the on-board navigator.

Porsche was candid about its plans for the Boxster from the first. Yes, there would be a production version, and, yes, it would look much like the show car. It would definitely be fun but civilized, too. As Research & Development chief Horst Marchart told John Lamm: "We are looking for features for the driver who wants to be happy when he drives the car. It is not important to have the highest maximum speed. . . . If the driver wants to lower the top, it should be easy. It needs good ergonomics. A good noise. A sporty car, but it can also be comfortable. It must not be hard riding . . . that is the direction we are going."

The heart of any car is the engine, and that's something Marchart and other Porsche people would not discuss. The reason, we suspect, was that they hadn't made up their minds when the Boxster was unveiled, even though they'd already frozen the design of the production 986. Perhaps that's why the concept car was a motor-less "pushmobile."

Ultimately, informed sources confirmed that two engines were in the works: a four and a six, both horizontally opposed "boxer" types in the best Porsche tradition. (The Boxster name hinted at that, being a blend of "boxer" and "speedster.") European moles managed to divine that the four

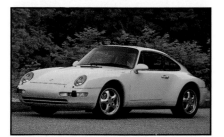

Until the next-generation 911, code-named 996 and coming for model-year 1997 or '98, Porsche rolled on with variations of the familiar 911 known and respected around the world. Whether a 1995 Carrera 2 Cabrio (top) *or a '95 Carrera 4 Coupe* (above), *the 911 remained at the pinnacle of the automotive arts.*

would be a 2.0-liter generating about 170 horse-power, the six an equally fresh 2.4 with 240 bhp. Yet many questions remained. The engines must certainly be related to save development money, but would Porsche offer the four, the six, or both? Reports were conflicting. On the one hand, design chief Harm Lagaay told *R&T*'s Lamm that the "main goal is . . . to maintain the price," the approximately $40,000 already decreed by Wiedeking. "Price is absolutely crucial," Lagaay insisted, "especially in America." That seemed to imply a four-cylinder 986, at least to start. Yet PCNA chief Fred Schwab told *AutoWeek* in late '93 that the car would debut with a six.

There was as much curiosity about cooling medium. Would it be air or water? On that score, Schwab cryptically told *AutoWeek* that "future emission control rules are more easily met with a slight alteration of the engine." Lagaay was more specific with *Motor Trend*'s Don Sherman: "Whatever the variation will be, it'll have to be a Porsche engine. With future emission controls and the need for more than two valves per cylinder, you're talking about water cooling for certain."

Other details began to emerge as the calendar marched toward 1996. As *AutoWeek* relayed from European sources in April '94, the production Boxster "will be built using several components from the next 911 (the 996), including the entire nose substructure and perhaps even the front door panels. Porsche has already announced that sheet metal . . . will be produced in the former East Germany at a BMW-owned facility." Both decisions seemed logical in view of the target price, but how to explain a forecast "Mercedes-style built-in roll bar system"? Something that complex would surely be too expensive even for a $40,000 car. Perhaps the overseas spies forgot to say it would be an option. For the same reason, costly show-car features like the TV screen, on-board navigator, and those petite fans wouldn't make it all.

However, the 986 would retain the Boxster's basic size, according to *AutoWeek,* which also predicted first-year production of 18,000 units, rising to 30,000 a year by the end of 1997. Interestingly, no one seemed to have a clue about suspension—but then, the concept Boxster didn't have that, either. Still, most observers assumed the setup would be all-independent at least. Anything else would be distinctly un-Porsche.

Overriding all technical matters was deep concern among press and public alike that the show car's pretty, nostalgic styling be preserved to production. Early spy photos gave cause for worry by depicting development prototypes that looked like cobbled-up amalgams of new Boxster and old 968. On the other hand, everyone knew the Boxster's lines would have to change somewhat because the concept car wasn't engineered for "crash" standards.

Yet maddeningly, rumors on that score conflicted, too. *AutoWeek* quoted Horst Marchart in late '93 as saying the 986 would "look more like the Boxster than many people expect." The magazine also paraphrased a comment from PCNA's Fred Schwab: "Major changes to the Boxster's looks are modifications to meet international safety laws and the enlargement of the front wheel wells so the car can be steered. The Boxster," he said, "had such small front wheel wells that the tires couldn't be turned." Yet five months later, *AutoWeek* reported this tip from a "company insider" to Britain's *Autocar and Motor:* "You will recognize the 986, but it is less Boxster than you might expect and the detail styling will be much closer to other Porsche models."

In August 1994 *Road & Track* published a set of computer-altered Boxster photos that purposed to show how the production 986 should look, all things considered. These illustrated a thicker, sturdier windshield frame; a longer and flatter nose (for better impact absorption); a larger, more rounded front bumper (again, for crash protection); a wider nasal air intake for proper engine cooling; deeper, stronger rocker panels; longer doors; a more fulsome rear end with simpler taillights; dual exhaust outlets instead of the show car's single central port—and bigger wheel wells. Though *R&T* hesitated about the cockpit, they logically assumed it would be simpler and more conventional than the Boxster's. But the magazine promised that the winsome basic look of the concept car would survive. So, too, would the Boxster's "modular" headlamps combining separate high/low beams and ellipsoid foglamps into a single flowing unit. And, oh yes: Badges would definitely read 986, not Boxster.

Much of this forecast was confirmed by a later 986 prototype snapped in early 1995 by world-famous spy photographer Hans Lehmann. Looking at this picture, it seemed about the only changes *R&T* had missed were rear brake cooling scoops moved higher up the flanks than on the Boxster, plus a large flap on the right front fender, likely for the fuel filler. (The Boxster had a racing-style filler on the left side of the front hood, near the cowl.) *AutoWeek* was one of many publications to run this photo in March '95. By that point, *AW*

The 1996 911 Turbo (seen here in European trim) has 4-wheel-drive, twin turbos with two intercoolers, and a thumping 402 bhp. Acceleration is ferocious (0-60 mph in less than 4.5 seconds), and promised top speed is 181 mph. German price is $142,725.

tradition, but one that underlined the production car's mission of rebuilding the U.S. sales base. Porsche termed the Boxster "a futuristic sports car study," yet in its "rear mid-engine" layout and smooth, compact two-seat convertible package it recalled the pioneering 356/1 that Ferry Porsche and Erwin Komenda had built over 40 years before. And though the Boxster's lines were completely new, there was a clear stylistic link with the great competition 550 Spyder and RSK/RS60 of the mid-Fifties.

The similarity was precisely the intent of designer Grant Larson, Montana-born but raised in Mequon, Wisconsin, where he sometimes dusted cars in the museum of industrial designer Brooks Stevens. After studying at the famed Art Center College of Design in Pasadena, California, Larson launched his professional career with Audi. A few years later he moved to Porsche, working under chief designer Harm Lagaay. As Larson told *Road & Track*'s John Lamm, the Boxster was influenced by many things, but most of all by "Porsche history."

It was thus no surprise that for all its newness the Boxster—with its sloped nose, curving flanks, and neatly rounded tail—was unmistakably a Porsche. Press releases termed the proportions "concise" and called particular attention to the relatively long wheelbase and short overhangs dictated by the mid-engine configuration. Most everyone else just thought the Boxster looked terrific.

R&T's Lamm noted a close size similarity between the Boxster and its illustrious racing forebears. Compared to the 911, the Boxster was shorter overall by 6.9 inches (at 162), lower by 3.2 inches (48.8), and wider by 3.5 inches (68.5), but five inches longer in wheelbase (at 94.5). Front/rear track dimensions were 57.9/58.5 inches, up 3.6/4.4 inches from those of the evergreen rear-engine Porsche.

The Boxter hunkered achingly close to the ground on 17-inch wheels with chrome outer rims and copper-tone five-spoke centers. Wheel wells tightly embraced Z-rated tires (205/50s front, 225/45s rear) to enhance the ready-for-action air.

As the template for a new production Porsche, the Boxster was more functional than most concept cars. Its manual soft top, for example, was fully engineered to fold neatly out of sight beneath a hinged hard cover behind the cockpit. Yet this was no Spartan 356 Speedster, as Porsche fitted power windows, dual airbags, air-conditioning, even a cellular telephone, trip computer, and on-board navigation system.

Still, there was no shortage of fanciful ideas. The

Until the next-generation 911, code-named 996 and coming for model-year 1997 or '98, Porsche rolled on with variations of the familiar 911 known and respected around the world. Whether a 1995 Carrera 2 Cabrio (top) or a '95 Carrera 4 Coupe (above), the 911 remained at the pinnacle of the automotive arts.

instrument cluster, for instance, was a five-dial type *a la* 911, but the gauges were nearly impossible to read with their gold numerals and cream-colored backgrounds (at the least the pointers were legibly black). A center console held the shifter, as well as a pair of individually adjustable fans with protective mesh over exposed blades that looked incapable of generating anything more than a puff. A similarly tiny fan winked from the leading edge of each upper door panel. Interior door handles were leather-wrapped tubes—real "retro," though Porsche said they were part of a modern side-impact protection system.

More thoughtful were the twin bucket seats that looked alike but weren't. The driver's was more heavily bolstered for better lateral location and thigh support, while the passenger's chair was wider, flatter, and given a greater range of adjustments, plus a zippered storage pocket on the back. Luggage space was sparse in the tail, but a useful pair of fitted travel cases could be stowed behind the seats. A real high-tech touch was the LCD dashboard screen for displaying trip data, clock, and additional operating instruments, as well as controlling the cell phone, audio system (complete with CD player and graphic equalizer), and the on-board navigator.

Porsche was candid about its plans for the Boxster from the first. Yes, there would be a production version, and, yes, it would look much like the show car. It would definitely be fun but civilized, too. As Research & Development chief Horst Marchart told John Lamm: "We are looking for features for the driver who wants to be happy when he drives the car. It is not important to have the highest maximum speed. . . . If the driver wants to lower the top, it should be easy. It needs good ergonomics. A good noise. A sporty car, but it can also be comfortable. It must not be hard riding . . . that is the direction we are going."

The heart of any car is the engine, and that's something Marchart and other Porsche people would not discuss. The reason, we suspect, was that they hadn't made up their minds when the Boxster was unveiled, even though they'd already frozen the design of the production 986. Perhaps that's why the concept car was a motor-less "push-mobile."

Ultimately, informed sources confirmed that two engines were in the works: a four and a six, both horizontally opposed "boxer" types in the best Porsche tradition. (The Boxster name hinted at that, being a blend of "boxer" and "speedster.") European moles managed to divine that the four was forecasting overall length of 163.6 inches, height of 48.9 inches—and a choice of four- and six-cylinder four-valve engines.

But forget all this fervid prognosticating. The 986 is coming soon, and it will be the first completely fresh Porsche since the 928 was introduced over 20 years ago. That's great news no matter who turns out to have been the best guesser. Still, the car's success is by no means assured. Since the 1989 introduction and subsequent worldwide success of the Mazda Miata, the automotive marketplace has exploded with sporty roadsters. The 986 will face some tough competition in BMW's American-built Z3, Mercedes's new SLK, and the recently launched mid-engine MGF, all of which are being pitched in the hotly contested $30,000-$40,000 price bracket.

But if any car can bring needed new customers to the Porsche fold, the 986 is it—assuming, of course, its price is on the right side of that promised $40,000. You can bet that Porsche is doing everything it can to deliver. After all, as *Car and Driver* observed: "If that price becomes a reality, the [986] will be the hottest-selling Porsche since the 944 came to market . . . in 1982. If Porsche's future is to be secure, nothing less will do."

Details of the 968 are less than complete at this writing, and even less is known about the next 911. Though the 996 isn't likely to be as vital to total sales as past 911s, Porsche is much more secretive about its first really new rear-engine car in over three decades—understandable given company pride and the 911's long-standing legendary status.

Nevertheless, various sources provided a peek at the 996 as this book was going to press. According to *AutoWeek,* among others, the next 911 will have a water-cooled six-cylinder boxer engine sitting firmly behind the rear axle—no surprise there—and it could well be derived from the 986 power-plant in line with Wiedeking's plans to maximize future engineering and tooling expenditures. Horsepower is whispered to be 300, which Porsche could easily achieve with a displacement of around 3.0 liters, a reasonable enlargement of the 986's 2.4. If all this proves true, the 996 would be the first "volume" 911 with more than two valves per cylinder.

As for the rest of it, the 996 looks to be a considered evolution of familiar 911 precepts inside and out. A photo of a partly disguised prototype snapped by *Herr* Lehmann suggests a somewhat wider, more angular body with longer front/rear overhangs, yet it appears to preserve most all of the beloved design cues initiated by Butzi Porsche.

Departures may include ventless front door glass, ovoid headlights *a la* the Boxster/986, and a more compact flip-up spoiler in the engine lid. The interior will probably be completely redesigned, with truly modern ergonomics (a 911 weakness for years) and a continuation of "+2" rear seating.

AutoWeek reported in March 1995 that the 996's introduction has been moved back to 1998, a year later than first thought. The reason is not development problems but resurgent demand for the current 993 Series. Whenever it arrives, the 996 should continue to offer the familiar coupe and Cabriolet body styles with rear- and all-wheel-drive. It's unknown whether they'll still be called *Carrera.* The 986 would seem to preclude another 911 Speedster, but a new 996 Turbo is almost assured, though it may not appear before the year 2000.

Until then, thrill-seekers will have to content themselves with the 1996 Turbo, which was wowing crowds at the Geneva Salon as this book was being finished. Based on the new 993 platform, the '96 marks a first for 911 Turbos in using the all-wheel-drive system of the normally aspirated Carrera 4, plus a manual gearbox with six forward ratios instead of five. Wheel/tire diameter has grown another inch (to 18), and the trademark wide-body rear has been freshened with a reshaped whale tail curving gently down at its outboard ends.

Drivers will appreciate the all-wheel traction, for the familiar 3.6-liter engine has been muscled up to no less than 402 horsepower via twin blowers—another first for the model—plus other changes. Top speed is a blistering 181 mph—ample justification for announcement ads that said the '96 Turbo is "Like your own portable amusement park." But then, great rides have always been Porsche's stock-in-trade.

Some may argue that Porsche strayed from greatness with the 914 and 924, but there's never been a doubt about the pedigree of the 944, the 968, and even the posh 928. And the 911, as always, remains in a class of one. Now, with the 986 and a new 911 at hand, Porsche's future looks infinitely brighter than just a few years ago. It's our hope to be back a few years from now with another book about this legendary marque, a book chronicling Porsche automobiles and accomplishments as yet undreamt of. We know of no nicer way to leave you than that.

Porsche aficionados speculate on whether spy photos of 996 clays such as these are suggestive of the true configuration of the next-generation 911. Whether a legitimate proposal or simply a conscious attempt at misdirection, the shape seen here has been nothing if not controversial. Note the severely sloped rear roofline and discrete taillights. The "body panels" of these clays have been covered with Di-Noc to simulate metal; window areas carry black sheet plastic.